Women, Equality and Europe

Edited by

Mary Buckley
Lecturer in Politics
University of Edinburgh

and

Malcolm Anderson
Professor of Politics
University of Edinburgh

MACMILLAN
PRESS

First published 1988.

Published by
THE MACMILLAN PRESS LTD
Houndmills, Basingstoke, Hampshire RG21 2XS
and London
Companies and representatives
throughout the world

Typeset by Wessex Typesetters
(Division of The Eastern Press Ltd)
Frome, Somerset

Printed in Hong Kong

British Library Cataloguing in Publication Data
Women, equality and Europe.
1. Sex discrimination against women—
Europe
I. Buckley, Mary   II. Anderson, Malcolm
305.4′2′094   HQ1587
ISBN 0–333–42413–1 (hardcover)
ISBN 0–333–42414–X (paperback)

Contents

Notes on the Contributors

Malcolm Anderson is Professor of Politics at the University of Edinburgh and chairperson of the University Association for Contemporary European Studies. He is author of *Government in France*, *Conservative Politics in France* and *Frontier Regions in Europe* (editor).

Ursula Barry is Lecturer in Economics/Sociology at the College of Technology, Dublin. She is author of *Lifting the Lid: A Handbook of Information on Ireland* and joint-editor of *Information Technology: Impact on the Way of Life*.

Mary Buckley is Lecturer in Politics at the University of Edinburgh and Honorary Research Fellow of the Institute of Soviet and East European Studies at the University of Glasgow. She is editor of *Soviet Social Scientists Talking: An Official Debate About Women*.

Angela Byre is a lawyer and a Research Fellow at the Policy Studies Institute. She was the first co-ordinator of the EEC's monitoring network on European Community equality laws established under the 1982–5 Action Programme.

Michelle Coquillat was a university teacher in the USA and Paris prior to being a member of the cabinet of Madame Yvette Roudy, the first Minister of Women's Rights (1981–6) in France. She now holds a position in the French Ministry of Industrial Redeployment and Foreign Trade.

Jennifer Corcoran is a Principal Lecturer in Law at Manchester Polytechnic and part-time chairperson of Industrial Tribunals. She was formerly legal adviser to the Equal Opportunities Commission.

Catherine Hoskyns is Lecturer in International Relations at Coventry (Lanchester) Polytechnic. She is doing research on the development of the European Community's policy on women's rights and is a member of Rights of Women (London) and the European Network of Women.

Pauline Jackson is a social researcher with special interest in women's employment in Ireland. She is co-editing a book on gender with the Sociological Association of Ireland and is currently a postgraduate student in the Social Science Department of University College, Dublin. Her thesis is on the place of women in multinational manufacturing plants in Ireland.

Joni Lovenduski is Senior Lecturer in Politics in the Department of European Studies at Loughborough University. She is author of *Women in European Politics* and co-editor of *The Politics of the Second Electorate* and *The New Politics of Abortion*.

Pippa Norris is Senior Lecturer in Government at Newcastle Polytechnic. She is author of *Politics and Sexual Equality* and Secretary of the Women and Politics group of the Political Studies Association.

Joyce Outshoorn is Senior Lecturer in Politics at the University of Amsterdam and editor of *Socialisties Feministiese Teksten*. She is author of *De Politieke stryd Rondom de Abortuswetgering in Nederland 1964–1984* and co-editor (with Joni Lovenduski) of *The New Politics of Abortion*.

Odile Quintin is Head of the Equal Opportunities Bureau in the Commission of the European Communities, responsible for European policy on equal opportunities.

Margherita Rendel is Reader in Human Rights and Education, a political scientist and lawyer. She was active in the struggle for the Sex Discrimination Act 1975, initiated the first Women's Studies MA course in Britain and edited *Women, Power and Political Systems*.

Ina Sjerps works at the Emancipatieraad (council for women's emancipation) in The Hague. Prior to that she was an assistant in International Law at the University of Amsterdam.

Elizabeth Vallance is Head of the Department of Political Studies at Queen Mary College, University of London. She is the author of *Women in the House: a study of Women MPs*, (with E. Davies) *Women of Europe: Women MEPs and Equality Policy*, and (with

Lisanne Radice and Virginia Willis) *Member of Parliament: the Job of a Backbencher*.

Giovanna Zincone is Associate Professor in Political Science at the University of Turin. She is author of *Gruppi Sociali e Sistemi Politici il Caso Donne* (*Social Groups and Political Systems: The Case of Women*).

Acknowledgements

Ten of the contributions to this book were first presented as papers at a conference on 'Women, Equality and Europe' held in the Centre of European Governmental Studies at the University of Edinburgh on 31 May and 1 June 1985. The conference was organised under the joint auspices of the Centre and the University Association for Contemporary European Studies. We wish to record grateful thanks for the assistance given by Margaret Ainslie of the Centre, Eva Evans of the Association and Richard McAllister of the department of Politics of the University of Edinburgh. The editors are grateful to the European Parliament and the British Council for financial support which made the conference possible and to Catherine Hoskyns and Joni Lovenduski for advice concerning speakers.

Invaluable help in preparing the final manuscript for publication has been provided by Jenny McDonald. Her careful and thorough work frequently speeded up unforeseen delays. Mona Bennett and Hilary Johnston also deserve our special thanks, as do Keith Povey and Muriel Hampson for their meticulous copy-editing.

Edinburgh   MARY BUCKLEY
                                                       MALCOLM ANDERSON

Introduction: Problems, Policies and Politics[1]

Mary Buckley and Malcolm Anderson

What are the problems of equality in contemporary Western Europe? Have policies been devised to resolve them? What are the obstacles to progress? These are the questions we address in this volume. The chapters which follow discuss policy initiatives in the European Community (EC) and responses to them by governments and by the women's movement. Here in the introduction we place these assessments in a broader context.

Our starting-point is the view that the politics of women's rights is more complicated than generally acknowledged. A comprehensive examination of how different problems have been isolated for treatment in Western Europe, how policies have been conceived and how they have been implemented can only be achieved through the pooled research of lawyers, economists, political scientists and sociologists. This is because policy-making in this field has legal, economic, political and social aspects. Scrutiny of law alone would offer a partial and inadequate analysis of the position of women in Western Europe. Legal provision, nevertheless, contributes a necessary foundation for equality policies.

THE NOTION OF EQUALITY

The nature of the claim for equality has not been fully worked out and awaits rigorous sharpening and more serious discussion. The notion of equality of the sexes emerged rather late in the history of ideas after philosophers had for many centuries been reflecting upon other 'great themes' such as the meaning of political stability, democracy, rhetoric, oligarchy, rights, duties and freedom. If the position of women was addressed at all, it was generally related to other political arguments. Women's roles did not constitute a central focus since most political thinkers set out to explore the characteristics of actual and/or ideal political systems. Some were preoccupied with a description and evaluation of the operation and decay of different forms of

1

government; others were concerned how best to achieve Good, Harmony or Justice. So what was said about women tended to be defined by allegedly broader concerns. Woman's place in society was either fitted into a prior argument about the polity or else empirically derived from the customs of the day. Plato, Aristotle, Hobbes, Locke and Rousseau all mentioned or discussed women, but not in their own right.[2]

It was not until the end of the nineteenth century that the position of women in society became more central for some writers. This was largely because 'liberal' notions of rights and justice implied changes in female roles. For Harriet Taylor and John Stuart Mill, for example, the good society was essentially one of education and liberty. They argued that so long as actions do not harm others, or interfere with others' liberties, one should be free to follow one's own desires and wishes. Liberty here had three dimensions: firstly, an inward domain of liberty of consciousness and freedom of opinion; secondly, liberty of tastes and pursuits; and lastly the liberty of combinations of individuals to unite. For women to enjoy these liberties alongside men, a radical change in their subordinate position was necessary.[3]

The Marxist tradition also gave greater prominence to women's roles. It was held that not only were working women, like working men, exploited in the labour force, but women suffered a double oppression because of their slave status within the family. Although Bebel's *Woman and Socialism* and Engels's *Origin of the Family, Private Property and the State* go some way towards it, the Marxist classics did not provide a systematic treatment of the various ways in which one sex was subordinate to the other.[4] More-enquiring and sensitive feminist works such as Simone de Beauvoir's *Second Sex*, Germaine Greer's *The Female Eunuch*, Sheila Rowbotham's *Women's Consciousness, Man's World*, Juliet Mitchell's *Woman's Estate*, Kate Millett's *Sexual Politics*, and Anna Coote and Beatrix Campbell's *Sweet Freedom* were written in the relatively recent past.[5] These and many other works began to explore the forms, extent and subtleties of female subjection. A more thorough probing into what the notion of equality of the sexes entails is therefore a pursuit of the twentieth century, notwithstanding nineteenth-century tracts on emancipation published in Russia, Britain, the United States of America, France and elsewhere.

EQUALITY AND POLICY

The claim for equality of the sexes came relatively late to political thought, and policies to promote this equality are even more recent. Although the political genesis of contemporary issues goes back at least to the time of the French Revolution, the Declaration of the Rights of Man of 1789 deliberately overlooked women. Women did not win the vote in European countries until the twentieth century, and only in the inter-war period did some political parties begin to support aspects of equality of the sexes. Although the principle of equality had found its way into a handful of constitutions after 1945, in the 1980s many politicians still hesitate seriously to embrace it and some argue against it. Yet an increasing number feel constrained to pay lip-service to it, either out of conviction, the pressure of electoral competition or the desire not to appear behind the times.[6]

The lack of political importance attributed to equality of the sexes is illustrated by the neglect of the gender dimension, even though it is present in most areas of policy. This was especially the case in the decades which followed the winning of votes for women – a development which occurred at different times in different countries. Economic depression, war, cold war and reconstruction effectively kept gender issues off the agenda. The Second World War did not have the same stimulating effect which the First World War had in the recognition of women's rights, because of the widespread but erroneous assumption in the 1940s that these rights had been achieved. More women were drawn into the labour force, but economic activity did not automatically lead to an increase in social and political status. When issues of equality gradually re-emerged in the 1950s and 1960s there was genuine uncertainty about their precise nature. The lines of disagreement are now much clearer.

There are four central theoretical arguments about equality relevant to a discussion about policy. First, there is the liberal notion of equality of opportunity, often challenged by those who stress the greater importance of equality of results. Equality of opportunity is the attempt to create conditions which give individuals equal access to education, training and jobs. It is then up to individuals to make the best of these opportunities. Critics, however, question whether this is real equality, if the result of the competition between individuals results in very unequal outcomes for different groups in society. Why is it, they ask, that apparent equality of opportunity in education does not result in women attaining top jobs, commensurate with their proven abilities? Equality of opportunity, it must be concluded, is just one step towards genuine equality of the sexes. Margherita Rendel pursues this theme further in Chapter 12 of this volume, 'Women's Equal Right to Equal Education'.

Second, there are the arguments (which have a family resemblance to those about equality of opportunity) that equality means treating everyone in the same way. According to this position identical treatment puts an end to discrimination. If minorities or the underprivileged can enjoy the same rights as others, then the sources of conflict will disappear. Critics of this position claim that in order to establish real equality, different categories of people must be treated differently: identical treatment reinforces inequality. Since women and men are socialised in different ways and physiological differences exist, they belong to different gender groups with different characteristics. To treat the unlike in like ways will not produce like results. The exponents of identical treatment have a ready rejoinder – to discriminate between different groups in society creates both privileges and resentments.

Third, there are the unequivocal anti-egalitarian arguments. These are various, but two are particularly relevant to contemporary Europe. One maintains that inequalities are derived from and sanctioned by a divine or a natural order. Put simply, women might be described as naturally inferior to men in strength and intellectual capacity and endowed by nature for motherhood alone. Such a view is found in various parts of the Bible and in the Koran. It is a position found in a country like the Republic of Ireland and among immigrant Muslim groups. A very different anti-egalitarian outlook is that of the 'New Right'. This school of thought holds that political liberty and economic efficiency are best or even only promoted by free markets and these inevitably produce inequalities. Inequalities are here justified as by-products of the correct way of running an economy and society. They may not be desirable in themselves but they have much less importance than prosperity and liberty (defined as the absence of constraints imposed by public authorities).

Fourth, there is the continuing debate within the women's movement about whether a concentration on the goal of equality of the sexes in a man's world means acceptance of a status quo that overlooks important differences between the sexes. Over the last decade some feminists have contended that women's values, lives and traditions are significantly different from those of men. Therefore equality in a patriarchal world cannot be achieved and is not the important goal.

Instead, more attention should be devoted to the situation, needs and values of women. Policy-makers should take seriously flexible working hours, childcare facilities, abortion, rape victims and shelter for battered women. Whether to focus on 'equality' or 'difference' or whether to attempt to combine elements of both approaches carries broad implications for feminist strategy and tactics.

These four sets of arguments are not merely 'academic' but have direct policy implications. They have to be clarified in order to legislate effectively and for the courts to administer law in a consistent manner. Those who support equality of the sexes in policy matters find that their definitions differ and consequently that their policy priorities vary. Those who take different sides on the second set of arguments will often clash on policy questions and each side will be convinced that they are the true defenders of equal rights. All schools of thought agree that the law has a role to play in achieving equality but will differ about its importance.

How best to lay the foundation of equality of the sexes through law is inevitably controversial because discriminatory practices are sustained by a complex of values, attitudes and behaviour. Equality must be far more than the statement of a legal principle that individuals should not be discriminated against on the grounds of sex. Legislation is required in many areas of social policy, embracing pay, working conditions, access to education, health provision and eligibility for social security benefits. The questions raised by these policies have become very familiar. What is the use of equal opportunities for women and men in education and employment if it does not produce equality of results? Does the content of education or the nature of recruitment and work practices benefit one sex at the expense of the other? At the basis of such questions lies the unresolved philosophical questions concerning the concept of equality.

EQUALITY AND THE EUROPEAN COMMUNITIES

There was a happy coincidence of the establishment of the European Economic Community and the growth of second wave feminism. The Treaty of Rome was the acknowledgement by European politicians that the nationalist and militarised state acting independently had become an anachronism. The states were, and have remained, important as managers and promoters of social and economic interests: one of the primary roles of the state is to defend these interests beyond its frontiers. Before 1945 military and strategic interests allied to nationalistic assertion dominated government policy. In this situation female roles were inevitably regarded as subordinate to those of men. In the new circumstances emerging at the time of the establishment of the EC, women had greater opportunity to develop a political programme. But the setting-up of the EC was just part of the broader context in which second wave feminism emerged. Improvements in the standard of living, increased job and professional possibilities as a result of economic expansion, expanding educational opportunities, changes in techniques of birth control, increased incidence of marital breakdown and the impact of the media (in particular television) all played a part in the shift in values and attitudes which took place in the 1960s.

The women's movement in Europe has many roots and took different forms. Its various contemporary expressions and actions are discussed in Joni Lovenduski's chapter below. However, one characteristic of the movement worth stressing is its marked absence of parochialism. The literature of the women's movement is international in character. Women in one country have been very ready to learn from the experience of women in others. The United Nations and European Communities have therefore been able to play important supporting roles. The UN, for example, declared 1975 to be International Women's Year and in 1985 organised a conference in Nairobi to mark the end of the decade for women. The EC has developed equality policies, initiated debates and sponsored research on women's issues, produced the bimonthly publication *Women of Europe* and other reports, compiled statistics and has arranged special seminars such as one on women in the European Community held in Madrid prior to Spanish entry. The European Communities have been and remain important in developing gender policy – much more so than the vast majority of women in the member states realise. Although the Communities are little more than the sum of the states which compose them, the governments of those states have committed themselves to some important common endeavours. One of these was to promote equality of the sexes.

All the theoretical and practical problems that the aspiration of equality for women entail are exemplified in the history of gender policy in the EC.[7] Before highlighting key developments for women in Europe some basic information about the Communities is necessary. The Treaty of Rome was signed in 1957 and the full implementation of the industrial common market was 1 January 1967. The original membership was six (France, Germany, Italy, Belgium, the Netherlands and Luxembourg), which became nine in the early 1970s (with the inclusion of Britain, Ireland and Denmark) and, finally, in the 1980s, twelve (with the accession of Greece and, more recently, Spain and Portugal). The original treaty contained one clause in Article 119 which referred specifically to the equal rights of women in employment.[8] There are two other Articles (100 and 235) which have a part to play in developing women's rights.[9] Article 100 provides for Directives to be issued to approximate provisions in the member states which 'affect the establishment or functioning of the Common Market'. The Equal Pay Directive of 1975, referred to below, was adopted under this Article. Under Article 235, the Communities can legislate when action is needed to fulfil the objectives of the EC when the necessary powers have not been conferred by another Article. The Equal Treatment Directive of 1976 was passed under this Article.

The main institutions for policy-making are the Commission, the Council of Ministers, the Court of Justice and the European Parliament.[10] The Commission is a European civil service which was initially intended to be the core of a 'supranational Europe'. It has, however, become more of an independent adviser to the Council of Ministers. The Commission is made up of 17 commissioners, each with their own departments known as Directorates General, such as Agriculture, Economic and Financial Affairs and Regional Policy. They are appointed by agreement of the member governments for a four-year renewable term of office. The United Kingdom, France, Italy, the Federal Republic of Germany and Spain all have two commissioners. The other seven smaller states each have one. Despite their particular responsibility, Commissioners are required to act independently of national interest and for the Community as a whole. Until the recent changes which divided Employment and Social Affairs, the Directorate-General for Employment, Social Affairs and Education (D-G V) has conducted various important enquiries into the position of women. Because Article 119 refers specifically to the equal rights of women in employment, it was this Directorate which played the leading role within the Commission on equality for women. In Chapter 4 below, Odile Quintin, Head of Directorate A4 (Bureau for questions concerning employment and equal treatment for women) of D-G V, gives a personal rather than official view of its work.

Unlike the Commission, the Council of Ministers is composed of members who officially represent national governments. Each member state has a permanent representative in Brussels and there are also ministerial meetings in the major policy areas such as finance, energy, transport and agriculture. The Council for the most part sanctions rather than initiates legislation since it is often engaged in responding to proposals from the Commission. The Council also has the authority to request the Commission to undertake any studies which the Council considers desirable to attain common objectives. It is in the Council of Ministers and in the European Council (the meeting of heads of government) that the vital decisions about resources are made.

The Council of Ministers can enact Regulations, Directives, Decisions or Recommendations and Opinions. Directives have been particularly important in the promotion of legislation to achieve equality, such as the Equal Pay Directive of 1975, Equal Treatment Directive of 1976 and Social Security Directive of 1978. Directives are legally binding but individual states are free to select the most suitable form of implementation in their own legal system. Angela Byre's chapter in this volume explores legal aspects of the monitoring, enforcement and interpretation of the women's directives, and in two case-studies Catherine Hoskyns discusses the way in which the Federal Republic of Germany and the Republic of Ireland have responded to the Equal Pay and Equal Treatment Directives. The reaction of the Dutch government to the Social Security Directive is described in Ina Sjerps's contribution, which also offers one feminist response to EC and national initiatives. By following the spirit of Directives, member states are supposed to bring national legislation into line with Community law. Frequently, however, deadlines are not kept and procedures are adopted which evade Community intent.

Unlike Directives, Regulations are both binding and have direct legal force in member states. Decisions are more narrowly addressed to a specific government, firm or individual and are binding on the parties concerned. Much weaker are Recommendations or Opinions which are purely advisory and therefore have no mandatory authority.

While the Commission increasingly takes action to further equality of the sexes in keeping with its view of general Community interests, the Council of Ministers has to approve all changes. When legislation has been passed both the Commission and Council of Ministers are formally responsible for its implementation. Yet it must be stressed that the success of EC policy depends upon the compliance and support of national governments. Enforcement takes place through the legal systems of the member states. In this sense, enforcement is voluntary. However, infringement proceedings can be taken by the Commission and cases are referred to the Court of Justice. Angela Byre's chapter also examines selected cases and their outcomes.

Disputes between the Commission as a watchdog of Community law and a member state are referred as a last resort to the Court of Justice for adjudication. States which fail to adhere to EC equality policies can therefore be brought to court. The Court has eleven judges and five advocates-general who are appointed for renewable six-year terms. Judgements are independently reached and not biased in favour of the interests of any one member state. The Court's decision is final and binding. To date, the majority of cases brought by the Commission have won verdicts in the Commission's favour. Cases can also be brought against member states by other member states. Another major role performed by the Court is that of interpreting points of EC law referred to it by courts in the member states.

Just as the Commission can refer infringements to the Court, so individuals in the member states have recourse to their own national courts and to the European Court if they consider that breaches of community law have taken place. A recent change in retirement policy in Britain was brought about in this way. Helen Marshall, a dietician, wished to continue working until the age of 65, but had been dismissed at 62. She took her case to an industrial tribunal which decided in her favour. Subsequently the health authority won an appeal and then the Court of Appeal referred the case to the European Court of Justice. Marshall won a ruling from the Court of Justice in February 1986 which stated that the British system of compulsory retirement for men and women was discriminatory.[11] Yet individual actions have been rare on issues of equal pay and equal treatment. Jennifer Corcoran's contribution to this volume focuses on why this is the case and pays particular attention to enforcement procedures in Belgium and Greece.

The European Parliament, which has been directly elected since 1979, has a limited but potentially crucial role. The first European elections produced six main political groups: Socialists; European People's Party; European Democrats; Communists; Liberals and Democrats; and European Progressive Democrats. Members of the European Parliament (MEPs) sit in trans-national groups according to party affiliation. Plenary sessions are held on average one week in every month and take place in the Palais de l'Europe in Strasbourg. Parliament cannot formally initiate bills (this is the job of the Commission) but it can refuse its consent. Parliament has therefore

limited legislative powers but this does not mean that the work of the
Parliament is insignificant.

The importance of the Parliament for the promotion of equality of
the sexes lies in the questions it raises, the debates it initiates, and the
research reports it commissions. The Parliament has advocated
adoption of an ambitious policy to promote equal opportunities, and in
January 1984 called upon the institutions of the EC and its member
states to make new efforts in this direction. Parliament's detailed work
is conducted in eighteen specialised committees. One of these carries
special responsibility for the position of women in the Community and
this helps to broaden the debate on discriminatory practices.[12]
Interestingly, more women are elected to the European parliament
than to national parliaments. This raises the question of whether this
higher female profile works to the advantage of women. In asking 'Do
women MEPs make a difference?', Elizabeth Vallance argues in
Chapter 8 that while they do not make a great deal, their presence must
be a positive factor in promoting awareness of the position of women.

FROM THE TREATY OF ROME TO THE SECOND ACTION PROGRAMME

Although equality policies have developed in the EC, the promotion
of equality of the sexes was not a major aim of the founders of the EC
or of the governments which committed their states to membership of
it. Despite this, much legislation which champions equality has
resulted in the member states, precisely because EC regulations make
this necessary. This gain for women has stemmed from the inclusion in
the Treaty of Rome of Article 119. In short, Article 119 bound states to
the principle of equal pay of equal work. This article was not included
out of a serious attempt to establish equality of the sexes in the states of
Western Europe. Rather, it was inspired by the desire to ensure equal
competition between states. One aspect of this was the guarantee that
women would not be paid at lower rates than men in the member states
to avoid any state gaining competitive advantage over others. From
this modest starting-point many issues have been put on the agenda.
The responsibility of the EC for equality of the sexes has expanded
beyond the initial intent. An important landmark came in October
1972 when, after a Paris summit meeting, the Commission presented
the Council of Ministers with a Social Action Programme. One of the
aims was:

to bring about a situation in which equality between men and women obtains in the labour market throughout the Community, through the improvement of economic and psychological conditions and the social and educational infrastructure.[13]

This broad goal extended the narrow confines of Article 119. It recognised that there were social, educational and psychological preconditions for the achievement of equal pay. Thus the EC has seriously contributed not just to research into the position of women, but has made, and is continuing to make, efforts to broaden the brief of the Community's responsibility for women and to define more explicitly what this commitment entails.

Increasingly, the broad prerequisites for successful equality initiatives are being recognised. A recent review of the Community Action Programme on the Promotion of Equal Opportunities for Women 1982–5 realistically acknowledged that 'much remains to be done' and concluded that 'comprehensive and diversified policy is needed to achieve concrete results in the equal opportunities field'.[14] The buzz words and phrases of the 1980s appear to be 'more action' of a 'diversified', 'intensive' and 'full-scale nature'. The boundaries of what is relevant to the promotion of equality are being drawn wider by researchers and feminists.

Nevertheless, since the European Community is essentially an economic Community, the crucial dimension of equality in which it is currently involved is access to jobs in conditions of high unemployment. Although most feminists define the key issues for women as much broader than job access, it remains a very basic issue, especially with the increase in the participation of women in the labour market. Women seeking employment, and holding jobs, has risen sharply since 1970. However, women in employment are not equal with men for several reasons. First, a large number of women work part-time. This ranges from 46 per cent of working women in Britain down to 17 per cent in Italy and Luxembourg. Second, there are relatively few women in posts of responsibility which have higher salaries. Third, women are frequently subordinated to men in the family because of a traditional division of labour or because of a persistence of traditional attitudes. Fourth, equal pay is not yet a reality despite Equal Pay acts. In their contribution to this anthology, Ursula Barry and Pauline Jackson examine the significance of part-time labour for women in the north and south of Ireland and point out that the majority of such workers are unskilled, low paid and lack the protection of labour legislation.

So the fundamental importance of the EC is the treaty-based assertion of the right to equality in employment. On this much has already been built and can still be built. The Community is cumbersome and likely to become more so with the increase in the number of members, and it is accused of being bureaucratic, but it is nevertheless one vital motor for change in women's condition. In addition to making a positive contribution on issues such as equal pay, equal treatment at work and equality in social security systems, the European Communities have shown that they have the potential to stimulate change in several related, but distinct, areas. For example, the substance of education and training was tackled in the Communities' Social Action programme of 1974 and in the New Action Programme on the Promotion of Equal Opportunities for Women 1982–5. Equality in education and training is a necessary, if not a sufficient, condition for equal access to jobs.

The EC is also encouraging changes in social attitudes. These are vital both for a non-sexist content to education and for the results of equal opportunity in education to lead to equal and fair access to jobs. Men are often still regarded as having priority for jobs on the breadwinner principle and some men still object to their wives working or to having female colleagues. Progress in this area is necessarily slow but the Communities are making some impact by sponsoring surveys on social attitudes, through publications and by information meetings.

In addition, the Communities have drawn attention to the fact that the traditional division of labour has forced women into occupations such as secretarial work, textile manufacture and the 'caring' professions. While the Commission cannot change this situation it can highlight its significance for levels of pay and attitudes towards 'women's work'. The EC has also underlined the point that systems of work often make women's working lives more complicated and arduous than those of men. Flexible hours, flexible working week, parental leave and other facilities which can help women are now also on the European agenda even if they have low priority.

There are, of course, issues which many feminists believe should have a more prominent place on the political agenda of the 1980s. These include: the position of immigrant and black women in Europe; violence against women; and forced prostitution and traffic in women. It is easy to pay lip-service to the importance of these issues. But channelling resources into research and action is another matter. They are problems with low political salience and therefore remain neglected.

However, past policies are re-examined by the institutions of the EC and 'new' issues are tabled. The Commission, for instance, has just submitted a Second Action Programme 1986–90, which calls for more intensive action in the areas named by the first Action Programme 1982–5, and backs the broader goal of developing a 'citizen's Europe' or a 'people's Europe'.[15] Described as a medium-term Community Programme, it adopts many aims, including: improvement of the application of existing legal provisions in member states; intensification of a consciousness-raising campaign to reach a wider target public and also relevant professionals such as lawyers and labour inspectors; and examination of the position of women in the new member states of Greece, Spain and Portugal.

The Second Action Programme views education and training as the 'root' of the promotion of equality and so singles these out for continued attention. This is associated with concern about the significance of the new technologies for women's employment. But education and training facilities do not guarantee equality. A *sine qua non* of equality in the workplace is the sharing of family and occupational responsibilities. In keeping with this the Commission has reviewed its commitment to changing attitudes and has also given its support to positive action in certain sectors, such as banking, with a view to the desegregation of employment. In addition, it proposes that guidelines for future community actions be drawn up to address the problem of single-parent families, single women, immigrant women, self-employed women, women wishing to return to the labour force after a career break, and physically and mentally handicapped women. This broadening of the Community brief to include different categories of women reflects a growing recognition of the various needs and problems which different groups of women face, on top of their common disadvantages in education and employment.

CULTURE, WORK AND POLITICS

There is a subtle interaction between the culture (the attitudes and values) of a society, the economic role performed by a certain category of the population and relative access to political power. Culture, economic roles and political power influence one another in different ways in different historical periods. In the 1980s, political action can have important effects both on the labour market and on social attitudes.

The attitudes and values which support and constrain female roles and the perception of those roles by both women and men have been changing in recent years. However, Europe is a large and complex cultural area and generalisations which refer to the whole continent are hazardous. Until recently, there was indeed little comparable evidence for the individual European countries – the classic survey of political culture by Gabriel Almond and Sidney Verba published in 1963 did not dwell on the connections between women's attitudes and their social roles.[16] Almond and Verba admitted that the extent to which women tended to 'live in' the community and polity, affected in an important way the politics of a country. Their survey, which covered the United Kingdom, Germany and Italy (as well as the USA and Mexico), was not sufficiently detailed on women to form any firm conclusions. Of more significance are the recent surveys by Eurobarometer on behalf of the European Communities on the position of women in all the member states. The results of these are interesting, but should be used with caution because the questions are not very refined and may not carry precisely the same meaning for respondents in different countries.

The whole field of cultural attitudes is, therefore, one which allows for considerable speculation. It has been assumed, until recently, that there has been a North–South 'gradient' of attitude – there was a greater readiness to accept political equality, access to prestigious professions and a changed role in the family for women in the North than to the South of Europe. Men in Southern Europe had a more 'macho' self-image and a greater determination to dominate in relations with women than was the case in Northern Europe. All the indications in terms of social policy were that until the 1970s this was, broadly speaking, correct. The situation since has become more complex. The struggles over divorce and abortion in Italy and the fundamental changes which have taken place in Spain are making an impact on values in these countries. Zincone, in Chapter 10 of this volume, is undoubtedly correct in characterising Italy as a 'middling' country now with regard to women's access to political arenas, and this represents a significant development. By contrast, a North European country, the Republic of Ireland, manifests the least openness to women's autonomy and independence. But there are changes in attitudes affecting the position of women in Ireland. According to one opinion poll, 57 per cent of Irish voters in the month before the June 1986 referendum supported the Dublin government's proposals to introduce divorce; 36 per cent claimed they would vote against divorce and 7 per cent were undecided.[17] Yet in the referendum on divorce, 36.5 per cent voted in favour of change and 63.5 per cent against, in a turnout of just over 59 per cent.[18] Even though this result reversed the views expressed in early opinion polls, it was consistent with the anti-abortion referendum of 1983 which was supported by a two-to-one majority. The strength of the Church persists in the Republic of Ireland and along with it the pervasiveness of traditional attitudes.

There are, therefore, significant changes, but old attitudes still die hard all over the continent and are frequently given an extended life by highly practical concerns. Some changes in legislation that is based on the old attitudes involve increases in public expenditure at a time when governments regard them as inexpedient. This is particularly the case with attempts to change social security systems.

The most important changes still to take place are in the values and attitudes of both women and men. Political demands for equality and legal rules enforcing equality have limited impact. When legislation is based on an inaccurate assumption of acceptance of equality in everyday social relations, it is unlikely to be successful. More equal social relations can only come about by a complex educational process. Part of this process is an awareness of the need for changes in the tasks performed by women in society. At the moment, women are in subordinate positions in the labour market. Despite some exhortations by governments in the other direction, there is more pressure by women and on women to take up paid employment. Eurostat statistics show that, of the 88 million women in Europe between the ages of 15 and 65, 32 million are in paid employment. This amounts to just over one-third of the female population in this age group.[19] National variations, however, are quite marked. While 58 per cent of Danish women between 15 and 64 work, only 15 per cent of Greek women fall into this category. Research indicates that this immense variation across the member states cannot be explained by women deliberately deciding not to work. Survey data show that most women, if given the choice, would enter paid employment.[20] Yet despite the great increase in the last twenty-five years of the number of working women and the number seeking work, equality of access to jobs is still far off. Women are much more likely than men to be without employment, or in low-paid jobs, or in jobs without significant responsibility.

This lack of equality in part reflects a lack of aspiration on the part of women, and a defensiveness on the part of men. It is also an expression of women's relative lack of power in society. As women acquire better education and more qualifications, their position on the labour market should improve. Yet there is unlikely to be radical change without organised and determined pressure. Lovenduski, in her chapter, makes the telling point that the women's movement can rally very successfully on single issues such as abortion, but it is less effective in the sense discussed by Zincone – that of forcing access into influential political arenas. Even committed and concerted action by women on single issues does not inevitably lead to success, since it can result in an effective reaction on the part of the establishment. Joyce Outshoorn's discussion of the politics of abortion, in Chapter 13, illustrates this point.

Women are divided on the utility of gaining access into political arenas. Some back off from 'male-dominated' areas, characterising them as hierarchical, competitive, aggressive and ultimately unconstructive. Others maintain that there are powerful interests and political sentiments which bind groups of men and women together. Women have therefore to force access to the male preserves of political parties, trade unions and the legal profession. The women's movement, they contend, can heighten the consciousness of women and encourage public awareness of the under-representation of women in political parties, in legislatures and in public authorities. But change within political parties depends in part on individuals and relatively small groups persuading their male colleagues that women have the competence, public acceptability and both a valid and an important contribution to make as women. This applies to the appointment of individual women as well as to the setting-up of particular institutions to further the interests of women. An example of the latter was the establishment in 1981 of a ministry for Women's Rights in France. Its life was, however, shortlived, as it was abolished in 1986, with minimal protest, by the incoming right-wing government. It is now timely for its successes and shortcomings to be analysed. In Chapter 11, Michelle Coquillat, formerly a member of the cabinet of Yvette Roudy, the Minister for Women, tackles part of this task by reviewing its main achievements from the point of view of an 'insider'.

The closure of the Ministry gives additional credence to Pippa Norris's argument in Chapter 9 that political parties play an important role in the promotion of women's interests. Set up in France under Mitterrand, a Socialist President, the Ministry was closed under the 'cohabitation' of a Socialist President, and a Gaullist Prime Minister, Jacques Chirac, supported by a right-wing National Assembly. Norris examines the effects of political parties upon women's earnings and position, and concludes that Socialist governments have reduced pay differentials and promoted legislation on sex discrimination. Some political parties are therefore more likely than others to show practical as well as rhetorical commitment to women's rights.

Space and the unevenness of research limit the breadth of topics which can be covered in this volume. The editors regret that analyses of the position of immigrant women, black women, handicapped women and battered women are absent. Discussions of the role of trade unions and women's informal groups are missing too. These areas were omitted not by choice but because of difficulties in finding authors. A second volume is surely needed to supplement this one and to provide a more exhaustive assessment of the lives of women in Europe and a more thorough appraisal of the way forward for equal rights.

However, the chapters which follow elaborate further the legal, economic, political and social dimensions to the promotion of equality of the sexes introduced here. These contributions show the interrelatedness of policy areas, the extent of the EC's success and what inhibits further progress. They are intended to give greater depth and seriousness to policy debates. These take place too infrequently in the political arenas that really matter. As Ann Clwyd (Labour) observed in the House of Commons on 14 May 1986: '[since] I have been a Member of this House there have been few debates on equality between men and women, and they have always been greeted with ridicule by Conservative members. This is a serious subject which ought to be debated properly.'[21] We wholeheartedly agree.

Notes

1. We thank Catherine Hoskyns and Richard McAllister for their comments on this chapter.
2. See Rosemary Agonito, *History of Ideas on Woman: A Source Book*, Capricorn Books, New York 1977; Susan Moller Okin, *Women in Western Political Thought*, Princeton University Press, Princeton, New Jersey, 1979.
3. Max Lerner (ed.), *Essential Works of John Stuart Mill*, Bantam, New York, 1965; John Stuart Mill, *The Subjection of Women*, D. Appleton and Co., New York, 1870; John Stuart Mill and Harriet Taylor, *Essays on Inequality*, University of Chicago Press, 1830. Expression of an earlier liberal view can be found in Mary Wollstonecraft, *Vindication of the Rights of Woman*, Penguin, Harmondsworth, 1978.
4. August Bebel, *Woman Under Socialism*, Schocken Books, New York,

1971; Frederich Engels, *Origin of the Family, Private Property and the State*, Pathfinder Press, New York, 1972.

5. Simone de Beauvoir, *The Second Sex*, New English Library, London, 1970; Germaine Greer, *The Female Eunuch*, Paladin, London, 1971; Sheila Rowbotham, *Women's Consciousness, Man's World*, Penguin, Harmondsworth, 1973; Juliet Mitchell, *Woman's Estate*, Penguin, Harmondsworth, 1976; Kate Millett, *Sexual Politics*, Virago, 1977; Anna Coote and Beatrix Campbell, *Sweet Freedom*, Picador, London, 1982.

6. There is a growing literature on women and politics. Key contributions include: Joni Lovenduski and Jill Hills (eds), *The Politics of the Second Electorate*, Routledge & Kegan Paul, London, 1981; Vicky Randall, *Women and Politics*, Macmillan, London, 1982; Janet Siltanen and Michelle Stanworth (eds), *Women and the Public Sphere*, Hutchinson, London, 1984; Joni Lovenduski, *Women and European Politics: Contemporary Feminism and Public Policy*, Wheatsheaf, Brighton, 1986.

7. How the EC affects women is discussed in Rights of Women Europe, *Women's Rights and the EC*, published by Rights of Women Europe, 1983.

8. Article 119 states:

> Each Member State shall during the first stage ensure and subsequently maintain the application of the principle of equal remuneration for the same work as between male and female workers.
>
> For the purpose of this Article, remuneration shall be taken to mean the ordinary basic or minimum wage or salary and any additional emoluments whatsoever payable directly or indirectly, whether in cash or in kind, by the employer to the worker and arising out of the worker's employment.
>
> Equal remuneration without discrimination based on sex means:
>
> (a) that remuneration for the same work at piece rates shall be calculated on the basis of the same unit of measurement;
> (b) that remuneration for work at time-rates shall be the same for the same job.
>
> (*Treaty establishing The European Economic Community*, Rome, 25 March, 1957, Her Majesty's Stationery Office, London, 1962, p. 45.)

9. Article 100 states:

> The Council shall, by a unanimous decision, on a proposal of the Commission, issue directives for the approximation of such legislative and administrative provisions of Member States as directly affect the establishment or operation of the Common Market.
>
> The Assembly and the Economic and Social Committee shall be consulted in the case of directives the implementation of which would involve amending legislation in one or more Member States. (Ibid, p. 38)

Article 235 is as follows:

> Where action by the Community appears necessary to achieve one of the objectives of the Community, within the framework of the Common

Market, and where this Treaty has not provided for the necessary powers of action, the Council shall adopt the appropriate provisions by a unanimous decision, after consulting the Assembly. (Ibid, p. 73)

10. A useful introduction to the EC is provided by Juliet Lodge (ed.), *Institutions and Policies of the European Community*, Frances Pinter, London, 1983.
11. *The Sunday Times*, 2 March 1986.
12. Useful publications include: European Parliament, *The Situation of Women in Europe*, May 1984; European Parliament, Secretariat Directorate-General for Research and Documentation, *The Position of Women in the European Community*, June 1981.
13. Supplement No. 15 to *Women of Europe*, Commission of the European Communities, Brussels, March, 1984, X/118/84-EN, p. 3.
14. Supplement No. 23 to *Women of Europe*, X/77/86-EN, p. 1.
15. Ibid.
16. Gabriel A. Almond and Sidney Verba, *The Civic Culture*, 2nd edn, Little, Brown & Company, Boston, 1965.
17. *Guardian*, 6 May 1986.
18. *Guardian*, 28 June 1986.
19. Supplement No. 20 to *Women of Europe*, Commission of the European Communities, Brussels, 1985, X/149/85-EN, p. 5.
20. Supplement No. 16 to *Women of Europe*, Commission of the European Communities, Brussels, 1984, X/220/84-EN, p. 22.
21. *House of Commons, Parliamentary Debates*, 14 May 1986, columns 813–14.

1 Applying Community Standards on Equality
Angela Byre

It is often argued that the law can achieve little in terms of countering discrimination at the workplace, and that positive actions and policies are the real means of remedying discriminatory practices and righting the balance of opportunities in employment. However, as a means of providing a floor of basic rights for the individual and identifying the types of practices which should no longer be regarded as generally acceptable, the law can act as an initial catalyst to change. This chapter takes as its basic framework for discussion the EEC's efforts to establish common legal standards on equality across a Community of West European countries with widely differing traditions and legal frameworks. Community legislation on equal pay and equal treatment is discussed and a number of problems of application and interpretation are considered. The Community's approach to the key issue of indirect discrimination is also briefly examined.

LEGAL FRAMEWORK

The basic Community-level provisions on equal pay are in the 1957 Treaty of Rome which established the European Economic Community (EEC). Article 119 of the Treaty provides that during a first stage (expiring on 31 December 1961 for the original six member states of Belgium, France, West Germany, Italy, Luxembourg and the Netherlands; and binding on Denmark, Ireland and the United Kingdom from 1 January 1973, on Greece from 1 January 1981, and on Portugal and Spain from 1 January 1986, on their accession to the Community): 'Each Member State shall ensure and subsequently maintain the application of the principle that men and women should receive equal pay for equal work.' The Article continues (with perhaps unintentional use of gender-based language) as follows:

> For the purpose of this Article, 'pay' means the ordinary basic or minimum wage or salary and any other consideration, whether in cash or in kind, which the worker receives, directly or indirectly, in

20

respect of his employment from his employer. Equal pay without discrimination based on sex means: (a) that pay for the same work at piece rates shall be calculated on the basis of the same unit of measurement; (b) that pay for work at time rates shall be the same for the same job.

As with other elements of the founding Treaty, the equal pay provisions were originally prompted by economic factors and, in particular, a concern to ensure that competition in the member states was not distorted by the employment of women at lower rates than men for the same work. The social significance of such provisions soon became recognised too, and plans for specific Community legislation to amplify the Treaty provisions and assist the elimination of continuing national disparities and the harmonisation of national laws implementing the equal pay principle were included as 'priority actions' in the Social Action Programme adopted by the EEC's Council of Ministers in February 1974.[1] By early 1975, in International Women's Year, an Equal Pay Directive had been approved, based on the premise (expressed most clearly in the Directive's original draft Preamble) that it was necessary to improve and harmonise national laws 'in order that the growing number of female workers may benefit equally from progress in regard to workers' living and working conditions as part of a balanced social and economic development of the Community'.

The Equal Pay Directive[2] enlarges upon the Article 119 provisions of the Treaty in a number of ways. Most notably, the principle of equal pay is clarified as meaning:

> for the same work or for work to which equal value is attributed, the elimination of all discrimination on grounds of sex with regard to all aspects and conditions of remuneration. In particular, where a job classification system is used for determining pay, it must be based on the same criteria for both men and women and so drawn up as to exclude any discrimination on grounds of sex. (Article 1)

The Directive further provides (in Article 2) that member states should introduce into their national systems such measures as are necessary to enable employees who consider themselves wronged by failure to apply the equal pay principle to pursue their claims by judicial process after possible recourse to other competent authorities.

In theory at least, the introduction of the 'equal value' concept here enlarges the scope of the equal pay principle by allowing for broader comparisons across jobs and not simply between those doing identical work. The problem of job segregation, however, in a world in which, in practice, work is still commonly segregated into men's and women's work, has proved a considerable obstacle to full implementation of the equal pay principle. This has been the case even with the aid of the Directive's broader provisions – especially since the courts have required actual comparisons to be made and have not accepted any 'hypothetical male' comparisons (i.e. consideration of what a man would have been paid had he been employed in the particular job in question). As it stands, therefore, the Directive even with its 'equal value' extension can only be effective in areas where both men and women are employed. The status of this and other equality Directives is also an issue of difficulty and some uncertainty, since although it has been established that certain basic Treaty provisions are directly enforceable by individuals irrespective of national implementing legislation, the question of such 'direct effect' for a Directive has not been so definitively answered by the European Court. There are also added complications when 'direct effect' in the private sector is in issue, as elaborated below.

The Article 119 Treaty provisions and the 1975 Equal Pay Directive provide the basic framework at Community level for establishing equal pay rights and obligations. The legal framework for guaranteeing other aspects of equality in employment has been established in subsequent Directives – the 1976 Directive on equal treatment for men and women as regards access to employment, promotion, vocational training and working conditions;[3] and the 1978 Directive on equal treatment for men and women in matters of State social security[4] – and further measures are in the pipeline (notably for a Directive relating to equality in occupational social security schemes to complement the 1978 Directive).[5] Each of these Directives is self-contained, and though building on the same basic principle of equal treatment each has been subject to separate interpretation by the courts.

MONITORING, ENFORCEMENT AND INTERPRETATION

Having established a legal framework for equality rights and obligations at Community level, questions then arise as to how these provisions are to be implemented nationally in the context of widely differing traditions and legal systems, how they are ultimately to be enforced, and whether the Community provisions themselves require further interpretation in order to be fully effective.

The European Commission is itself charged with the general duty of monitoring and ensuring implementation of Community legislation. In the area of equal pay and equal treatment, this has taken the form of: (a) an initial monitoring activity, via questionnaires to and reports from member states' governments on the application of the basic Treaty and Directive provisions in their particular countries; and (b), on the basis of this feedback and analysis (and also, more recently, of practical researches undertaken by the special independent network of national lawyers and practitioners set up within the context of the EEC's 1982–5 Equality Action Programme), action by the Commission against individual governments, via formal infringement proceedings before the European Court, to secure full implementation of the Community law requirements. Such actions against the UK government recently prompted the introduction of belated regulations on equal pay for work of equal value, and have led to new government proposals to enable women to continue working until the same age as men.

In addition to enforcement by the Commission, Community law also creates basic rights which are not dependent on the content of detailed national legislation and the promptings of the Commission in this regard, and which are directly enforceable and may be relied upon by individuals before their national courts. It has, for example, been clearly established that the principle of equal pay in Article 119 of the Treaty applies 'directly' in this way, and without the need for more detailed implementing measures on the part of the Community or the member states, in respect of all forms of direct and overt discrimination which may be identified solely with the aid of the criteria of equal work and equal pay referred to in Article 119. This ruling was given by the Luxembourg-based European Court in the second of three cases taken by an ex-air hostess from Belgium (*Defrenne* v. *Sabena*).[6] The Court had been asked for such a ruling under the 'preliminary reference' procedure, which enables national courts to refer issues of interpretation of the Treaty and the Directives to the Court for a preliminary ruling. The Court was, however, careful to draw a distinction between cases of direct and overt discrimination where the Treaty could be directly applied, and those involving indirect and disguised discrimination which could only be identified 'by reference to more explicit implementing provisions of a Community or national character' rather than the bare Treaty provisions themselves.

This in turn raises the question of whether the more extensive provisions of Community Directives can be of direct effect irrespective of national implementing legislation. The issue is of particular importance given the variety of ways in which Directives are (or in some cases are not) implemented nationally – member states being obliged only to implement Directives 'as to the result to be achieved' and able to choose the 'form and methods' of such implementation.[7] The issue of Directives' direct effect has been raised before the European Court on a number of occasions, especially in references from the UK courts, but has not as yet been fully answered. In a recent German case, however, the European Court indicated that direct effect was a possibility where some or all of a Directive's provisions were sufficiently precisely drafted to be relied upon in themselves (*Harz* v. *Firma Tradax*).[8] The particular Directive provisions under consideration in this and a parallel German reference (*Von Colson and Kamann* v. *Land Nordrhein-Westfalen*)[9] were not, however, deemed to be sufficiently precise to be of direct effect. The *Harz* case concerned a business studies graduate who was not considered for a vacancy for which she applied with an agricultural supplies firm on the grounds that only male applicants would be considered. The local Hamburg Labour Court found that there had been discrimination on grounds of sex in the selection process, and asked the European Court for a preliminary ruling as to the sanctions required under the 1976 Equal Treatment Directive where there was proven discrimination in access to employment. German law provided only for those discriminated against in such circumstances to receive nominal damages linked to the costs of filing a complaint. The Court ruled that the Directive did not require a sanction of engagement to be imposed; nor did it 'include any unconditional and sufficiently precise obligation which, in the absence of implementing measures adopted within the prescribed time limits, may be relied on by an individual in order to obtain specific compensation under the Directive where that is not provided for or permitted under national law'. The Court added that although the Directive gave member states the freedom to choose between different solutions appropriate to its objective, it did require them to reflect adequately any damage suffered and to go beyond a mere symbolic sum if they chose to penalise breaches of the prohibition on discrimination by an award of compensation. When the issue returned to the German courts, the complainant was awarded compensation amounting to six months' pay.

The Court's line of argument on the direct effect issue in the German cases has been confirmed most recently in a UK reference to the Court (*Marshall* v. *Southampton & South West Hampshire Health Authority*).[10] The Court reiterated its view that where the provisions of a Directive appear to be unconditional and sufficiently precise as far as their subject-matter is concerned, they may be directly relied upon by individuals. Unlike the provisions tested in the German cases, the specific Directive provisions in issue here (prohibiting discrimination on grounds of sex with regard to working conditions, including the conditions governing dismissal) were held to be sufficiently precise and unconditional to have direct effect in this way. The complainant in the case had been dismissed by the local health authority which employed her solely because she had passed the retirement age for women applied by that authority, namely the qualifying age for a state pension which was 60 for women as compared with 65 for men. The Court held that this general policy on dismissal linked to different state pensionable ages was discriminatory and contrary to the relevant provisions of the 1976 Equal Treatment Directive, and that these Directive provisions in turn could be directly relied upon by the complainant against her employer. The Court added that Directives essentially impose obligations on the member states to whom they are addressed and not on individuals. Thus while Community provisions which have direct effect may be relied upon by individuals against a member state or a state authority acting in its capacity as employer (as in this case), the same would not necessarily be true against private individuals and employers. This apparently arbitrary distinction between private- and public-sector employments could be avoided if Community provisions were correctly implemented in national laws in the first place.

As the above discussion makes clear, the enforceability of Community standards and their interaction with differing national laws involves a considerable degree of interpretation by the courts. Below, some of the leading rulings from the European Court in interpretation of the equal pay principle (in the Treaty, in the Directive and in national laws) are discussed, as a means of further illustrating the scope for interpretation and the ambiguities of the Community legislation itself, and the sometimes less than clear-cut answers to preliminary questions given by the Court.

The principle of equal pay for men and women, outlined in Article 119 of the Treaty, is defined in the 1975 Directive as meaning: 'for the same work or work to which equal value is attributed, the elimination of all discrimination on grounds of sex with regard to all aspects and conditions of remuneration'.[11] Where a man and a woman are doing equal work for unequal pay, there is a presumption that the inequality in pay is due to the sex of the worker concerned. It would seem that this presumption can be rebutted if the employer can adduce evidence to show that the difference in pay between the workers doing equal work is due to 'the operation of factors which are unconnected with any discrimination on grounds of sex' – a comment made by the European Court in one of the early UK references to the Court (*Macarthys Ltd* v. *Smith*).[12] The case had been brought by a stockist manageress, who claimed equal pay on the basis of comparing her work and pay with a male predecessor in the job who had received higher pay. The Court ruled that such comparisons could be made and that the 'equal pay for equal work' principle should not be restricted by any requirement of 'contemporaneous' comparisons. A central question for interpretation regarding the equal pay principle concerns the nature of the justification that is required from the employer in order successfully to rebut the presumption of sex discrimination which arises whenever a man and a woman are paid unequally for doing equal work.

'Discrimination on grounds of sex' appears to cover both the treating of one worker less favourably than another on the ground of his or her sex – direct sex discrimination – and situations where an employer treats men and women alike in a formal sense as regards their pay but imposes conditions or requirements which exclude or impede workers of one sex from receiving equal pay for equal work and which are not objectively justifiable – indirect discrimination. This interpretation of indirect discrimination is based on the Opinion given by Mr Advocate General Warner in another UK reference to the European Court (*Jenkins* v. *Kingsgate Clothing Productions Ltd*).[13] No definition of indirect discrimination has yet been given by the Court, though this is clearly an area of increasing concern since, in practice, discrimination is moving to a less direct level either intentionally or otherwise. The interim Opinion of the European Court's Advocate General rather than the final ruling of the full Court is referred to in the *Jenkins* case, since the Court itself was somewhat ambivalent on a number of key issues – not least the nature of the employer's justification and the question of whether the principle of equal pay applies to cases of unintentional as well as intentional indirect discrimination. The Court's equivocation ultimately led the Employment Appeal Tribunal to decide the case in the complainant's favour without relying on Community law. The case concerned a female employee who worked on a part-time basis at a clothing factory and brought a claim for the same hourly rate of pay as a male employee doing like work on a full-time basis who received a higher hourly rate of pay. It was claimed that, even if unintentional, the adverse impact on women at the factory of the employer's policy regarding rates of pay for full- and part-time workers was indirectly discriminatory and contrary to the principle of equal pay unless it could be objectively justified.

The term 'equal work' essentially means work which is regarded as comparable for the purpose of entitling the workers who do that work to receive equal pay. At its narrowest, it includes identical work and broadly similar work. It also covers work which is not the same or broadly similar but to which equal value is attributed. The process of attributing equal value to dissimilar work is commonly done by means of a job evaluation scheme. However, if there is no job evaluation scheme, the European Court has held (*Commission* v. *United Kingdom*)[14] that there must be other means whereby a worker who considers that her work is of equal value to another's may pursue her claims by judicial process.

The purpose of an employer's justification is to rebut the inference that unequal pay is based on sex discrimination. Thus once a worker has shown that her or his work is equal to the work being done for the employer by a worker of the other sex, the employer has to show that the reasons for paying unequal remuneration are not directly or indirectly based on the sex of the workers concerned: for example that the inequality is not due to some sex-based generalised assumption such as that men are more capable than women of doing the work or that men deserve to be paid more because they are the natural breadwinners for their families. The employer should also show that there is an objective justification for the pay inequality. On the narrowest view, such a justification would be confined to factors personal to the workers concerned in doing the job – for example, greater length of service or higher qualifications. A broader view would enable an employer to justify the inequality if it could be shown that it was objectively necessary in terms of the needs of the business – for instance, that it was necessary to require workers to be full-time before receiving the standard hourly rate of pay since machines had to run continuously and be fully utilised. The broadest view would enable an employer to justify the inequality on the basis of so-called market forces: for example, situations in which an employer pays a man more than a woman because the man earned more in his previous job and will not work for less; or where the employer cannot afford the cost of paying men and women equally; or where the better-paid job has traditionally been highly rewarded because of the shortages of workers with the requisite skills in the particular area of employment.

The Community law position here has not yet been clarified, given the somewhat equivocal pronouncements of the European Court in the *Jenkins* case cited above. However, on the basis of the more specific Opinion of the Court's Advocate General in that case, the position would seem to be as follows. The argument that equal pay is too expensive for the employer is not a legitimate justification for unequal pay, because it would frustrate the central purpose of the equal pay principle. Arguments based on the 'going rate' are also no defence, if the 'going rate' reflects sex discrimination within the labour market. The employer should therefore give a justification that is objective (not merely based on good intentions and the absence of a discriminatory motive) and that is free from indirect as well as direct sex discrimination. The justification need not, however, be confined to factors personal to the workers concerned, but may include commercial benefits to the employer.

Another key issue for interpretation is that of comparability. In the *Macarthys* case referred to above, it was argued that a woman is entitled to claim not only pay equal to the pay received by a man who previously did the same work for the employer, but also (in the absence of an actual male comparator) the pay to which she would be entitled were she a man, the so-called hypothetical male comparison. However, the European Court held that the hypothetical male comparison was to be classed as indirect and disguised discrimination, the identification of which implied comparative studies of entire branches of industry and therefore required, as a prerequisite, the elaboration by Community and national legislative bodies of criteria of assessment. No such elaboration has yet been made. The Court's ruling would therefore appear to mean that, for the time being at least, Community law can only ensure equal pay for equal work where men and women are working in the same establishment or service. A woman would thus be prevented from receiving equal pay if there was and had been no man doing equal work in the establishment, even though the employer may have admitted that the woman would have been paid more if she had been a worker of the opposite sex.

A further area of uncertainty under Community law concerns the actual concept of 'pay'. In another UK reference to the European Court concerned with the question of whether contributions to private occupational pension schemes, or pension rights and benefits under such schemes, could constitute 'pay' within the meaning of Article 119 of the Treaty (*Worringham* v. *Lloyds Bank Ltd*),[15] the Court confined itself to the narrow facts of the particular case. It thus remains unclear whether and to what extent retirement contributions or benefits in occupational pension schemes fall within or outside the principle of equal pay. Similarly, the distinction between state social security schemes and occupational pension schemes has not yet been satisfactorily clarified.

As this brief review of some of the leading European Court rulings concerning equal pay shows, the overall Community framework here (and similarly that for other equal treatment provisions in the employment field) is still developing, as are the varying national frameworks which apply the Community provisions. Further EEC-level guidance and reappraisal of the basic provisions will therefore continue to be needed for some time to come.

INDIRECT DISCRIMINATION

The issue of indirect discrimination is now a key concern at both the legal and practical levels. The issue is briefly considered further here, as a means of illustrating the way a basic concept included in the Community law framework but not specifically defined there is being monitored and elaborated on at national and Community levels. The equal treatment principle in the Directives states merely that 'there shall be no discrimination whatsoever on grounds of sex either directly or indirectly by reference in particular to marital or family status', and no further definitions are given.

In an effort to clarify the general position regarding indirectly discriminatory practices at national level and the way in which Community law could be applied here, the European Commission asked a special network of national lawyers and practitioners from both sides of industry (which I have had the privilege of co-ordinating) to draw up a 'typology' of such practices which could ultimately lead to a definition of indirect discrimination. No generally agreed definition has yet emerged from this process. However, we have drawn up a draft typology of commonly found practices which, in the view of the various network members, may be considered as constituting indirect discrimination. The following are a few of the traditional employment practices and working conditions which we have been led to question in terms of their potential discriminatory effects.

As regards access to employment, indirect discrimination might arise from the way in which jobs are described and advertised (with neutral wording accompanied by pictures or texts indicating sex bias); or from recruitment and selection criteria based on factors such as age, height, mobility and educational qualifications which are not essential requirements for the job in question and which the majority of women cannot satisfy (such factors may also be invoked in relation to promotion). As regards working conditions, discrimination may arise from the way in which certain work schedules and training sessions which could be arranged more flexibly are organised at times of day especially difficult for workers with family responsibilities; or, in the pay field, from the application of systems determining basic pay levels (with job classifications often neutral in form but discriminatory in application, and jobs largely done by women consistently undervalued). In terms of promotion, the linking of opportunities for advancement to actual service on the job may disadvantage those with career breaks of only short duration to have children; and the generally more limited promotion opportunities for part-timers will impact most heavily on women and may also constitute a form of indirect discrimination. Similarly, the selection of part-time workers first for redundancies or of those with most unbroken service may also give rise to discriminatory effects.

These and many other examples show that it is the effects of particular measures, apparently neutral in form but which as applied predominantly affect and disadvantage workers of one sex (usually though not always women), which tend to raise a presumption of indirect discrimination. The question then arises as to the extent to which such a presumption should be rebuttable – for example, on objective grounds and irrespective of intention, and perhaps linked to the essential requirements of the job or the particular workplace. Whatever the final shape of the much-needed Community-level guidance here, it will be important to ensure that permissible justifications are not drawn so widely as seriously to dilute the basic equality principle. The main practical message which emerges from the EEC's work so far is that traditional practices should be re-examined to see whether they could be producing discriminatory effects – albeit unintentionally.

CONCLUSIONS

As this brief overview of recent developments at Community and national levels indicates, the mere formulation of Community standards for equal pay and equal treatment will not of itself create firm rights which can be relied on by individuals in the various member states without further interpretation by the courts and often action by the national authorities. Moreover, aside from the ambiguities of the legal formulae chosen, legal provisions will only be effective if used by those they are aimed at assisting, and at a time of recession individuals may be reluctant to press their claims and risk their job security unless assisted by some outside body such as the Equal Opportunities Commission in the UK. Positive action to encourage egalitarian policies in practice is also a necessary complement to basic legislation, and both legislation and other initiatives in the area of equality should be regarded as part of an overall anti-discrimination/equal-opportunities programme covering all aspects of employment and working life.

The Community's first Equality Action Programme (1982–5)[16] has gone some way towards achieving these ends by bringing together many aspects of discrimination within a single action framework. The Programme is now being extended for a further period up to 1990,[17] again with an emphasis on a multi-faceted approach. The continuation of the Programme points to the fact that much still remains to be done, in particular in ensuring that the legal framework is fully understood and made as effective as possible. As far as equality in employment is concerned, however, if the current activity, first, provides the basis for a clear definition and guidance on indirect discrimination to be formulated and relied on by the courts, second, identifies the main areas where discrimination is still to be found, and, third, alerts those who are closest to the real situation on the ground (i.e. employers and unions and individual workers) to the type of practices which should be reviewed and the traditional assumptions which should now be questioned, the Community initiative will have achieved a good deal.

Notes

1. *Official Journal* C 13/74.
2. *Official Journal* L 45/75.

3. *Official Journal* L 39/76.
4. *Official Journal* L 6/79.
5. *Official Journal* C 134/83.
6. (1976) 2 *Common Market Law Reports* 98.
7. Article 189 of the basic Treaty.
8. Case No. 79/83.
9. Case No. 14/83.
10. Case No. 152/84.
11. Article 1, paragraph 1 of the Equal Pay Directive.
12. (1980) *ECR* 1289.
13. (1981) *ECR* 936.
14. (1982) *ECR* 2601.
15. (1981) *ECR* 767.
16. *COM*(81) 758 final.
17. *COM*(85) 801 final.

Note: this chapter was originally written in April 1985, and was updated to include material to April 1986.

2 'Give Us Equal Pay and We'll Open Our Own Doors'[1] – A Study of the Impact in the Federal Republic of Germany and the Republic of Ireland of the European Community's Policy on Women's Rights

Catherine Hoskyns

This chapter looks at the impact of the European Community's policy on women's rights on two countries – the Federal Republic of Germany and the Republic of Ireland. These two have been chosen as providing a contrast – in size, in length of membership of the Community and in political structures – and as having some particular problems in the implementation of Community measures in this field. The aim of the chapter is to estimate the effect that this new level of policy-making is having on the way the issue of women's rights is handled at the national level, and at the same time to relate these developments to the aims and practice of the women's movement across Europe.

CHARACTERISTICS OF THE EUROPEAN POLICY ON WOMEN

The content and development of the European policy on women is discussed in the introduction to this book. I should like at this point, however, to make some observations on those aspects of the policy which seem important in determining how it is received at the national level – and how women respond to it.[2]

As has been pointed out many times, Community social policy, of which the women's policy is a part, is really an employment policy. It springs out of the concern in the Treaty of Rome to liberalise the labour market, create a situation of fair competition and improve working conditions. The Community has some competence to deal with the situation of people as workers but not with citizens as such.

The policy on women reflects this emphasis. Research and rhetoric at the Community level may go beyond the employee status of women but, so far, legislation and funding has been strictly limited to this area. For women, whose position at work is so closely tied to their situation at home, this distinction makes little sense. It also prevents the Community from dealing with issues around which women have mobilised most strongly – particularly those to do with reproductive rights and male violence. Some of the indifference and suspicion of the women's movement towards the policy and towards the Community itself, derives from these factors.

The policy on women is also deeply rooted in the concepts of equality and equal treatment. This again springs from the ethos of the Treaty of Rome where equal treatment – whether of goods, services or nationals – is one of the principles upon which the Community is founded. The Community has, however, been much less willing to legislate, in any policy area, for interventionist measures or for special treatment to help weak or disadvantaged groups.

As the draft of the Equal Treatment Directive moved through the negotiating process, quite strong measures encouraging positive action were watered down to the point of virtual exclusion. Similarly, when the Commission produced a draft for a Community instrument encouraging the adoption of national positive action programmes, this was eventually adopted as a Recommendation – which creates no legal obligation – and not, as originally intended, a Directive. The Directives adopted contain few provisions obligating states to make support and advice available to help women claim their rights. A proposal from the European Parliament that the Equal Treatment Directive should include a provision for independent bodies in each country to monitor and support the implementation of equality laws was not accepted by the Council of Ministers. Given the strongly patriarchal nature of Western European society, equality legislation is unlikely to be effective unless strong mechanisms are established for its implementation.

The women's movement in most European countries has been sceptical about equality as an objective – especially when measures purporting to produce equality are not accompanied by strong provisions on positive action and for effective implementation. For many feminists the demand for equality is seen as leading to co-option and implying an acceptance of the values and structures of a patriarchal society. Since 1970 much of the activity of the women's movement has been directed not at achieving equality but at celebrating and consolidating women's 'difference' and at creating an alternative space for women. When demands have been made for legislation or changes in administrative procedure, these have usually been concerned with issues that deal more directly with the actual situation of women – for example, the legalisation of abortion and the reform of procedures and sentencing in rape cases.

Given that the Community has shown some concern about sex discrimination and the integration of women in the labour market, it is interesting that no comparable provisions exist at Community level with regard to racial discrimination and the integration of ethnic minorities. These issues are subsumed in the Community's policy on migration, which in different contexts covers both internal Community migrants and migrants from third countries. Nowhere does Community policy seem to recognise the existence of black Europeans. As far as the policy on women is concerned, the 1982–5 Action Programme talks of women immigrants but not of black or ethnic minority women as such. The gaps and anomalies in Community policy on these issues are likely to become increasingly contentious, particularly as more black people enter politics in Britain and elsewhere.

THE IMPACT OF THE POLICY

Despite these problems and limitations, however, there is no doubt that the policy on women has proved to have considerable (if unexpected) strength. As the case-studies show, both Germany and Ireland were forced to adopt equal treatment legislation because of the necessity to comply with European Directives. Such legislation would have come much later, if at all, without this intervention. Similarly, the British government, following a ruling from the European Court of Justice, has been forced to make a quite radical amendment to the Equal Pay Act despite its avowed hostility to 'social engineering' of this kind.[3] One of the characteristics of European policy in this field is the long time-lag between adoption and implementation. In this particular case, legislation which has its origins in the 1960s, and was adopted by member states in the 1970s, is now being applied in the 1980s when circumstances are quite different. Thus one of its main effects is to help keep the issue of women and employment on the agenda, at a time when governments would much prefer to let it drop.

The strength of the policy derives principally from the type of Community measures which exist to enforce compliance at the national level with Community legislation, and to monitor progress in this direction. Both the European Commission and the European Court, until recently at least, have adopted a broad interpretation of the legislation on women, and have taken a severe attitude towards infringements by member states. The flow of references from the national courts on the interpretation of Article 119 and the Directives remains steady. Originally it seemed to be only the British courts that were making use of this mechanism: now German, Dutch and Irish courts are taking it up.

All of this seems to have taken policy-makers and bureaucrats in the member states by surprise. Both German and Irish officials claim that there was little understanding at the time the Equal Treatment and Social Security Directives were adopted of what their domestic consequences would be. It was much later that the extent and ramifications of the legislative change necessary became apparent. Officials are now very aware of the effects of this kind of legislation and this may be one of the main reasons why further Directives in this field have been so strongly resisted by member states.

THE INVOLVEMENT OF WOMEN

One of the consequences of the adoption of policy and legislation on women at the European level has been the creation of special groups to deal with these issues both within the Community institutions and in conjunction with the member states. One of the first manifestations of this was when women civil servants and experts in employment questions came together in 1974 over the negotiation of the Equal Treatment Directive. Since then two women's bureaux have been established in the European Commission. The Commission has also set up on a permanent basis the Advisory Committee on Equal Opportunities, which brings together women from the different member states who deal with women's employment issues at an official or semi-official level. The European Parliament also now has a permanent committee on women's rights.

The Community's own institutions and decision-making structures are male-dominated and patriarchal in the way they operate – there has never yet been a woman Commissioner and there are few women in the top grades. The setting-up of these permanent and semi-permanent groupings begins to institutionalise the concern with women's issues, and gives those involved a vested interest in maintaining the policy and achieving some success.

The Women's Information Bureau of the Commission has as one of its tasks the informing and contacting of women's organisations in the member states. This contact is mainly with the more 'official' and better-structured women's organisations. The Bureau also produces a useful Bulletin, *Women of Europe*. A seminar held by the Bureau in March 1985 for these organisations adopted a surprisingly radical tone. The theme of the seminar was the reorganisation of working time, and the precise demands formulated suggest that the recession and women's unemployment are having a radicalising effect on these organisations and that contact through the Bureau is producing a useful means of co-ordination.

At a more feminist and grassroots level, the Centre for Research on European Women (CREW) has tried to bring together independent and autonomous women's groups and has helped to set up the European Network of Women (ENOW).[4] *CREW Reports* and *Network News* spread information of interest to feminists about developments at both the European and the national level. The aims of the Network are to create links between women's groups, to develop joint campaigns, and to lobby both in Brussels and in the member states. The linking together of grassroots groups across Europe – extremely demanding in terms of organisation and resources – creates a powerful force and generates a view of the European policy which both takes it seriously and worries at all of the objections and limitations discussed in the first part of this chapter. If this movement consolidates it is likely to inject into the European debate a whole new level of demands based on the real emotional and material needs of women.

All of this suggests that at very different levels and in different forms the interest and involvement of women in the European policy is gradually increasing. Ironically, this is happening at a time when most governments are showing themselves increasingly reluctant to implement the policy effectively and develop it further. There has in fact been no new Directive on any aspect of social policy (except health and safety at work) since 1978.

Community policy in any field does not develop in a vacuum. It is the product of a complex interplay between Community and national preoccupations and processes. In the rest of this chapter I shall look, therefore, at how this interplay has operated in respect of the policy on women in Germany and Ireland.

GERMANY AND THE POLICY ON WOMEN

According to the French sociologist, Evelyn Sullerot, Germany was responsible for the inclusion of Article 119 on equal pay in the Treaty of Rome. In response to the French demand for a broad range of social issues to be included in the Treaty, the German delegation agreed to equal pay (and a small number of other provisions) presumably on the understanding that the Articles in the Treaty were not likely to be directly applicable and that equal pay was in any case covered by the German Constitution. This view would have been confirmed by the fact that in 1955 the Federal Labour Court had ruled that the equality provisions in the Constitution were binding on parties to collective agreements, and that they would be in breach of the Constitution if they continued to set different rates for women workers.

The Constitution (adopted in 1949) provides in Article 3(2) that 'men and women shall have equal rights' and in Article 3(3) that 'no one may be prejudiced or favoured on account of sex'. The Constitution, however, also guarantees other basic rights which taken together have been interpreted as establishing freedom of contract and the autonomy of trade union and employers in concluding agreements in the labour market.[5]

The German Constitution is the basic document of the Republic and all government acts and statutory provisions can be overturned by appeal to the Constitutional Court. Within the constraints of the Constitution, however, the German system allows as much autonomy for social groups as possible, preferring to establish the details of legal norms through case law rather than by passing statutes and legislation. Such a system is hard for women to influence since it depends so crucially upon prevailing social norms, the power and influence of interest groups and the attitudes of the judiciary. In all of these areas women and women's interests are poorly represented.

In the 1960s approximately ten million German women worked outside the home, representing 36 per cent of the labour force. This figure has remained relatively constant. Women in general were employed in services rather than production, in low-level, low-status jobs, and had significantly less training than men. An increasing number of women were working part-time, which gave them less security and fewer benefits.[6] In 1969 in response to the expansion of the economy the Labour Promotion Act was passed. This identified women as a disadvantaged group needing help to enter the labour market and improve skills. As the need for labour declined in the 1970s or was met elsewhere, these provisions were whittled away. During the 1960s little progress was made in achieving equal pay despite the 1955 court decision. In general, women's wage groups were replaced by 'light work groups' which were largely female and occupied the same place in the wage scale. The discrimination involved in evaluating women's work in this way was not seriously taken up by the trade unions until the 1970s.[7]

1969 was a point of social and political change in Germany. For the first time since 1949, the Christian Democrats (CDU) lost power and were replaced in government by a Social-Democrat/Liberal coalition (SPD/FDP). This occurred in the aftermath of the uprisings and unrest of the late 1960s, and brought the SPD leader, Willy Brandt, who was known to be more sympathetic to social movements and underprivileged groups, to the position of Chancellor. These developments coincided with the establishment of the new women's movement. Feminist women in Germany in general came out of left politics and the student movement, but formed autonomous groups when they found it impossible to develop new forms of political action or change personal relationships within the existing left.

The first campaign initiated by these groups was over the legalisation of abortion. In 1971 there were demonstrations in the streets, and on 2 June *Der Stern* published an article in which (following the French example) prominent German women announced that they had had an abortion. After much dispute and political wrangling a bill legalising abortion was introduced by the SPD in 1974 and a more restricted bill was finally adopted in 1976. Over the same period, marriage and family law was also reformed, repealing provisions which had enshrined in law the woman's domestic role in marriage and had given the husband some control over the wife's right to work. The main thrust of the women's movement in the early 1970s was therefore not for equality as such but for the repeal of laws which seemed crudely to predetermine the role of women and for the creation of alternative structures and values.

From 1974 on, this second theme became dominant, resulting in a proliferation of organisations, the setting-up of women's centres, refuges, bookshops and journals, and the development of a wide variety of women's courses. Activity was more low profile and decentralised but by no means quiescent. Concerted efforts were also being made by women in the SPD and in the trade-union federation (DGB) to establish a stronger women's presence and to get women's issues given a higher priority. Although a network of women's sections and women's committees now exists in both organisations, the political environment and the core of decision-making in each still seems to be predominantly male.

THE IMPACT OF THE DIRECTIVES

During the early 1970s Germany was also involved at the European level in negotiations on the Equal Pay and Equal Treatment Directives.[8] In 1974 a women's unit had been set up in the Ministry for Youth, the Family and Health to co-ordinate and advise on all policy to do with women. The members of the unit had a watching brief over the negotiations but were not the experts directly involved. In the drafting of the Equal Pay Directive, the main concern of the German delegation seems to have been to clarify the juridical basis, and to emphasise that nothing should be adopted which would affect the 'autonomy of the social partners' (the trade unions and the employers). The German delegation was very reluctant to accept the expansion of the definition of equal pay to include equal pay for work of equal value, on the grounds that this went beyond Article 119. They eventually conceded after pressure from the European Commission, other states, and their own women's unit.

The progress of these negotiations raises a more general point – by no means confined to Germany. This concerns the different attitudes of men and women civil servants towards negotiations of this kind and the substantive issues with which they deal. Men on the whole, even if sympathetic, tend to see issues concerning the position of women as peripheral, and the problems which they present as technical. Women, on the other hand, even if not 'feminist', understand the totality of the problem and are likely to take it seriously. As one German woman put it:

My male colleagues say the law is OK – there is no discrimination. But I see it everywhere; it is systemic. The problem in Germany is that work is over-identified with men.

The general view in the Ministry of Labour and among German lawyers was that the two Directives did not require Germany to pass any further legislation. The Constitution was seen as conferring the basic rights and it was 'assumed' that the Courts would take the European provisions into account when dealing with equality cases. This was not the view of one of the women who had been involved at an early stage in the negotiations. She commented:

The rights were clear juridically but not socially. The process of law-making would actually be important in raising consciousness. It would make the rights more useful – and more used.

By 1977, news of the European Directives and what was happening in other countries began to filter through to German domestic politics, and the issue was taken up by the women's sections (ASF) in the SPD. The debate then began as to whether a comprehensive anti-discrimination law with an equality agency to enforce it – on the US/British model – should be adopted in Germany. The issue was raised at a seminar for women's organisations (traditional and feminist) held in Berlin in September 1977 and organised by the Berlin State Government and by the Women's Information Bureau of the Commission. According to reports, the feminist women at the seminar showed doubts about a law based on equality with men and argued for a special 'law for women' which would support positive action and self-help – a significant example of the instinctive feminist mistrust of the implications of equality. The traditional women showed themselves more in favour of a comprehensive law.

In general the trade-union movement (the DGB) was against a comprehensive law, seeing it as pre-determining issues which should be settled through negotiation. In addition, the conferring of special rights on women was seen as likely to divide the labour force. The DGB was also firmly opposed to an independent equality agency, in the belief that such an agency could only take over rights and duties 'properly the responsibility of the trade union movement'. The senior women in the women's committees were also doubtful about a broad law – preferring to press for women's issues to be given a higher priority in negotiations rather than for legal rights. These doubts linked in with objections from employers about the costs of an extension of equal rights legislation and the effect it would have on freedom of contract.

Since the trade unions (with extensive influence in the SPD) and the employers (with strong links to the FDP) were both against a comprehensive law, and since there was no consistent pressure from women, there was no chance of a consensus within government developing for it. The debate on the issue, however, did convince policy-makers that some legislation was necessary, and this view was reinforced in 1979 when the European Commission wrote officially to the German government requesting information about the implementation of the Directives.

In the end, a 'piecemeal compliance' was made with the Directives by inserting into the already existing Civil Code the provisions felt to be essential. This new legislation was adopted in August 1980 and was subtitled 'Labour Law to Comply with European Community Provisions' ('Arbeitsrechtliches EG – Anpassungsgesetz').[9] Unlike other governments which have often tried to conceal the European origins of equality legislation, the German government deliberately drew attention to this link, saying in effect: 'We didn't want to do this; we've been forced into it.' To officials, the 'piecemeal compliance' was a satisfactory compromise. It incorporated Community obligations in a way that was considered to be 'in tune with the German legal system' and involved 'no slavish imitation'.

LAW AND CASES

Four equal-treatment provisions were inserted into the Civil Code by the law of 1980. The first and most important (Section 611a) makes it unlawful for an employer to discriminate in a work relationship, especially in respect of hiring, promotion, working arrangements and dismissal. However, the employer can still argue 'technical reasons' other than those of gender for limiting jobs to people of one sex. The other provisions cover sex-neutral advertisements, equal pay for work of equal value and protection against victimisation. These provisions seemed to be a somewhat sketchy application of the Directives since they did not cover: indirect discrimination, equal treatment in vocational training, the need for sex-neutral job classification schemes or the possibility of positive action – all matters spelled out in the European texts. The possibility of exclusions under Section 611a also seemed extremely broad. Moreover, it was pointed out that the provisions prohibiting discrimination in hiring were unlikely to be effective, since under German law no real damages or compensation could be paid unless a contract of employment had already been signed. The Commission made clear very quickly that it was not satisfied with these provisions and that an infringement action was being prepared.

Although the idea of a separate equality agency had been abandoned, the women's unit in the Ministry for Youth, the Family and Health was considerably enlarged and given the new name of 'Arbeitsstab Frauenpolitik'. Its job was to monitor all developments at governmental level with regard to women, to intervene where necessary and give advice. It had no responsibility for representing women in negotiations, or supporting cases before the courts. The first head of the unit was Marlies Kutsch, a woman with long experience in the trade-union movement. Some equality units were also set up at state level (for example in Berlin in 1978, in Hamburg in 1979 and in Bremen in 1981) usually as a result of pressure from SPD women. The effectiveness of these units seems to have varied enormously – depending on the precise resources and responsibilities they were given and the vigour of the staff.

In the context of these developments anti-discrimination cases were given more publicity and became politically sensitive issues. The Heinze case first brought to court in 1979 is a good example. In this case, the issue concerned overtime allowances being paid to male workers only. The Regional Labour Court found that the freedom of the employer to pay workers what 'he' liked (and it was a 'he'!) was a more important principle than the equal treatment of women. This judgment was decisively overturned in the Federal Labour Court which ruled that the equality provisions must apply to allowances and bonuses as well as to basic rates of pay.

European law seems not to have been used in these cases although it was clearly relevant. In 1983, however, in a quite new development, two anti-discrimination cases were referred to the European Court from the local labour courts in Hamm and Hamburg.[10] These cases both concerned the inability of the German courts to award any real damages even if employers were found guilty of discrimination in the hiring of workers. In the Von Colson and Kamann case, two women social workers were refused employment at a male prison although they seemed clearly the most competent applicants. The Hamm Labour Court found the discrimination blatant but could apply no effective sanction against the employer. In making the reference, the

Hamm Court in effect asked whether the terms of the Equal Treatment Directive *required* states to apply effective sanctions to enforce its provisions. In its ruling of 10 April 1984, the European Court found that although member states had discretion as to what kind of sanctions they applied, these 'should ensure real and effective legal protection and have a genuine deterrent effect on the employer'. In light of this, the Hamm Court in December 1984 awarded damages amounting to six months' pay plus interest at 4 per cent going back to November 1982 to both the women. The Hamburg Court followed suit.

Although German cases are not normally seen as establishing precedents, it seems likely that this ruling will be followed in other similar cases. Effectively, therefore, German law has been amended by the European provisions. The publicity surrounding the cases may also have some effect in deterring similar practices.

These developments seemed to underline the inadequacy of the German law, and pressure increased at both state and federal level to change it. However, this movement received a setback in May 1985 when the Commission's infringement action against Germany was finally heard in the European Court. In a surprise judgment the Court accepted only one of the Commission's five complaints. It is possible to argue that the Commission was ill advised in some of the points raised, but the Court's judgment is unusual in the generally hostile tone it adopts towards the Commission's case.[11]

German officials were 'relieved' at the judgment and saw it as justifying their 'piecemeal compliance'. Given this experience with the first two Directives, it seems highly unlikely that the present German government will agree to any new Directives in the field of women's rights – unless they are clearly covered by provisions already existing in German law.

THE WOMEN'S MOVEMENT IN THE 1980s

All these developments seem somewhat to have changed the attitude of German feminists toward the law, and in 1982 both the main feminist journals, *Emma* and *Courage*, came out strongly for a comprehensive anti-discrimination law. This represented a substantial change from the views expressed in 1977.

The change, however, has only been marginal. In the 1980s, the main concern of the feminist movement has been with the broader peace movement and with combating all forms of male violence. This has involved consolidating the women's presence in the peace movement and setting up support systems for women affected by violence. Another trend has involved a return to a more inward-looking personal politics and a new emphasis on the importance of women's ability to have children and capacity for human relations. All of these tendencies concentrate on the 'difference' of women and the establishment of alternative structures. The demand for equality seems irrelevant, if not actually damaging to these concerns.

The conflict between the ideals of 'equality' and 'difference' was brought to a head in Germany in the late 1970s over the issue of whether women should be allowed to serve in the armed forces. This caused a deep and lasting division within the women's movement between those who saw it as important to establish the principle of equality everywhere, and those who saw equality in structures which appeared to be so totally devoted to the interests of men as being a trap for women.

In October 1982 a CDU/FDP Government replaced the SPD/FDP coalition. It is difficult now in Germany for any government to ignore the situation of women (women form an important pressure-group within the CDU), but the present government has taken the line that enough has been done for women at work and that more needs doing for women in the home and to improve the status of the wife and mother. This is ideologically a rather subtle line which takes up (but with very different political intentions) the idea of women's 'difference'. The debate about equality legislation has therefore been down-played, and serious review and amendment is now less likely given the overall failure of the Commission's infringement action.

German women have not on the whole been very active in the contacts and links among women being created around the European policy. In general, the attitudes adopted and the types of activities undertaken by German feminists have not been such as to make the Community seem a particularly relevant institution. And even the more formal and official women's organisations seem to find participation in European-level activities time-consuming and 'not always relevant'. German women MEPs, however, especially Marlene Lenz (CDU) and Heidemarie Wieczorek-Zeul (SPD), have been extremely active in the various women's committees of the European Parliament.

CONCLUSIONS

Germany has the reputation of being the country which has done least to implement the European policy and where the situation of women shows least change. The above account suggests that this is perhaps too negative an assessment. Over the last ten years the issue of what kind of an anti-discrimination policy is appropriate has been hotly debated and a change of emphasis is apparent. In particular, the European provisions present a challenge to the German preference for 'unfettered negotiation' in the labour market – a system which has not worked well for women in the past. In addition, as the German experience shows, the existence of the European policy and the ramifications of applying it do make it harder for governments to return to a more traditional attitude towards women at work.

Despite this, the effects of the European policy in Germany have been limited, mainly it would seem because it has not so far connected with any real mobilization by women. As has been shown, the main emphasis in the German feminist movement has been on creating the radical alternative and establishing the 'difference' of women. There has been much less emphasis on operating through the institutions and taking on the state apparatus. When this has been attempted, as in the trade unions and in the SPD, the resistance of the patriarchal core has been extremely strong. As a result of these particular circumstances, issues such as whether women should serve in the army seem to divide women in Germany more deeply than has been the case elsewhere.

These particular circumstances also make the European policy appear less directly relevant. The areas of greatest mobilisation in the early 1970s, over abortion law reform and family policy, are not within the competence of the Community. Community procedures both for negotiating and enforcing policy seem distant and arcane. Some German women also in their hearts seem to share the view of most German officials: that it is really 'inappropriate' to receive provisions of this kind from external sources. If they are needed they should be fought for within the domestic environment.

Over the past ten years there has been a slight narrowing of this gap. Some feminist women are more interested in law and institutions than they used to be and the European policy has become somewhat more transparent and accessible. In Germany, however, the gap between what the Community policy says and what women feel they want and need remains large. This enables the government to get away with a very partial application of the European provisions and a negative attitude to further developments.

IRELAND AND THE POLICY ON WOMEN

The early 1970s was also a time of change in Ireland. The new women's movement 'came out' in 1970–71 influenced by developments in the United States and Britain. From 1970 to 1973 Ireland was in the process of entering the European Community, and in February 1973 a Fine Gael/Labour Party coalition came to power ending sixteen years of Fianna Fáil rule.

The nucleus of women who formed the new women's movement came from the media and from small left political groupings. Their aim was to 'blow the cover' on the position of women in Ireland, and expose the anomalies in a society where in formal terms the role of wife and mother was honoured and protected, but where in actual fact the numbers of deserted wives, pregnant teenagers and illegitimate children were growing yearly. They also wanted to show that there were 'new women' around capable of playing an active and independent role in politics and at all levels of decision-making. Since Ireland, despite deep political and ideological differences, is a small close-knit society, this exposure and the attitudes of the 'new women' caused embarrassment and shock.[12]

The Irish Constitution, adopted in 1937, guarantees in Article 40 equality before the law to all citizens, but assumes that different social groupings have 'differences of capacity, physical and moral, and of social function'. In Article 41 the 'function' of women is set very clearly within the family and in the home, and the Constitution undertakes that mothers 'shall not be obliged by economic necessity to engage in labour to the neglect of their duties in the home'. The same Article protects marriage and the family and prohibits divorce. Attitudes deriving from this view of the role of women, together with continuing high levels of unemployment, led to relatively small numbers of women taking up paid employment. By 1971 women formed only 26 per cent of the labour force. In the early 1970s women in the civil service and in certain other sectors were still obliged to resign their posts on marriage. It was these kinds of attitudes and restrictions which the women's movement sought to challenge.

The situation of women was also on the political agenda for other reasons. In the 1960s the trade-union movement had begun to challenge the use of different pay scales for men and women and it was also becoming clear that entry into the Community was likely to involve the adoption of legislation on equal pay. In 1970 the influential 'Commission on the Status of Women' was appointed. Its report in 1972 contained a broad range of proposals including recommendations on equal pay legislation and on the removal of the marriage bar in the civil service.

EQUALITY LEGISLATION

During 1973 and 1974 the Ministry of Labour was involved both in drafting Irish legislation on equal pay and in conducting negotiations on the Community's Equal Pay Directive. The link with the Community was close because Patrick Hillery, a former Fianna Fáil Minister of Labour, had been appointed Commissioner for Social Affairs in Brussels and was thus responsible for European policy in this field. The Irish legislation in fact preceded the Directive but care was taken to see that it complied with all the provisions likely to be included in the European legislation. The law provided for the appointment of equal pay (later equality) officers who would investigate complaints and make recommendations. Only if these recommendations proved unacceptable would there be an appeal to the Labour Court. Though the system has some obvious problems and defects (it is at present under review) it has proved to be relatively open and accessible to women claimants.

The equal pay legislation was not introduced without traumas. In the aftermath of the oil crisis, employers reacted in panic and demanded that the government delay national legislation and apply to Brussels for a derogation from the obligations of the Directive. The Commission refused the derogation, after some effective lobbying by women, and the employers then subsided. This incident both encouraged women to look to Brussels and demonstrated Community authority in these areas.[13]

Equal pay legislation would probably have been introduced in Ireland at some point in the 1970s. Given the onset of recession, however, it is highly unlikely that any further provisions would have been adopted in the field of women's rights at work. Nevertheless, because of the need to comply with the European Equal Treatment Directive, the Employment Equality Act was adopted in 1977. This Act has proved to be particularly important in Ireland because, following the Directive, it prohibits discrimination based on marital status. It was only possible to adopt the legislation, however, by excluding certain sectors (like the police and the prison service) from its provisions and by extending the circumstances where sex can be considered an 'occupational qualification' well beyond what is permitted by the Directive.[14] These exceptions are gradually being reduced under pressure from the European Commission. The Act provides for the establishment of an Employment Equality Agency (modelled on the British Equal Opportunities Commission but without its powers of legal representation) and is enforced through the system of equality officers set up for the equal pay legislation.

Between 1976 and 1984, 570 cases were referred to the equality officers under the equal pay provisions alone. Of these, 223 were settled or withdrawn and of the rest 182 were won by the complainants.[15] On the whole very little direct reference to European law seems to be made in the Labour Court – perhaps because the terms of the Irish and European legislation are so close. No equality case has yet been referred from the Labour Court to the European Court. However, two such references are now being considered in the light of judgments made in 1984.[16]

THE INVOLVEMENT OF THE WOMEN'S MOVEMENT

After its ebullient start in the early 1970s the Irish women's movement began to diversify and decentralise. Some women went into pressure group activity; others set up women's aid centres and a variety of support groups. A more recent development has been the setting-up of a women's information centre and publishing co-operative. In the mid-1970s an onslaught was made on the political parties, and in the 1977 elections Nuala Fennell (now Secretary of State for Women's Affairs) stood as an independent when her party Fine Gael refused to adopt her as a candidate. In the trade unions an attempt was made to establish a stronger women's presence and challenge the view still widely held that 'work and work related activities were essentially a male preserve'.[17] In 1976 the Trade Union Women's Forum was established, which among other things helped to ensure that Sylvia Meehan – a feminist and trade-union activist — was appointed as head of the Employment Equality Agency. Because of the closeness of Irish society, all of these activities tended to end up with demands being made on the state and some involvement with institutions.

One important area of state regulation which the women's movement took up towards the end of the 1970s was the policy on social welfare. Irish social welfare hinges on the family and at that time all married women were regarded as dependants whatever their situation. This led to them receiving a lower level of unemployment benefit for a shorter time and to discriminatory treatment over a range of other benefits. In 1981 the Women's Social Welfare Campaign was set up specifically to work on these issues.[18]

The European Directive on Equal Treatment in Social Security was adopted in 1978 and came into force in December 1984. Although it only covered employment-related benefits its implications for the Irish system described above were obviously considerable. Both the payment of different levels of unemployment benefit to married women and the automatic payment of the dependant's allowance to married men were seen as infringing the Directive and requiring amendments to the Irish provisions.

Political confusion in Ireland (there were three changes of government between 1978 and 1982) caused delays in implementing the Directive. Civil servants were taken aback by the complexity of the issues. One remarked:

We didn't realise the full implications of the Directive when it was passed. The concepts of dependency and equal treatment just don't mix. What is needed is a full overhaul of the system with more emphasis on individualisation.

Such an overhaul never took place. Instead the government hastily carried out a piecemeal reform: proposing that married women should receive equal benefit rates and that the dependant's allowance should only be paid to a person (male or female) whose partner was totally occupied in the home or unable to work. This second proposal caused an outcry since the loss of the automatic allowance was seen as likely to cause hardship in quite a range of low-income households. It also seemed likely to put a further weapon in the hands of men who were anyway reluctant to see their wives go out to work.

Both the women's movement and the Fianna Fáil opposition campaigned against this proposal. Irish feminists were particularly incensed that equality in a downwards direction, or put into effect in a way that disadvantaged women, seemed to be considered both in Brussels and in Dublin in an adequate implementation of the Directive. In response to this pressure the government announced that 'alleviating measures' would be introduced, to the effect that anyone whose partner was earning less than IR£50 a week or working for less than 18 hours would still be entitled to the allowance.

A Bill was finally introduced into the Dáil in December 1984 and adopted in July 1985.[19] At the time of writing, implementing regulations had still not been produced – more than a year after the final date for the application of the Directive. Early in 1985 a case was brought in the High Court on behalf of Ann Cotter and Norah McDermott, arguing that their rights under the Directive had been infringed, since as unemployed married women they had still been receiving a lower rate of benefit after the December 1984 deadline had passed. They claimed arrears of pay since that date. The case has now been referred to the European Court – the first Irish reference on an equality issue.[20]

Although Irish women have been critical of certain aspects of the Directive, the whole issue of social welfare in Ireland seems to be one where, overall, the European provisions have operated to support a campaign already initiated by women. As a result some real changes have been effected. Irish women have recently become much involved in the contacts and links being established among women at the European level. Sylvia Meehan was chair of the European Commission's Advisory Committee between 1983 and 1985 and Irish feminists are active in both CREW and the Network. Irish women seem to have few of the complexes about the Community which exist in other countries and are willing to use it as a lever against what they see as the hypocrisy and patriarchy of the Irish political system. This may be because in the case of Ireland there seems to be a rather closer connection than elsewhere between the European provisions and the real needs and concerns of women.

This has, however, had the effect of creating a backlash, and in 1983 in a move which ran counter to the developments discussed above a prohibition on abortion was inserted into the Irish Constitution by means of a referendum. As a result, abortion cannot now be legalised in Ireland through a vote in the Dáil. It would take a two-thirds majority in a further referendum – something much harder to achieve. This can be seen as an attempt to shore up the defences of Irish society against 'unacceptable' changes in the status of women being brought about by a combination of internal pressure and external influences.

CONCLUSIONS

The case-studies in this chapter show that at a certain level the European policy on women is having a considerable effect. It is forcing a common form of legislation on the member states and is keeping the issue of women's employment on the political agenda. Provisions adopted to comply with European obligations are harder to repeal and change at the national level and have so far held their place even in a time of recession and unemployment. The application of European law in equality cases is gradually being accepted as part of judicial procedure in these member states and, as a result, both the rights guaranteed and the forms of legal redress are being drawn closer together.

These developments have undoubtedly been of benefit to women, first because the establishment of formal rights is important to disadvantaged groups and second because the input from Europe has helped to keep the issues on the agenda at national level. At the same time, the existence of common policy and legislation has begun to create a fragile network which at different levels and in different forms is creating links between women across the Community. Despite these advantages, however, the policy has remained limited in its application and of only marginal relevance to the interests of most women in the Community. The concern with equality rather than positive action, the limitation to the field of employment, the emphasis on getting the wording of the law right rather than on giving practical assistance to women to apply it, all contribute to this. So does the generally arcane and perplexing nature of Community procedures and institutions. As the Irish example shows, there is a marked and substantial difference where Community policy connects with the real concerns of women, and where individuals begin to benefit directly.

There are now clear indications that a watershed has been reached in the development of the women's policy at the European level. The prevailing ethos among Community governments is against social legislation of this kind, and the emphasis is on reducing public expenditure, deregulating business and 'freeing' the labour market. Politicians and civil servants in the member states have been alarmed by the implications of existing Directives and are reluctant to open the door to further legislative upheaval. As a result no new Directives on women's rights have been adopted since 1978 – the most recent example of the deadlock being the failure of governments in

December 1985 to agree to even a watered-down version of the Directive on parental leave.

Only a clear commitment from the Community institutions and strong mobilisation among women in the member states is likely to unblock the situation. This seems unlikely to materialise. The Commission is giving a far higher priority to industrial restructuring than to social policy, and some of the recent decisions of the European Court seem to reflect this emphasis. As for mobilisation, there is little awareness among women in the Community of developments at the European level. And although cross-Community links among women are beginning to develop, the costs of consolidating them or of lobbying effectively in Brussels are far beyond what grassroots organisations or informal groupings can afford. So despite efforts by the European Network of Women it proved impossible in 1985 to co-ordinate an effective campaign in favour of the proposed parental leave Directive.

The institution which now gives most support and backing to the women's policy is the European Parliament, through its women's committee. Parliament has recently intervened to prevent the down-grading of the two women's bureaux in the Commission and has insisted that the European Social Fund should continue to monitor the money spent on women's projects. Parliament's women's committee has also refused to allow itself to be limited by the competence of the Treaty of Rome and has spent much of 1985 preparing a substantial report on women and violence. In the end, it may be the Parliament, in its long-running fight to increase its power *vis-à-vis* the other institutions of the Community, that will prevent the women's policy from being either down-graded or quietly dropped.

The problem for the women's movement in Europe, therefore, is to decide how seriously to take the fragile structures which have been established over the last fifteen years at the European level. Obviously nothing like the national political process yet exists, and national issues and preoccupations continue to have more immediacy and more relevance. Nevertheless, European policy does provide levers which can and have been used to the benefit of women, and the existence of a common legislative and institutional framework has undoubtedly helped to develop more solid contacts between the women's movements in the different countries.

Perhaps it is this last factor which should carry most weight. If, as seems likely, the economic structure of the individual states and a large part of economic policy is going to be determined at the European level, then in the end labour and social movements will have to follow suit. The framework of the women's policy offers a chance for the women's movement to move in this direction. The experience of the Network, limited as it has been, provides a glimpse of the strength that would be gained by adding onto the existing local, national and separatist dimensions of the women's movement, a multiplicity of contacts across Europe and a stronger co-ordination at the European level.

Notes

1. The title of this chapter is taken from a (possibly apocryphal) Irish story. In 1974 the Minister of Labour, Michael O'Leary, went to address women shop stewards on the subject of equal pay. After the discussion he politely opened the door for some of the women. Instead of going through, it is said that they gathered round him chanting: 'Give us equal pay, Michael, and we'll open our own doors.'
   I should like to thank Hanna Beata Schopp-Schilling and Matthias Reute for help with the German section of this chapter, and Padraic Doyle, Caroline McCamley and Ann Wickham for help with the Irish section. None of them is responsible for my views and interpretations. I am also grateful to the Nuffield Foundation for help with the travel costs associated with this research.
2. I have discussed the characteristics of the women's policy and its relation to feminism in more detail in an article, 'Women's Equality and the European Community', *Feminist Review*, Summer 1985, pp. 71–88.
3. In July 1982 the European Court ruled that the British legislation did not adequately confer on women the right to claim equal pay for work of equal value. The subsequent amendment to the British Equal Pay Act has produced a flood of new cases on this issue.
4. For information on CREW and ENOW contact CREW, 38 Rue Stevin, 1040 Brussels.
5. See R. Nielsen *Equality Legislation in a Comparative Perspective – Towards State Feminism?*, mimeo, Women's Research Centre in Social Science, Copenhagen, 1983. For an authoritative review of German anti-discrimination law, see the chapter by Heide Pfarr and Ludvig Eitel in G. Schmid and R. Weitzel, *Sex Discrimination and Equal Opportunity*, Gower, Aldershot, Hants, 1984.
6. See M. Laufenberg, 'Female Employment in the FRG 1950–78', in *Strategies for Integrating Women into the Labor Market*, Copenhagen, 1982, and H. Daubler-Gmelin, 'Equal Employment Opportunity for Women in West Germany Today', in R. Ratner (ed.), *Equal Employment Policy for Women*, Temple University Press, Philadelphia, 1980.

7. For a discussion of this issue, see Alice Cook's chapter on Germany in Cook, Lorwin and Daniels (eds), *Women and Trade Unions in Eleven Industrialised Countries*, Temple University Press, Philadelphia, 1984.
8. The material in this section is based on interviews in Bonn in May 1983 and in Brussels in June 1983 and September 1984.
9. The full title is 'Gesetz uber die Gleichbehandlung von Mannern und Frauen am Arbeitsplatz und uber die Erhaltung von Anspruchen bei Betriebsubergang (Arbeitsrechtliches EG – Anpassungsgesetz) 13th August 1980'.
10. ECJ Case 14/83 *Von Colson and Kamann* v. *Land Nordrhein-Westfalen*; ECJ Case 79/83 *Harz* v. *Deutscher Tradex*.
11. ECJ Case 248/83 *Commission* v. *Federal Republic of Germany*, 21 May 1985. See also *V. Hoffman* v. *Barmer Ersatzkasse*, 12 July 1984.
12. A very vivid account of these years is given in June Levine, *Sisters*, Ward River Press, Dublin, 1982.
13. Padraic Doyle of Trinity College, Dublin is making a detailed study of the derogation issue as part of his Ph.D. thesis on Ireland's experience of equal pay legislation. I am grateful to him for this information.
14. Employment Equality Act, 1977. Sections 12 and 17.
15. Figures supplied by the Labour Court.
16. See *Arthur Guinness* v. *Rita Murtagh* EP17/1983 (equal pay for work of equal value), and *North Western Health Board* v. *Catherine Martin*, judgment in the Irish High Court 19 December 1984 (indirect discrimination over age limits).
17. Deborah Schuster King, 'Ireland', in Cook, Lorwin and Daniels (eds), *Women and Trade Unions*, ch. 7.
18. For an excellent analysis of the Social Welfare Code, see *Irish Feminist Review*, 1984.
19. Social Welfare (Amendment) (No. 2) Bill, 1984.
20. ECJ Case 286/85 *McDermott and Cotter* v. *Minister for Social Welfare and the Attorney General*.

Note: this chapter was originally written in April 1985, and was updated to include material to May 1986.

3 Enforcement Procedures for Individual Complaints: Equal Pay and Equal Treatment

Jennifer Corcoran

There are many ringing declarations of equality in constitutional documents and legislative texts. The practical consequences, however, have been disappointing. The crucial question to ask is what are the instruments and procedures for implementing the principle of equality because without effective enforcement these documents can remain empty formulae. In the field of equal pay and equal treatment in the EC there is much room for improvement in these procedures.

All member states of the EC now have legislation implementing the principles set out in the Equal Pay and Equal Treatment Directives.[1] In all member states the legislation gives individuals the right to complain if they think that there has been a breach of those provisions. Thus the individual plays an important role in ensuring that the principles of the Directives are implemented in practice. But with the exception of the UK and Ireland there have been very few individual actions. The European Commission has expressed concern about this, especially since it is obvious that inequalities in pay and treatment still exist. Indeed the position of women within the Community has remained largely unchanged over the last few years. Although there are several reasons for this limited individual action, just one of them is examined here: the difficulties faced by the individual in pursuing a complaint through the legal system. References to the systems operating in Belgium and Greece have been made, wherever possible, to afford the opportunity for a more detailed comparison between two member states with similar court systems and administrative agencies.

There are several peculiarities about equal pay and equal treatment cases. First, the complainant has no power in relation to the employer – she may fear the loss of a job, retaliation in some other way or the prospect of continuing to work in an atmosphere of suspicion and resentment. Second, the concept of discrimination is complex and very difficult to express simply in legislative terms. Sex discrimination, whether it is intentional or not, is the overt expression of a prejudice. Such prejudice is often irrational and always subjective and because of this it may not be recognised as such by the courts or other enforcing authorities. Third, Community law *and* national law may have to be taken into account. Gabrielle Defrenne's case, referred to the European Court of Justice in 1971 by the Belgian Conseil d'Etat, was the first to demonstrate the importance of the Community law.[2]

These peculiarities necessarily complicate equal pay and equal treatment cases. It is therefore important that the system through which the complaint is processed should not add to the difficulties but rather should seek to support the complainant and facilitate the approach to the court. If the procedure is full of technicalities, involves high costs and delays, then it may prove a barrier to justice. It is particularly important that there should be no unnecessary barriers, since it is left to the individual to take the initiative: there are very few positive requirements for employers to take action to ensure equality of treatment and pay and few administrative bodies with investigative or enforcement powers. To discover whether the procedures in use in the member states are a help or a hindrance to the complainant was the subject of a comparative analysis made in 1983 as part of the Community's Action Programme. A wealth of information was supplied by the respondents which has formed a basis for this chapter.[3] An examination is made of certain key factors which are perceived to be relevant to determining whether an individual will make a complaint. Of immediate importance for the individual is knowledge of whether the law makes certain conduct unlawful and if it provides her with a remedy.

INFORMATION ABOUT THE LAW AND THE PROCEDURES

The Directives recognised the importance of individuals being informed about provisions made in relation to equal pay and treatment. To this end, both Directives contain provisions that 'Member States shall take care that the provisions adopted pursuant to this Directive . . . are brought to the attention of employees by all appropriate means, for example at their place of employment.'[4] Greece implemented this requirement in the equal treatment law of 1984, giving unions a right to inform their members about the contents of that law and the steps being taken in the workplace to implement it. Employers have a duty to facilitate this activity and the Minister of Labour must in his turn make available to the unions and workers all relevant information.[5] Comments have been made that this law is not likely to have much effect since it will be very difficult to monitor and enforce. The unions envisaged in the recent laws have not yet been established in many workplaces.[6]

Equality agencies now exist in all member states and have produced guides to and information about the law. In Belgium, the Commission on Women's Employment, an advisory body, has produced a guide to the laws and publicity material. Recently an Equality Council has been set up in Greece with powers to provide information. But much depends in all member states upon how many resources the government is willing to allocate in providing and distributing such information. Voluntary organisations and trade unions may also provide publicity material.

The task of finding out what procedure must be followed in making a complaint is not made easier by the existence of differing procedures according to one's status as an employee. In both Belgium and Greece public employees process their complaints through internal administrative procedures, through the lower administrative courts and ultimately to the Conseil d'Etat, although in Belgium they have a choice and may proceed through the ordinary civil courts. In Greece, if civil servants wish to claim compensation, they must proceed through the ordinary civil courts and do not benefit from the simpler labour court procedure. Without advice it may be difficult to find out which is the right avenue to take. In addition to this uncertainty, potential complainants may be unsure whether what has happened is covered by the legal provisions or not.

There are few people who would wish to proceed with a complaint if it is not well founded. The potential complainant will wish to ascertain whether the grievance amounts to a claim in law and what making a claim will involve. The rare person may be able to sort this out for herself but it is much more likely that help will be sought from someone more knowledgeable.

PRELIMINARY ADVICE

The only mechanism provided specifically for clarifying the preliminary issue was a prescribed form in the United Kingdom.[7]

There are standard questions on the form to which the complainant may add her own. This Question and Answer Procedure does not apply to equal pay cases and contains no questions which might elicit information indicating indirect rather than direct discrimination – perhaps signifying official recognition of the complexity of the concept. Skill is needed in the drafting of the optional questions, otherwise the employer would be able to answer 'Yes' or 'No' to the questions without giving supporting information. In Belgium a precondition to any legal proceedings is the exhaustion of the workplace internal grievance procedure. The complainant must provide proof that this has been done. This may result in assistance and clarification of the issues by workplace representatives. It may on the other hand discourage an individual from making a complaint in the first place. Spontaneous industrial action may be preferred instead.[8] There are also internal grievance procedures which may be used in Greece, but the complainant could, if she wished, proceed straight to the court or make a complaint to the Labour Inspectorate.

There are labour inspectors in Belgium, Denmark, the Federal Republic of Germany, France, Greece, Italy and Luxembourg. They are potentially of great help to the complainant. They may investigate a complaint and suggest whether it has any foundation in law. They have powers to inspect documents, have a right of entry and may require witnesses to make statements. If they decide that an offence has been committed they then present their report and dossier of evidence to the relevant prosecuting Departments. Although they can use their powers in relation to equal pay and equal treatment, their main and traditional functions relate to safety, health and pay. In Greece their main purpose is 'to intervene between employers of wage earners to resolve peacefully the disputes arising from their work, using a conciliation procedure in order to establish social peace'.[9] Both parties to the dispute are summoned, and if they reach an agreement a conciliation report will be issued which has the status of a labour agreement or a no-conciliation report giving the statements made by the parties.

But in all cases the inspector has discretion whether to submit a prosecution report. In Belgium the report will go to the Board of Labour Relations. If the Board decides to prosecute in the criminal court, Article 1382 of the Civil Code provides that any individual who has suffered a loss as a result of the infringement may join in the criminal action and be awarded damages. If there is no prosecution, then the individual has no choice but to proceed straight to the Labour

Court. But, unlike the system in Greece, she may nevertheless have access to the dossier compiled by the inspector. If there has been no investigation of the complaint, then she is on her own in collecting evidence. There are no other means provided in the Belgium system to assist her. Both in Belgium and in Greece the inspectors may take action even though no individual has complained. The Belgian Committee on Women at Work and representatives of workers may also make a complaint to the labour inspectors.

This system of inspectors receiving and investigating complaints with the possibility of a criminal prosecution to which the complainant may join her action for compensation, has much to commend it. It removes the burden from the individual of having to face her employer alone and leaves it to experts with adequate powers to collect the evidence. In practice its effective use, however, is dependent upon many factors, not least that it be available to all employees whether public or private, wage-earners or salaried. There must also be sufficient inspectors to carry out the duties in relation to equal pay and treatment. In addition they must be trained to recognise discrimination and know what kind of evidence will be required by the courts to support allegations. The Belgian Committee on Women at Work pointed out that because of the vast range of duties imposed on the inspectorate, specialisation was essential. But out of a group of sixty-two inspectors only one was a specialist in equal treatment between men and women, whereas three had specialised in pay for the handicapped. Little use has been made of the powers and most of the reports related to job advertisements in the media or offers of employment by employers. In 1981 there were six authorised official reports drawn up. Three gave rise to prosecution. In 1982 only three reports were drawn up. In Greece no proceedings have been initiated by Labour Inspectors.[10]

THE PREPARATION AND PRESENTATION OF THE CASE

Labour inspectors, if they choose to use their powers in relation to equal pay and equal treatment cases, could be of great assistance in preparing and presenting a case. Without their help a complainant would have to present the case herself or find funding to pay for the services of a lawyer. Except in Greece, the unions are frequently seen as a source of funding for legal advice and representation. This help is confined to union members, although in Italy it was thought that help would be given to a non-member – provided she joined the union! State legal aid is available in all member states except Greece. In the United Kingdom it is available on appeal from the first-level hearing. But no one would claim that the availability of legal aid made any significant difference, since the granting of it is subject to a means test set so low that few people who are in paid work would qualify. For married persons, the assessment in Denmark, the Netherlands and the United Kingdom is based on the family income.

The complainant in Greece would have to pay for legal representation out of her own pocket. The only other possibility is to find a lawyer to act on a contingency-fee basis. A statutory order permits barristers to do this provided that a written contract is drawn up and a copy filed at the Bar.[11] No more than 20 per cent of the compensation awarded may be paid to the barrister in this way. The median award in Great Britain in Sex Discrimination Act Industrial Tribunal cases was about £300;[12] so 20 per cent of that would scarcely be adequate payment for a lawyer's services. In addition, if the success rate runs at, say, one-third of the cases, such work would be viewed as a bad risk. There has been only a handful of cases in Greece so far and the contingency-fee provision was not used for them.

The difficulty of funding legal representation is partially solved in the United Kingdom by the power of the Equal Opportunities Commission (EOC) to grant assistance, which may take the form of legal representation.[13] The presence of a statutory body also provides moral support for the complainant. Test cases on matters of important principle can be assisted and taken through to a court decision to establish the interpretation of a particular provision. There is no obligation to apply for this assistance; trade unions and other bodies continue to support cases and individuals may proceed unaided to the industrial tribunals. But recent research has shown that their chance of success is not as high as for those who are represented.[14]

Not everyone who applies to the EOC will be granted assistance.[15] The EOC has a discretion, within the statutory guidelines, whether to grant assistance or not. It is also within the EOC's discretion how much of its budget should be allocated to the granting of assistance. The cost of supporting cases increases with the general increase in legal costs and as the cases go on appeal to the higher courts. References to the European Court of Justice under Article 177 also have to be paid for. This is made more serious since in the Court of Appeal and the House of Lords the other side's costs may be awarded against the complainant. It is said that if this had happened in *Worringham and Humphries* v. *Lloyds Bank Ltd*, then more than half of the EOC's legal budget would have been used on that one case.[16] Thus the existence of this power in the UK, which is the envy of other member states, is not the panacea for individual access to the court system. Help is available in Denmark, the Netherlands and Ireland in the preliminary stages of a complaint but not usually for legal representation.

Even if there were more resources allocated by member states to provide for legal representation, one of the major difficulties for complainants and their representatives would remain – the gathering of evidence to prove that they have been treated less favourably on the grounds of sex.

THE COLLECTION OF EVIDENCE

The burden of proof is generally placed on the complainant: evidence to prove that her employer has treated her less favourably than he would a man must be produced. There are intrinsic problems in discrimination situations since the employer will be in possession of much of the evidence. The complainant may not know, for example, who else was interviewed for the job she applied for, what qualifications they held or what the determining factors were in the final decision. Rarely will there be direct evidence of discrimination. There is the additional problem that employers may not keep records of interviews, may not define the criteria for the job and may not know the incidence of women in their workforce. This is one of the reasons why the introduction of some form of positive action programme is important. In 1982 some limited requirements were introduced into French law for employers to keep and make available to Works Councils information and statistics relating to men and women within their workforce.[17] The European Commission's proposal for a Directive on positive action has not been accepted by the Council of Ministers,[18] and reliance must continue to be placed on the voluntary introduction of positive action by employers and public authorities.

There are already three instances where the burden of proof is on the employer. In Belgium, the initial burden is on the employer in dismissal and victimisation cases. A recent change in France requires the employer, in equal pay cases, to produce a full justification for the less-favourable pay. The benefit of any doubt will go to the complainant.[19] In Ireland, in victimisation cases, the onus is upon the employer to show a non-recriminatory reason for his action. There have, however, been so few cases that it is not possible to ascertain whether this reversal of the burden would ease the task of the complainant. The European Commission has continued to propose a reversal of the burden of proof, but on the existing evidence this seems unlikely in itself to encourage more individuals to make complaints.

To ease some of these problems enforceable powers are necessary to enable the complainant to obtain the necessary evidence. In addition, it is important that the person who requests evidence understands the legal concept of discrimination and what kind of evidence is needed to prove it. Where an inquisitorial system exists – Belgium, France, Italy and Luxembourg – the court or its officers will decide what further information, documents or witnesses are required from the parties before it can reach a decision. There will be penalties for refusal to respond to the court's request. But in the adversarial systems, where the court plays a passive role, it is up to the complainants to decide what is necessary and make a request for it to be produced. In Denmark, the Federal Republic of Germany, Greece and the United Kingdom, if the use of interrogatories and requests for further and better particulars fail, the court can be asked to make an order for the discovery of documents. In the United Kingdom the tribunal can prevent the party who refused to produce documents from pursuing or defending the claim. Non-compliance with a court order in Greece will result in the payment of the other party's costs and liability to be fined. But in the absence of labour inspectors or other officers, such as the Equality Officers in Ireland, with powers to enter premises and to examine records, the complainant has to know exactly what to ask for.

The burden on the complainant is eased somewhat where the courts are willing to shift the evidential burden from the complainant once a *prima facie* case has been established. The United Kingdom cases show, however, that there are widely differing opinions in the courts and tribunals about when a *prima facie* case is established. Without some guidelines by the European Court of Justice or the European Commission on this question, a complainant could not be sure what approach the court would take.

Direct evidence of discrimination is rarely available: few employers are going to state that they treated a complainant less favourably because she is a woman. The courts will often, therefore, be called upon to infer discrimination from the evidence that is available. The judge's understanding of what amounts to discrimination is consequently of vital importance. There is evidence to show that courts do not always understand the legal concept of discrimination and that this lack of understanding can adversely affect the outcome of a case.

JUDGES AND OTHER OFFICERS

Recent research in Great Britain has shown that the lack of specialisation in Industrial Tribunals (a Labour Court of tripartite composition, including a legally qualified chairperson, with an appeal to the Employment Appeal Tribunal) results in a poor understanding of and misapplication of the law in equal pay and treatment cases. This affects the number of cases in which a finding of unlawful discrimination is made. A recent study revealed that in Great Britain in a three-year period only seven chairpersons heard more than one equal pay or treatment case a year.[20]

Provision has been made in some member states for the court or tribunal to call upon experts in discrimination to give advice, an opinion or a recommendation. In Belgium, Article 135 of the law of 4 August 1978 provides for the court to seek advice on matters of equal treatment from the Commission on Women at Work. But the courts have been slow to make use of this expertise and so far only one request has been made. Similarly in the Netherlands the Committee for Equal Treatment must initially investigate a complaint and give an advisory opinion. The court, however, is not obliged to follow this opinion. It may also at any time ask the Committee for further information and advice.

In member states where it is possible to call upon such experts there is a demonstrable reluctance to do so. It may be that the courts fear causing a delay and making the proceedings more costly. Moreover, lawyers are professionals and are loath to admit that there are areas of the law which they may not understand or where their personal and traditional prejudices may affect their interpretation of the law.[21] But in all member states there are decisions, both in the civil and criminal courts and even in the more specialised labour courts and tribunals, which strike at the very principles on which the laws are based.[22] In a Belgian criminal case, both the magistrates' court and the appeal court[23] decided that there was no unlawful sex discrimination in a case where two members of an appointments board stated that they intended to appoint a man to a primary school post and did in fact do so. Those courts found that the freedom to express an opinion guaranteed in the Constitution outweighed the discriminatory act. The case had to go to the Court of Appeal, a third-level court, before the decision was quashed 'in the interest of the law' on the basis that the Law of 1978 relating to equal treatment modified the freedom of opinion enshrined in the Constitution.[24] It is argued by some Belgium lawyers that such unsympathetic decisions would be avoided if the criminal courts did not have jurisdiction to hear cases concerning civil and social rights. The evidence from other member states, however, does not support that conclusion.

A conviction is growing that to avoid decisions which show a complete misunderstanding of the Directives' aims, the judges should undergo special training, and the European Commission has accepted that training of the judiciary is important. Both the Decisional Arena Report and the Comparative Procedure Report recommended the training of the 'gatekeepers'.[25] In this context it is the judges who ultimately determine whether the principles set out in the Directives are implemented in practice. The European Commission's Colloquium, held in May 1985 in Louvain-la-Neuve, was one of the steps taken to encourage judges and experts in member states to initiate seminars and training programmes on the Directives and the related law in their own countries. The existence of such training or more specialisation would give the complainant greater confidence in the courts and tribunals. At present the fear of an unsympathetic hearing may be added to the other fears of victimisation by the employer and act as a very real deterrent to filing a complaint.

VICTIMISATION

There are real and practical dangers in making a complaint of discrimination, whether it be through workplace grievance machinery or to an outside authority or court. The complainant may be regarded as a troublemaker and not be offered jobs or promotion in the future. Her work may be scrutinised more often or more carefully than before. She may be moved to less-satisfying or lower-paid work. Where reorganisation results in redundancies she may be the one the employer chooses to dismiss. These are risks which all complainants of discrimination will have to weigh up before deciding whether to proceed or not. The economic recession and the general shortage of jobs make these risks even graver. The Directives require member states to 'take all necessary measures to protect employees against dismissal by the employer as a reaction to a complaint within the undertaking or to a legal proceedings aimed at enforcing compliance with the principle of equal treatment'.[26] This provision is, however, limited to victimisation by dismissal and does not direct member states to provide protection against the other forms of victimisation. Thus, in Belgium, only if there is a dismissal or a unilateral change in the terms and conditions of the job does the law provide a remedy. Some member states provide protection against victimisation short of dismissal. In Greece the protection stems from Article 281 of the Civil Code, which forbids 'the misuse of authority'.[27]

There is no requirement in the Directives for national laws to provide protection against victimisation for witnesses or others who may be involved in the pursuit of the complaint. Article 281 of the Greek Civil Code could apparently be relied upon by a victimised witness, but in Belgium the witness would not be protected. Leonard's research has shown that the presence of witnesses is the one factor which clearly improves the complainant's chances of success.[28] The evidence of witnesses is vital where documentary evidence is difficult or impossible to obtain. But the witness suffers from the same fears of victimisation as the complainant. These fears are added to the natural aversion of most people to becoming involved in formal legal proceedings. Most systems provide that a witness may be ordered to attend to make a statement or give evidence, but the complainant may be reluctant to demand this of an unwilling colleague.

Remedies and sanctions are particularly important in victimisation cases, since the law must be seen to be supporting the victim in pursuance of a complaint and ensuring that the employer does not gain any advantage in reacting in an oppressive and unlawful way to the original complaint. The strongest provisions are in Irish law.[29] In addition to placing the burden of proof on the employer the Labour Court may order reinstatement. A fine may also be imposed on a continuing basis of IR£10 a day until the employer complies with the court's order. This has not yet been used in relation to a reinstatement order. In other member states where there is a provision for the court to order reinstatement or re-engagement, the complainant must be satisfied with compensation if the employer refuses to reinstate.

In Belgian law, in victimisation cases, again the burden of proof is on the employer. The complainant will receive a mandatory award equivalent to six months' wages without having to prove actual loss. Alternatively she may prove the actual financial loss suffered. The complainant or her representative in the workplace must make a request for reinstatement – even though the employer may refuse – or, where there has been a unilateral variation of the working conditions, a request to revert to the previous conditions. This request must be sent to the employer by registered letter at any time up to 30 days after the dismissal or unilateral variation.

The now-infamous Beckaert–Cockerill case demonstrates the unsatisfactory nature and weakness of the Belgian law and other national laws in providing protection against victimisation.[30] In that case a redundancy situation arose, and after the whole workforce had come out on strike it was agreed between management and unions, with the official arbitrator giving his stamp of approval, that those women who were not head of their households would be transferred to temporary contracts on a part-time basis. The twenty-six women involved objected and went on strike. Thirteen of them, the most active, were then dismissed. Before they could commence legal proceedings they had to find out whether this was a normal dismissal or victimisation, since this determines which procedure is to be followed and what remedies are available.

Their request to the employer for reinstatement was refused and the case was eventually heard by the Charleroi Labour Court. The court awarded them the lump sum compensation, but what they wanted was their full-time jobs back. The court, however, has no power to order and enforce reinstatement. The women are reported to have said that they were 'too tired to go on. It's been too long.'[31] So not only was a discriminatory agreement negotiated by the union and the employer but it was given the official stamp of approval. The women were treated less favourably than the men, since most of the men were heads of households, and then the women lost their jobs because they protested against discriminatory treatment.

In contrast the Greek law places the onus of proof on the complainant, but provides that if she proves her case then the steps taken against her shall be void.[32] Thus if she has been dismissed, the dismissal is presumed never to have taken place. But although this is more satisfactory, there is no evidence of it happening in practice.

If member states are to be seen to have made any real attempt to provide protection against victimisation, then the burden of proving a non-retaliatory reason for the alleged victimisation should certainly be placed on the employer. Other people involved in the complaint should be protected and action short of dismissal should be made unlawful. At present it is too easy for the employer to victimise a worker at no great cost and sometimes, as in the Beckaert–Cockerill case, to great advantage. The basic weakness of present provisions lies not only in the remedies and sanctions themselves but also in the reluctance of the courts to use them to maximum effect.

CONCLUSION

There are in all systems good practices which might be adopted in other member states to assist the individual complainant. At present there are too many hurdles to be jumped, mainly without predictable assistance. This may discourage a complaint being made in the first place. No member state has adapted its system to include all of the practices which might encourage the individual to make a complaint. Where they exist very often they are not implemented or have little impact either on the number of complaints or on the successful outcome of cases.

One is forced to conclude that the political will to provide effective means for enforcing the principles contained in the Directives is absent: lip-service is paid but no real support is given. The legal provisions and procedures place a heavy burden on the individual – the weakest of all those concerned with removing inequalities on the grounds of sex in pay and treatment. While this remains so, it should come as no surprise that few complaints have reached the courts.

Notes

1. Council Directive, 10 February 1975 (75/117/EEC) and Council Directive, 9 February 1976 (76/207/EEC).
2. *Defrenne* v. *Belgium*, Case 80/70, *Common Market Law Reports* [1974], 494.
3. Jennifer Corcoran and Elaine Donnelly, *Report of a Comparative Analysis of the Provision for Legal Redress in Member States of the European Community in Respect of Article 119 of the Treaty of Rome and the Equal Pay, Equal Treatment and Social Security Directives.* V/564/84-EN Def., Commission of the European Communities, Brussels.
4. Article 7, Equal Pay Directive, and Article 8, Equal Treatment Directive.
5. Law No. 1414/1984. There has been a similar requirement in Greek law since 1912 which has never been enforced.
6. Article 6, Law no 1288/82. See also Sophia Koukoulis-Spiliotopoulos, 'Part VI. National Reports: Equality in Law between Men and Women in the European Community', European Conference, Louvain-la-Neuve,

22–24 May 1985, Commission of the European Communities and the Interuniversity Centre of Comparative Law, Catholic University of Louvain.

7. Sex Discrimination Act 1975, section 74.
8. See Angela Byre, *First Report of the Network of Experts*, p. 20, V/564/84-EN, Commission of the European Communities.
9. Article 2, paragraph 2, Presidential Decree, 1156/1977.
10. See Report of the Commission to the Council on the *Application of the principle of Equal pay for Men and Women in Greece*, *COM*(84), 667, final, Commission of the European Communities.
11. Bar Code, Statutory Order 3026, 1954, article 92, paragraphs 3 and 5.
12. See Alice Leonard, *The First Eight Years: A Profile of Applicants to the Industrial Tribunals under the Sex Discrimination Act 1975 and the Equal Pay Act 1970*, Equal Opportunities Commission, Manchester (forthcoming). I am grateful to Dr Leonard for permission to refer to this valuable study.
13. See Sex Discrimination Act 1975, section 75.
14. Leonard, *The First Eight Years*.
15. There were 353 requests for assistance for Industrial Tribunal cases in 1984 and 245 of these were given legal assistance. A total of 258 applications were made in 1984 to Industrial Tribunals for complaints to be heard. See *Ninth Annual Report*, Equal Opportunities Commission, HMSO.
16. Case 69/80, [1981], *Industrial Relations Law Reports*, 178.
17. Code du Travail L432-3-1.
18. The Social Affairs Ministers agreed on 13 December 1984 at a Council Session to issue a Recommendation Relating to the Promotion of Positive Action for Women. A proposed Directive was not accepted.
19. Code du Travail, L140-8.
20. Leonard, *The First Eight Years*.
21. The response from the English Law Society, the professional body governing solicitors, to a question put by the EOC 'Whether any guidance has been given by the Law Society to their members about the implementation of all the Sex Discrimination Act 1975 or the need to ensure equality of opportunity for male and female solicitors' epitomises lawyers' attitudes. The reply was, 'Solicitors are presumed to know the law. No guidance has been given.' Letter of 25 November 1977. See *Women in the Legal Services*, Equal Opportunities Commission, Manchester.
22. See, for example, *Turley* v. *Allders Department Stores Ltd* [1980] *Industrial Case Reports*, 66. The Employment Appeal Tribunal (EAT) in a majority decision concluded that for the purposes of comparison under the Sex Discrimination Act 1975, a pregnant woman was not a woman. See also *Kirby* v. *Manpower Services Commission* [1980] *ICR* 420 concerning a complaint of victimisation under the Race Relations act 1976, where the EAT considered that the first duty of Kirby, a Job Centre employee, was to respect the confidences of employers using the Centre even where an employer stated an intention to discriminate against ethnic-minority workers. Kirby was moved to less-interesting work after

he informed the relevant Community Relations Council of certain employers' discriminatory statements.

23. Cour d'Appel de Liege. Fourth Chamber. 17 November 1981. *Journal des Tribunaux*, 13 March 1982.

24. Cour de Cassation. Second Chamber. 11 May 1983. *Journal des Tribunaux du Travail*, 1983. See also E. Vogel-Polsky, Part I, National Reports.

25. G. de Santis and G. Zincone, *Decision-Making Arenas Affecting Women at Work in Four European Countries*, EC Commission for Employment, Social Affairs and Education, 1983; and Corcoran and Donnelly, *Report of a Comparative Analysis*.

26. Article 7, Council Directive, 9 February 1976 – the Equal Treatment Directive. A similar provision appears in Article 5, Council Directive, 10 February 1975 – the Equal Pay Directive.

27. See T. Mitsou, Part VI, National Reports.

28. Alice Leonard, *Judging Discrimination: Sex Discrimination and Equal Pay Cases in Industrial Tribunals*, Cobden Trust, 1987.

29. See sections 9 and 10 of the Anti-discrimination (Pay) Act 1974 and sections 25 and 26, Employment Equality Act 1977.

30. Decision of the Labour Tribunal, Charleroi, 12 November 1984.

31. See *CREW Reports*, volume V, no 2.

32. Articles 174 and 180 of the Civil Code.

4 The Policies of the European Communities with Special Reference to the Labour Market[1]

Odile Quintin

The European Community has been active for many years in promoting the equal treatment of women in employment. In so doing, it has been building on the sole commitment to women in the Treaty of Rome – that they should receive equal pay for equal work. It is on the basis of the principle of equal pay that, both at European and national level, the whole concept of equality of treatment for men and women at work has developed.

Article 119 was included in the Treaty of Rome in the section dealing with social policy. It was, however, adopted for economic motives. One member state (France) already had legislation establishing the principle of equal pay and it considered that it would be at a competitive disadvantage unless all member states applied the same principle. After the establishment of the European Communities, the Commission was concerned by the fact that implementation of Article 119 in some member states showed a tendency to adopt a minimalist approach. In order to solve some of the difficulties, the Council adopted a directive on 10 February 1975[2] to apply the principle of equal pay for men and women. This directive gave women workers the clear right to demand equal pay before the courts when they were doing the same work or work of equal value.

Although direct discrimination in pay became less apparent, this did not mean that equal pay was the norm across the Community. Women would only win equal pay when they achieved equal treatment on the labour market, and it was to ensure a legal framework for equal treatment in employment, training and working conditions that the 1976 directive[3] was adopted. This was followed two years later by a directive[4] extending the application of equal treatment to social security schemes. This directive only came into force in December 1984 at the end of a very long implementation period.

71

Purely legislative action, whilst it represents an important step by guaranteeing for women fundamental rights to equality in employment, is only the first step on the road to equal opportunities. Despite the economic crisis (and perhaps partly because of it), there is an increasing demand for work by women which must be regarded as an irreversible phenomenon. The Commission has tried in its policy for the first half of the 1980s, to take account of the needs of women in employment at all levels. The economic and social climate prevailing in this decade has hampered the underlying trend towards equal opportunities. This in turn reinforced the need for the Community to act as a prime mover in the field.

Two Action Programmes on the Promotion of Equal Opportunities for Women have been compiled since 1982. The first of these, the Action Programme[5] over the period 1982–5 was the direct outcome of a Conference that took place in Manchester in May 1980. The conclusions of this Conference were further developed in the European Parliament's Resolution of February 1981 on the position of women in the European Community.

In view of the need for even further action in the social, political and industrial spheres, the second 'Medium Term Community Programme'[6] for the period 1986–90 was recently drawn up to continue the work of the first. The present Programme is made up of two broad components, the first addressing itself to the question of consolidation of the legal rights of individuals, the second comprising a series of positive action programmes aimed at overcoming non-legal barriers to the achievements of equal opportunities.

LEGISLATIVE ACTION

Although all member states have legislation embodying the principle of equality, the Commission has found it necessary to take infringement proceedings against all member states (except Greece) because their legislation did not completely meet the requirements of the Community directives. It was also necessary to set up a group of experts in order to monitor the practical obstacles preventing women from claiming their rights, with particular reference to indirect discrimination. A separate study has been conducted into the system of legal redress in the member states.[7] Work is in progress in the social security field too. The Commission has adopted a draft directive to extend the principle of equal treatment to occupational social security schemes,[8] and the possibilities of extending the principle to areas not covered by the directive are currently being examined.

Tax regimes are related to social security problems. The Commission has studied the income tax systems of the member states from the point of view of indirect discrimination against married women. This study[9] reaches the conclusion that only systems of separate taxation have a neutral effect on the work of married women – a conclusion that has been emphasised again in the Memorandum adopted by the Commission in December 1984 on income tax and equal treatment for men and women.[10] Another area where we have studied the situations of the member states in some detail is that of protective legislation.[11] The equal treatment directive provides for the amendment of this form of legislation where the original intention to protect has become outdated.

The Commission is preparing new legislation in those areas felt to be particularly appropriate. In November 1983 the Commission adopted a draft directive on parental leave and leave for family reasons[12] to ensure that workers of both sexes have the right to a period of leave to look after their young children without losing their rights to employment. The Commission has also adopted a draft directive on applying the principle of equal treatment to self-employed women and women in agriculture,[13] particularly to ensure that self-employed women may receive the benefit of maternity leave.

PRACTICAL SUPPORT FOR EQUALITY

Directives alone cannot tackle many problems facing women which result from the economic recession. A major part of our work over the past few years has been concerned with the disquieting trend towards higher women's unemployment. The Commission's communication on this subject was followed by discussion in the Standing Committee on Employment and the adoption of a resolution by the Council in June 1985.[14] How far that resolution will change anything in practice is not clear, and we will need to pay close attention to monitoring developments. The particularly worrying problem of unemployment amongst young women is something we are taking into account in our new initiative on youth policy, timed to coincide with International Youth Year. On the positive side, an increasing proportion of young women are taking part in the exchange programme for young workers and we will be taking care to ensure that this trend continues.

The second part of the action programme relates to the promotion of equal opportunities in practice, particularly by means of positive action programmes. These programmes are intended to overcome the non-legal obstacles to equal opportunities, which are based partly at least on attitudes arising from the traditional segregation of roles in society.

The Commission has conducted a critical analysis of positive action measures undertaken in some member and non-member states. On the basis of this analysis and on the results of the seminar held on positive action in Athens in September 1983 (organised by the Greek government, the Commission and the European parliament) the Council of the European Communities has adopted a Recommendation on Positive Action.[15] While this does not impose any binding requirements on the member states, it is hoped that it will stimulate activities at all levels.

The Commission also supports positive action in other practical ways, such as sponsoring campaigns, seminars, and specific sector approaches. The banking sector, for example, introduced positive action programmes as a result of research and a co-ordination at the European level. This action now extends to the industrial sector and we are encouraging certain industries in the member states to pursue positive action programmes. There is evidence that women hesitate to assume a leading role in industrial firms but one area where women are able to gain experience of management is within small businesses and co-operatives. Since 1983 the Commission has been supporting the creation of women's co-operatives and other local initiatives for women; it has recently funded a project to investigate the numbers of women either participating in or running co-operatives across the European Community with a view to establishing links between them.

Following the Recommendation on Positive Action, we also intend to draw up a Code of Practice to assist those firms and organisations working with us or on their own to give their staff equal opportunities.

It is often said that education is the basis for achieving equality of opportunity at all levels of society. In response to many demands and also upon the initiative of the Irish Minister for Education, a conference was held in Brussels on 27–28 November 1984 on equal opportunities for girls at school. Following this conference the Council's Education Committee adopted the Resolution of 3 June 1985 establishing an action programme on equal opportunities at school.[16] This programme, which covers all forms and levels of education, aims primarily to promote awareness among all the participants in the educational process of the need to achieve equal opportunities for girls and boys – children, parents–inspectors, heads of educational establishments, teacher-training staff, teachers, educational counsellors, guidance officers and local authorities.

As regards the more specific problems of integration into working life, the European Community action programme on the Transition of Young People from Education to Working Life has a clear equal opportunities dimension. At all levels of the programme, from project management and staffing down to specific positive actions within individual projects, there is a clear commitment to finding practical ways to promote equal opportunities. Much material is being gathered during the programme which is exchanged and put together with a view to future publication.

In all our work in the field of education and training, we are placing great emphasis on the need to diversify the options available for girls. A network of equal opportunities advisers has been working on this problem since 1983 under the terms of the New Action Programme. This group, co-ordinated by Madame Sullerot, is now working on positive projects to encourage diversification of job opportunities in the member states. Special attention is being paid to the responsiveness of policy-makers and those with social responsibilities to achieve the desegregation of employment and to adapt social structures to take account of changing values. When we talk of changing values, we are really concerned with the question of the sharing of family responsibilities necessary to give a woman the same opportunity not only to take a job, but to plan a career, particularly in public life. Both women and men are clearly influenced by the images of themselves portrayed to us by the media. The Commission has completed two studies on this subject, one on the position of women in television organisations[17] and the other on the image of women as presented by television,[18] which formed the basis of a seminar in June 1985 in Brussels to discuss research and action. One of the recommendations of the seminar was the establishment of a Steering Committee on Women and Television which met for the first time in Brussels on 11 February 1986. The Steering Committee will encourage the exchange of ideas and experiences and the promotion of positive actions in television companies. This forms part of the Commission's intention to increase the awareness of both the general public and of special audiences of the positive aspects of changing attitudes towards women's employment. In addition to the specific field of television, the Commission supports information activities aimed at target audiences to try to speed up changes in attitudes. We intend to develop information services to reach all groups which may play a role in the promotion or follow-up of equal opportunities. To this end we have held a seminar on legal equality, bringing together lawyers from all the member states, whose role in the interpretation of legislation is fundamental.

The Commission's work does not proceed in isolation. Consultations take place at all stages of our work with the Advisory Committee on Equal Opportunities which is made up of equality bodies or their equivalents in the member states. We also consult the social partners, employers and trade unions, other interested parties, and maintain close contacts with women's associations and organisations. It should be observed that the European Parliament is a key body in stimulating equal opportunities policies at community level.

1985 was the year in which we drew up an evaluation of progress so far on equal opportunities in the Community. The Commission presented a report on the implementation of its Action Programme, both at Community level and in the member states. This report served as the basis for a contribution to the 1985 Nairobi Conference at the end of the UN Decade for Women. The Commission is convinced of the necessity to pursue and develop its equal opportunities policy. It is clear that work in this area has resulted in some achievements and also served to clarify those areas where particular attention was required under the Medium Term Community Programme.

The evaluations we made permit a clarification of those areas on which further action is required. They form part of the new programme for the promotion of equal opportunities over 1986–90. Our goal is to pursue and develop existing actions where further progress is necessary, and to pin-point areas where more concrete action is required.

Notes

1. Opinions expressed in this chapter are personal to the author.
2. Directive 75/117/EEC.
3. Directive 76/207/EEC of 9 February 1976.
4. Directive 79/7/EEC of 19 December 1978.
5. *COM*(81) 758 final.

6. *COM*(85) 801 final.
7. Corcoran and Donnelly, *Report of a Comparative Analysis of the provisions for legal redress in Member States in the European Economic Community in respect of Article 119 of the Treaty of Rome and the equal pay, equal treatment and social security directives*, V/564/84.
8. Proposal for a Council Directive on the implementation of the principle of equal treatment for men and women in occupational social security schemes, *COM*(83) 217 final.
9. Meulders *et al.*, *Implementation of equal treatment by revising income tax systems which appear to have an indirect adverse effect on women's employment, their right to work and their promotion in employment*, V/2798/1/82 final.
10. Memorandum on Income Taxation and Equal Treatment for men and women, *COM*(84) 695 final.
11. Halpern, *Protective measures and the Activities not falling within the Field of Application of the Directive on Equal Treatment – Analysis and Proposals*, V/707/3/82.
12. Proposal for a Council Directive on parental leave and leave for family reasons, *COM*(83) 686 final. Amended Proposal for a Council Directive on parental leave and leave for family reasons, *COM*(84) 631 final.
13. Proposal for a Council Directive on the application of the principle of equal treatment between men and women engaged in an activity, including agriculture, in a self-employed capacity, and on the protection of self-employed women during pregnancy and motherhood, *COM*(84) 57 final 2.
14. 85/C 166/01.
15. Council Recommendation of 13 December 1984 on the promotion of positive action for women (84/635/EEC).
16. Resolution of Council of the Ministers of Education, meeting with the Council of 3 June 1985 containing an action programme on equal opportunities for boys and girls in education (85/C 166/01).
17. Gallagher, *Employment and Positive Action for Women in the Television Organisations of the EEC Member States*, V/205/84.
18. Thoveron, *Place and Role of Women in certain Television Programmes in EEC countries*, V/751/85.

5 Women on the Edge of Time: Part-Time Work in Ireland, North and South

Ursula Barry and Pauline Jackson

This chapter compares the pattern of female employment in the North and South of Ireland. Material on Northern Ireland is usually submerged within general data for the British economy. However, the Equal Opportunities Commission for Northern Ireland has recently produced a series of bulletins compiled by Mary Trainor and Janet Trewsdale, *Womanpower*, which provide fascinating details of women workers in Northern Ireland.[1] This has provided a new opportunity for cross-border comparisons of women workers on this island. This is the first attempt, to our knowledge, to draw together such data for Northern Ireland and the Irish Republic. British employment legislation applies directly in Northern Ireland while many parts of the legislation in the South are modelled on the British.

There remain problems in carrying out comparisons due to gaps in the data for both economies and to different systems of compilation. However, this is similar to the problems involved in comparing data in any two economies. We have used the Labour Force Survey data since surveys are carried out on a European basis and provide the surest base for comparison. The latest data for Northern Ireland are for 1981. No Labour Force Survey was carried out in the South in 1981, so 1983 data have been used.[2]

Popular conceptions have viewed Northern Ireland as an economy which provides greater opportunities for women workers than are available in the South of Ireland. However, while the economic activity rate among women is higher in the North, this situation is changing and the pattern of employment is beginning to run on parallel lines.

We focus particularly on part-time workers, comparing the level and composition of such employment in the two economies. Our objective is to highlight the vulnerability of this significant sector of the female workforce and the inadequacy of current legislation, particularly the EEC Directive on Equality. We argue that those organisations which have successfully lobbied for equality legislation affecting pay, opportunity and social welfare should actively lobby for the implementation of the EEC Draft Directive on Part-Time Work.

WOMEN IN THE LABOUR MARKET: NORTH AND SOUTH

The pattern of labour force participation by women varies considerably between the North and South of Ireland – that is, between the Northern Ireland economy and the economy of the Republic of Ireland. Traditionally, the recorded activity rate among women has been higher in the North than in the South. The recorded activity rate refers to the percentage of women in the age group 16 to 65 years who are registered as employed or seeking employment. We recognise that many women work in areas of the economy which are unpaid and thus are officially classified as economically inactive. Available data deal only with the registered workforce and, while they are useful for comparative purposes and for an indication of trends, are not an accurate picture of the female workforce.

The most obvious contrast between North and South is the very different levels of recorded labour force participation among women. The 1981 Labour Force Survey showed a labour force participation rate of 43 per cent, made up of 37 per cent in employment and 6 per cent seeking employment, among women in the Northern economy. In the South, the 1983 Labour Force survey reveals a female participation rate of 31 per cent, made up of 28 per cent in employment and 3 per cent seeking employment. However, while this rate has been virtually static in the North, it is rising in the South, and the gap between the two economies is closing. The activity rate in the North was 41.5 per cent in 1975, 42.9 per cent in 1977, 42.4 per cent in 1979 and just over 43 per cent in 1981. In the South, the rate has risen from 27.3 per cent in 1971 to 29.7 per cent in 1981 to 31.5 per cent in 1983.

Although activity rates in both economies vary considerably according to marital status, this variation is particularly marked in the South. Tables 5.1 and 5.2 illustrate that it is the difference in activity rates among married women in the two economies which accounts for the higher level of recorded economic activity among women in the North. The labour force participation rate among single women is similar in both economies (57 per cent in North and 56 per cent in South).

Table 5.1   Northern Ireland: economic activity of females aged 16 and over
by marital status 1981 (percentages)

	Single	Married	Other	Total
Paid employment or	12	22.3	2.9	37.3
self-employed	(48.0)	(38.2)	(17.8)	
Unemployed	2.2	3.2	0.5	5.9
	(9.4)	(5.2)	(3.4)	
Full-time student	5.1	0	0	5.1
	(20.1)			
Retired	3.5	4.5	8.1	16
	(13.8)	(7.6)	(48.5)	
Housewife	1.2	26.9	4.5	32.7
	(4.9)	(46.1)	(27.3)	
Long-term sick or	0.8	0.9	0.4	2.1
disabled	(3.0)	(1.6)	(2.3)	
Other	0.2	0.6	0.1	0.9
	(0.7)	(1.1)	(0.5)	
Total	25	58.4	16.6	100
	(100.0)	(100.0)	(100.0)	

Figures in brackets refer to column totals.
Source: Labour Force Survey 1981.

Table 5.2   Republic of Ireland: economic activity of females aged 15 and
over by marital status, 1983 (percentages)

	Single	Married	Other	Total
Paid employment or				
self-employed	49	18	12	28
Unemployed	7	1	1	3
Full-time student	26	0	0	9
On Home Duties	7	79	71	53
Long-term sick or				
disabled	4	0	3	2
Other	6	1	12	4
Total	100	100	100	100
	(34.7)	(52.8)	(10.7)	(100)

Source: Labour Force Survey (calculated from table 7) 1983.

Among married women, however, the rate in the North is more than double that of the South. The activity rate among married women in the North was 43 per cent in 1981, whereas in the South the rate recorded among married women in 1983 was 19 per cent. A similar contrast emerges among women in the 'other' category (i.e. widowed, divorced or legally separated). Their activity rate was 21 per cent in 1981 in the North compared with a rate of 13 per cent in the South in 1983. It is important to point out that the activity rate among married women in the South has been rising fairly steadily from 7.4 per cent in 1971 to 17.4 per cent in 1981 and to 19.6 per cent in 1983. In the North, while the rate rose between 1977 and 1979, it fell back again in the 1979–81 period.[3]

The pattern of employment of women workers shows similar characteristics in the North and South. About three-quarters of women work in the services sector in both economies. Tables 5.3 and 5.4 give a breakdown of female employment in both economies highlighting largely similar areas of concentration.

Table 5.3 reveals that in the North the two categories of manufacturing employment together employ about 20 per cent of the

Table 5.3 Northern Ireland: industrial analysis of employees in employment, 1981 (percentages)

Industrial order	Females		
	Married	*Part-time*	*All*
Agriculture, forestry & fishing	0.2	0.4	0.4
Energy and water	1	0.2	1
Extraction/processing of minerals	0.7	0	0.7
Metal manufacture/ mechanical engineering	4.6	1.4	4.6
Other manufacturing	13.8	6.9	15.9
Building/civil engineering	0.7	0.8	1
Distributive trades	16.6	26.1	18.1
Transport & communication	1.5	1.2	1.9
Finance/insurance	3.7	3.1	4.8
Other services	55.7	58.8	50.4
Working abroad	0.1		0.1
No reply	1.3	1	1.2
Total	100	100	100

Source: Labour Force Survey 1981.

women workers, while the vast majority of workers are concentrated in the various services categories. By way of comparison, Table 5.4 indicates that while similar patterns are evident in the South, manufacturing employs a lower percentage – 16.5 per cent of women workers. Agriculture remains a significant source of employment in the South where just over 6 per cent of women work, whereas in the North less than 1 per cent of women workers are engaged in agricultural employment.

Table 5.4   Republic of Ireland: females at work by industrial groups and proportion of workforce, 1983

Industrial group	Women as % of total	% of female workforce
Agriculture, forestry & fishing	11.5	6.3
Mining/quarrying	5.2	0.1
Manufacturing	26	16.5
Electricity/gas/water	9.4	0.3
Building & construction	3.7	0.9
Commerce/distribution	35.9	16.8
Insurance/finance	47.3	6
Transport/communication	18.8	3.8
Public administration/defence	29	6
Professional services	59.5	30.5
Personal services	63.1	10.2
Other	36.7	1.7
Total	30.7	100

Source: 1983 Labour Force Survey (table 12) CSO 1984.

PART-TIME WORK – TACKLING THE SUBJECT

In 1984, the Southern government (Republic of Ireland) launched a part-time employment scheme. In return for signing-off at labour exchanges, long-term unemployed (over one year) are offered two and a half days 'socially useful' work for IR £70 a week. But is part-time work an answer to female unemployment? Unique to the scheme is its discriminatory attitude to women with children, the traditional holders of part-time jobs. Through administrative and eligibility requirements, men are the main beneficiaries of the new scheme and the marginal and secondary status of part-time work is expanded to embrace another deprived group – long-term unemployed men. The wage offered is significant. At IR £70 for two and a half days work it is double what part-time women cleaners could expect to earn.[4]

Over a short period of time, part-time work has been transformed from the Cinderella in the kitchens of the labour force to the Prince Charming of new employment initiatives. The published results of the 1979 LFS in the South do not even include the answers to the questions on hours of work. Even in the 1983 LFS the answers to the questions on part-time and full-time work are not provided. So what has happened in the interim?

In response to the crisis, European employers have accepted several restructuring strategies. In new technology, protectionism against Japanese and US imports is predominant. In heavy industries such as coal and steel, there have been closures of plants. In manufacturing, particularly in areas employing women, including shoes, leather, gloves, clothing, knitwear and textiles, outworking (homeworking) and subcontracting have been important in reducing big employers' social costs by transferring them to small employers (contractors) or employees themselves (outworkers). Policies to repatriate immigrant workers, combined with racism, have served to reduce labour market pressure in host countries but heightened tension in the labour-exporting regions like Ireland. Part-time work, casual work, fixed-duration contracts and temporary work all fulfil a similar purpose – the foundation of a floating pool of irregular workers, deskilled, de-unionised, demoralised and available for precarious work as the different branches of the economy and industry experience sporadic and short-lived upsurges in demand for labour. Mary Redmond's legal and statistical appraisal of the subject sums it up well:

> All too often temporary and part-time workers are regarded, not as an integral and auxiliary part of the labour force . . . but as an alternative workforce. They constitute a mechanism whereby cheap labour can be acquired, particularly cheap female labour . . . labour that may be hired and fired free from the constraints of employment legislation.[5]

The expansion of the concept and practice of part-time employment is found in new state employment initiatives. Work on such schemes is attractive to younger, unmarried, unemployed, both men and women, and typically involves work in the public domain: building and environmental restoration, cultural and leisure amenities. However, interestingly, we see part-time temporary work here offered to younger people and in areas which impinge on the public sector – age groups and sectors where part-time work in the South is not particularly prevalent. Such schemes may form the expectations of young people, young women in particular, of their future role in the labour force, accustoming them to part-time temporary work – via the state – as the only valid outlet for their energies and at an age when they still seek and hope for full-time jobs with the wages and purchasing power which goes with them.

The use of part-time temporary work as a means to combat unemployment will increase the proportion of workers engaged in part-time work in the South, bringing the situation closer to that which prevails in the North, though this will not appear in labour force measurements.

Part-time work is too often regarded as a form of work that women want, that fits in with their household and family situations. This emphasis on women's subjective attitudes presents part-time work as an almost exclusively 'supply' problem: women seek part-time work and employers benevolently provide it. One frequently hears remarks such as: 'It is not surprising that part-time jobs are especially popular with married women.'[6] Or 'The widespread preference of part-time work among housewives was consistently held across all of the eight countries.' However, it was particularly favoured in the Netherlands and Ireland.[7] In relation to the Netherlands, it might have been pointed out that hourly earnings for part-timers are on a par with those for full-timers.

By contrast, Paukert stresses employers' demand for part-time workers, rather than women's preferences. In her interpretation of the rising importance of precarious employment in the Western economies, she comments:

The greater flexibility and the low cost of part-time work have been . . . factors of interest to employers, particularly in times of fluctuating business. Changes in operating conditions (including the use of new technology) have led many enterprises to a restructuring of activity and to a redistribution of work tasks – hourly earnings of part-time workers are lower than those of full-time workers in most OECD countries.[8]

MEASURING PART-TIME WORK

There are two different ways of measuring the extent of part-time work using the Labour Force Surveys. The first way is by analysing the answers to the question on whether a person's job could be described by them as part-time or full-time. This is a subjective measure and reflects the respondent's own attitude to their job or their employer's attitude to them. The second way of measuring part-time work is by examining the answers to a series of questions on the hours worked by surveyed persons during the week prior to the interview, and in particular the question 'How many hours do you usually work at your job, including overtime?' Answers to these questions can be used to measure part-time work. For example, all those working under 18 hours a week, or even under 30 hours a week, could be considered part-timers for the purpose of analysis. While this second method seems more objective, it depends on adopting a threshold level of hours per week below which all those working such hours are regarded as part-time workers, and it varies according to which measure one uses. The first, more subjective, method, when applied, yields a greater volume of part-time workers than the second. In terms of measuring how many part-time workers might be covered by various pieces of labour legislation, the second method has its advantages. Daly, in her survey of West of Ireland part-timers, used a third, more qualitative, measure.[9] She and her team visited over 1,200 households both to enumerate and interview part-time cleaners. Her method has the advantage of providing vital information on the social and economic environment from which part-time workers are recruited.

PART-TIME WORK IN EUROPE

The proportion of women at work who are part-time varies considerably across the member states of the European Community. A first group of countries is comprised of those where less than 20 per cent of women in employment are part-timers: Ireland (South) (13 per cent), Luxembourg (18 per cent), Belgium (17 per cent), Italy (11 per cent) and France (17 per cent).[10] A second group of countries which are mainly highly industrialised encompasses Germany, the Netherlands, the UK, Denmark and the North of Ireland. In the second group, very high proportions of women are part-timers, ranging from 28 per cent in Germany to 46 per cent in Denmark.

With eleven million part-time workers in Europe in 1983, of whom nine million are married women, the debate over part-time work is shifting.[11] Previously regarded as a marginal phenomenon, it is increasingly seen not merely as an important quantitative phenomenon but a form of work to be encouraged to combat unemployment.

PART-TIME WOMEN WORKERS: NORTH AND SOUTH

There are about 120,000 women part-timers at work throughout Ireland, North and South. Of these, about 67,000 are to be found in the North and 53,000 in the South. This is somewhat paradoxical, since the North has a smaller economy and smaller labour force; however, the labour force participation of women is greater in the North than in the South. The proportion of women in employment who are part-timers differs considerably between the North and the South at 30 per cent and 15 per cent respectively.[12] However, there are convergent trends. While the proportions in the North remained static between 1979 and 1981, the proportions in the South are rising slightly, probably parallel to the growth of the labour force participation of married women, referred to earlier.

It is often erroneously presumed that all or almost all part-time workers are women. This is not the case. In the South, about 73 per cent of all part-time workers are women. However, the remaining 27 per cent are men, with a special characteristic – youth. A large proportion of male part-timers are under 24 years old. In fact, women and young men make up 82 per cent of all part-time workers in the South.[13] It is possible that with the recession, part-time working among unemployed young men may spread as it already is expanding among young unmarried women in the North.

The age profile of women part-timers is very similar North and South. In the North, about one-half are aged between 25 and 45, while the South just over half are aged 25 to 49 years old.[14] Full-time workers are much younger, especially in the South, where 42 per cent of full-time women in employment are under 25 years old. The similarity in age profile is matched by comparisons of marital status North and South. In the North 84 per cent of women (1981) part-timers are married, while in the South 75 per cent of part-time women are married (1983). These high proportions are all the more remarkable when one recalls the very low labour force participation of married women in the South. In the North, the proportion of married among part-timers fell between 1979 and 1981. Trainor and Trewsdale interpret this as the impact of deep economic recession on single women who are prepared to take a part-time job while awaiting a full-time position.[15]

The relationship between married women, dependent children and part-time work status is well established in Northern Ireland:

The proportion of women working part-time increases as the number of dependent children increase, up to a maximum of 70 per cent for 4 dependent children. The presence of 5 or more dependent children reduces the tendency to work part-time.[16]

As for hours worked, comparisons are difficult, but the magical threshold of 21 hours appears North and South of the border. In the North, 71 per cent of women part-timers work 21 hours or less, while in the South, O'Donovan estimates that 62 per cent work less than 21 hours.[17] Redmond, having studied the Dáil and Seanad (Parliament) debates at the time of the Redundancy Payments Bill, concludes that the 21-hours threshold was arrived at after discussions with employer and trade-union representatives who apparently hoped and believed it would exclude married women who worked in the evenings.[18]

This it did, excluding well over half the part-timers from the later Unfair Dismissals Act and Minimum Notice. The new threshold in the South is eighteen hours, and employers in the South are correspondingly reducing their part-timers' hours to seventeen or less to evade their obligations. The point is poignantly made by the part-time women contract cleaners at University College Dublin who went on strike during summer 1985. A change in contract altered their working conditions, and as members of the Irish Transport and General Workers' Union, they resisted.

A reduction in working hours was at the core of the strikers' grievance, as one of their leaflets explained:

It was as a direct result of this that the hours were cut again down from four to three [a day]. As we've explained, this meant the workers employed on the contract would not only lose money again but would also fall out of the PRSI system, and lose entitlement to sickness and maternity benefit, holiday pay, redundancy rights and the protection of the Employment Protection Acts. This was completely unacceptable to us.[19]

Their dispute is typical of the volatility of part-time jobs as employers play cat-and-mouse with hours' thresholds.

Where do part-timers work? In North and South, the services sector accounts for the majority of women part-timers. In the North, while full-time employment has been decreasing, part-time employment was increasing during the 1970s. The growth area was the services sector where part-time female employment almost doubled between 1971 and 1977.[20]

The role of agriculture in the economy of the South is more important than in the North and it correspondingly occupies a greater share (22 per cent) of part-time women workers.

Table 5.5   Distribution of women part-timers in the south by sector of economy, 1983

	(000)	%
Agriculture	12	22
Industry	5	9
Services	37	69
Total	54	100

Source: Eurostat, *Employment and Unemployment Bulletin*, no 2, 1985, table 8, p. 8, Luxembourg.

As Table 5.5 illustrates, 69 per cent of part-time workers are in services, as is also the case in the North.

An occupational analysis reveals the importance of part-time workers in certain jobs, trades and activities in the North (Table 5.6).

In some occupations, like catering, hairdressing and cleaning, over 63 per cent of women workers are part-time. In others, like shops (selling) and sport, 40 per cent or more are part-time. Interestingly, few managerial or well-paid jobs are part-time.

In the services sector, such as shops, we find married women with dependent children aged in their thirties and, in the case of the South, often with unemployed husbands.[21] There are also converging trends as the proportion of women who are working part-time in the South expands to approximate the proportion in the North. A second convergence is the expansion of part-time work out of the traditional spheres in both the North and South into state-funded part-time

Table 5.6   Proportion of all women workers who are part-time in selected occupations in Northern Ireland, 1981* (per cent)

Occupation		Full-time	Part-time
I	Managerial & professional & related supporting management & administration	100	0
II	Professional & related in education, welfare and health	76.6	20.2
III	Literary, artistic & sports	60.6	39.4
IV	Professional & related in science, engineering & technology	69.6	30.4
V	Managerial (excluding general management)	90.5	3.3
VI	Clerical & related	80.6	18.1
VII	Selling	51.9	44.4
VIII	Security & protective service	78.4	21.6
IX	Catering, cleaning, hairdressing & other professional services	34.5	63.4
X	Farming, fishing and related	68.7	31.3
XI	Material processing	87.6	11.1
XII	Processing, making & repairing (metal & electrical)	100	0
XIII	Painting, repetitive assembling, product inspection, etc.	87.2	11
XIV	Construction, mining, etc.	0	0
XV	Transport operating, moving & storing materials	74.4	25.6
XVI	Miscellaneous	32.3	57.7
	Not stated	25.1	0
	Column total	67.2	30.2

*Where full-time and part-time totals of individual occupations do not add up to 100, the discrepancy is due to the 'no reply' category.
Source: Trewsdale and Trainor, and EOC NI table 2.8 from LFS 1981.

employment initiatives for younger men and women. In the North, this is pertinent to the 'leisure industry' where, in the category of sports and artistic workers, almost 40 per cent of women workers are part-timers.

The growth of part-time work is economically and socially connected to the growth of temporary or fixed contract work. In the South, thousands of civil service jobs have remained unfilled over the past five years. In 1985 the state introduced a scheme to fill some of these posts by employing 1000 young people on temporary contracts. This scheme was renewed in 1986. The rate of pay for these young contracted workers was less than that available to unionised cleaning women. The trade unions continue to monitor the scheme very closely due to the hostility with which it is viewed by both the general membership and the leadership of the highly unionised civil service sector.[22]

Part-time work is just one facet of the casualisation of labour being imposed on the de-industrialised economy of Ireland in both North and South. In this context, increasing numbers of women find that the EEC Equality Directives, whose application supposes that workers are part of a 'guaranteed' work force, are no longer applicable.

Using quite a different method of calculation, a table somewhat similar to Table 5.5 was constructed for the South. Here, in Table 5.7, based on hours worked, all women working under 20 hours are categorised as part-time, and over 20 hours as full-time. This underestimates the numbers of part-timers, but enables us to discern trends.

Table 5.7   Proportions of full and part-time women at work by occupation, 1983, South (per cent)

Occupation	Full-time	Part-time*
Agricultural	80	20
Producers, makers	94.7	5.3
Labourers, unskilled	80	20
Transport, communications	89.7	10.3
Clerical	94.6	5.4
Commerce/insurance	88.5	11.5
Service	79	21
Professional/technical	75.2	24.8
Others	96.9	3.1
Total	86	14

*Women working 0–19 hours a week.
Source: Calculated from LFS 1983, tables 16 and 18.

In four out of the nine broad occupational categories, 20 to 25 per cent of women are part-timers using the nineteen-hour threshold – agricultural, services, unskilled occupations and professional and technical jobs. As in the North, clerical jobs are less part-time as are producer (factory) occupations.

EQUALITY LEGISLATION AND WOMEN WORKERS

In the previous section it has been demonstrated that part-time work is a significant and, in some areas, a growing trend among women workers in the North and South of Ireland. In the North, recorded part-time work involves nearly one-third of women workers, while available data in the South indicates that just over 16 per cent of women workers are working part-time. In the North, 84 per cent of female part-time workers are married women while the corresponding figure for the South is 75 per cent. Clearly, we are talking about a significant proportion of the female workforce, the majority of whom are unskilled, low-paid and excluded from the protection of labour legislation.

The majority of protective legislation both in Britain and the Republic of Ireland is based on an hours' threshold – i.e. the legislation only applies to those working a minimum number of hours every week. The threshold varies from sixteen to eighteen to twenty-one hours depending on the piece of legislation under question. The critical issue here is that thousands of part-time women workers are denied the protection of unfair dismissal legislation, are not entitled to sick pay, paid holidays or pension schemes, and very often receive no employment contract or statement of working conditions.[23] The implication of this is that part-time workers, the vast majority of whom are women, make up a vulnerable, unprotected and grossly underpaid section of the workforce. In this context, equality legislation in Europe must be viewed from a highly critical perspective, in particular in its relevance to this marginalised section of the female workforce. Furthermore, eligibility for social welfare benefits is also linked to the number of hours a person has been working, acting as yet another form of penalty on part-time workers.

Existing equality legislation outlaws both direct and indirect discrimination on grounds of sex and marital status. While the Equal Pay legislation covers pay and working conditions, the Equal Opportunity legislation covers such areas as advertising, promotion, training and work practices. Generally, one can state that these areas of legislation have a limited impact on the conditions of women workers. Each case must be based on a claim for equal treatment with a person of the opposite sex or in a different category of marital status. Under the Equal Pay legislation in the Republic of Ireland, 570 cases were referred for investigation between 1975 and 1984.[24] The most important year for cases was 1980, but since then the number of cases has been falling – averaging about thirty annually. About 65 per cent of the decisions favoured women employees. Under the Equal Opportunity Act (1977) in the Republic, 190 cases were reviewed between 1977 and 1984. In 115 cases, recommendations were made, and 53 of these favoured the employees involved. Under both Acts, the number of cases is small, affecting only a tiny proportion of women workers.

EXCLUSION OF PART-TIME WORKERS

The majority of the provisions under equality legislation are based on a specific period of employment (up to two years) and the establishment of discrimination between workers of different sexes. Many part-time workers are also casual workers and therefore unable to comply with the length of service requirements. Because the vast majority of part-time workers are women, there are very few occasions in which a case can be taken on the basis of sex discrimination. Test cases have been taken to utilise existing equality legislation in cases of discrimination between part-time and full-time workers within one establishment. In the case of *Carty and O'Reilly* v. *Dunnes Stores Ltd*,[25] an equality officer considered a case in which two part-time female employees were claiming equal pay with a male full-time employee, on a pro-rata basis. The equality officer recommended in favour of the employees, despite the fact that the employer argued that male and female part-timers were on the same rate. The employers appealed the case unsuccessfully.[26]

A similar case was brought in England and finally went to the European Court of Justice, following a negative decision in the English courts. In this case, the European court ruled that differential rates of pay between men and women workers could not be justified simply by showing that the women work part-time. The European Court of Justice further asserted that differential rates of pay between female part-timers and male full-timers could be justified by showing 'objective economic reasons'. This means that where employers show lower productivity levels or other such 'economic' factors, then differential rates can be justified.[27] While these cases show that equality legislation can be used to establish equal pay and conditions between part-time and full-time workers, this is only possible in limited circumstances. First, there must be workers of different categories of part-time and full-time. Second, only part-time workers who have satisfied a length of service requirement can claim under the Act. Finally, employers can justify differential rates on the basis of 'objective economic criteria'.

Adequate protection and working conditions for part-time workers require new legislation. The Draft EEC Directive on Part-Time Work, which was blocked by the Council of Ministers of the European Community, contained many provisions which would transform the position of eleven million part-time workers in Europe. It was proposed that the hours' threshold preventing part-time workers qualifying for protective legislation and social welfare provisions, be abolished. Thus, under this draft directive part-time workers would be entitled to the same rights as full-time workers on a pro-rata basis. Britain and W. Germany opposed the Draft Directive and Denmark and Ireland expressed serious reservations. The main stumbling-block in the discussions at Council level was the 'hours' threshold' – Britain argued to maintain a threshold of 12 hours.[28]

While the draft directive on part-time work is not technically part of equality legislation in Europe, our contention is that it is vital to a significant proportion of women workers. Amendments to both British and Irish legislation could be and should be implemented in the meantime, based on the principle of extending the rights and provisions covering full-time workers to part-time workers on a pro-rata basis. However, given the opposition and reservations expressed by both these governments within the Council of Ministers of the European Community, pressure at European level is essential. In our view, improvement in the conditions and pay of part-time workers is crucial to women's organisations in Europe and should be viewed as of equal importance as anti-discrimination and equal pay measures. At least 120,000 women workers are marginalised and vulnerable as part-time workers in the North and South of Ireland; their working conditions are dependent on real changes in pay and conditions.

Notes

1. Mary Trainor and Janet Trewsdale, *Womanpower No. 3: The Impact of Recession on Female Employment and Earnings in Northern Ireland*, Equal Opportunities Commission for Northern Ireland, Belfast.
2. Central Statistics Office, *Labour Force Survey*, Central Statistics Office, Dublin, 1984.

3. Trainor and Trewsdale, *The Impact of Recession*; Central Statistics Office, *Labour Force Survey*, Central Statistics Office, Dublin, 1982, 1984; Central Statistics Office, *Census of Population*, Central Statistics Office, Dublin, 1981.
4. Mary Daly, *The Hidden Workers – A Summary Report*, Employment Equality Agency, Dublin, 1985.
5. Mary Redmond, 'Beyond the Net – Protecting the Individual Worker', *Industrial Relations Review*, Dublin, 1983.
6. Eurostat, 'Employment and Unemployment', *Bulletin*, No. 2, Commission of the European Communities, 1985.
7. M. Fine-Davis, *Women, Work and Well-being in the European Community*, Commission of the European Communities, V/55/85-EN, 1985.
8. Liba Paukert, *The Employment and Unemployment of Women in OECD Countries*, OECD, 1984.
9. Daly, *The Hidden Workers*.
10. Commission of the European Communities, *Women of Europe*. Supplement No. 14. 'Women and Statistics', Commission of the European Communities, X/30/84-EN, 1984.
11. Eurostat, 'Employment and Unemployment'.
12. Trainor and Trewsdale, *The Impact of Recession*. Eurostat, 'Employment and Unemployment', ibid.
13. Eurostat, 'Employment and Unemployment', ibid.
14. Trainor and Trewsdale, *The Impact of Recession*.
15. Ibid.
16. Ibid.
17. P. O'Donovan, 'Workshop Paper to the Council for the Status of Women Forum', Royal Dublin Society, Dublin, 5 October 1985 (unpublished).
18. Redmond, *Beyond The Net*.
19. Mary Lenihan, Leaflet issued in September 1985 by No. 11 Branch of the Irish Transport and General Workers' Union, Dublin 1985 (unpublished).
20. R. W. Hutchison and J. Sheehan, *Demographic and Labour Force Structure in the Republic of Ireland and Northern Ireland*, Co-operation North, Dublin and Belfast, 1981.
21. Daly, *The Hidden Workers*.
22. National Manpower Services, Social Employment Scheme Brochure, Dublin, 1985.
23. Ursula Barry, 'Reduction and Reorganisation of Working Time – EEC Initiatives', Report to Employment Equality Agency, Dublin (unpublished) 1983.
24. Pauline Jackson, 'Female Labour Force Participation', *Report to the Bureau for Women's Equality*, Brussels (unpublished) 1984.
25. The Labour Court, *Thirty-Sixth Annual Report 1982*, The Stationery Office, Dublin, 1983.
26. Barry, 'Reduction and Reorganisation'.
27. House of Lords, *Report of Select Committee on European Legislation: Part-Time and Temporary Work*, HMSO, London, 1981.
28. Commission of the European Communities, Draft Directive on Part-Time Work, Commission of the European Communities, 1983.

6 Indirect Discrimination in Social Security in the Netherlands: Demands of the Dutch Women's Movement

Ina Sjerps

The objective of the women's movement in the socio-economic field can be summarised as the demand for economic independence. This demand, which dates from the beginning of this century, is based on the assumption that economic independence may help to change the present structures according to which women are subordinated to men.

A major part of public life is determined by the sphere of paid work. Money, influence and opportunities are distributed by it. Breaking through this pattern of distribution of paid and unpaid work between the sexes is one way of breaking out of the system of subordination of one sex to the other.

Making paid work available to women is not sufficient to meet these objectives. Economic independence means more, namely: being capable of providing one's own subsistence over the years, with the opportunities of shaping one's working and public life, in the same manner as men. If women were economically independent in this sense, contemporary problems such as the rise in single-parent families living in poverty on social security, might no longer exist.

Next to a right to paid work, equal pay and reasonable working conditions, women should have individual rights to transfer payments, from taxes to social security benefits. Furthermore, special measures are needed to redistribute paid and unpaid work in an even way, between the sexes. A massive reduction in waged working time is essential alongside an increase in childcare facilities and parental leave. Not only in society as a whole, but also on a microlevel, it is necessary to make women economically independent from men, since it is a prerequisite for emotional and psychological independence.

In this decade, one of the main demands of the Dutch women's movement has been the individualisation of the social security system. This is part of the overall demand for the economic independence of women. One of the reasons for focusing on the position of women in social security schemes is the existence of a European Communities (EC) directive on equal treatment of men and women. As EC Directives are legally binding, the Dutch government was forced to adjust the social security system to the principle of equal treatment.

In this chapter, the demands of the women's movement with regard to social security are compared with the effect of the EC Directive. It is argued that the Directive, in prescribing equal treatment, does not lead to a substantial improvement for women. This once again raises the question of the utility of the concept of equal treatment, and of its interpretation in the legal system of the European Communities.

An individual treatment with regard to social security and taxation is seen as essential for economic independence.[1] Individualisation of the social security system means that every adult should be entitled to benefits in his or her own right. The level of benefits should be high enough to make an independent lifestyle possible. No reference should be made to marital or cohabiting status. The individual, not the family, must be the unit to whom rights and obligations are attributed. The importance of an individual right to benefits is twofold: first, as a source of income and thereby financial independence, when no income or insufficient income can be obtained through paid work; second, as an important labour condition which may stimulate women to take up paid work by making it a more attractive and reliable source of income.

Individualisation of social security rights is also supported for reasons other than the quest for economic independence and equality. Under the influence of emancipation and ideologies of equality characteristic of post-war Western societies, equal treatment in the sphere of paid labour is a general expectation. When the same work is done, and when the same contributions and taxes are paid by men and women, it no longer makes sense to treat them differently in terms of pay, including in benefits (unemployment, illness or disablement benefits).

There are two main types of social security schemes: wage-related benefits, usually granted for a certain limited period in case of unemployment, disablement and illness, and means-tested benefits guaranteeing a minimum income in cases where no other income assets are available.

Wage-related schemes can also be regarded as insurance-based schemes. People find it more and more logical that when a man and a woman do the same job and pay the same contributions, they should also be granted the same wage-related benefits. This 'logic' has not always existed. The old notion was that even in wage-related schemes women needed less protection (in particular married women) because their income was less important than that of men. Women were not, or were not supposed to be, the breadwinner of the family. At the same time, making it possible for men to be family breadwinners by giving male incomes a better protection, even in wage-related schemes, was considered just.

The new notion, that it is just to treat people in the same way when they have paid the same contributions (insurance-thinking), finds support in the ideology of the critics of the welfare-state, which favours the (liberal) notion of insurance-based benefits, with a lesser 'solidarity' component. Therefore, the women's movement gets support for its demand of individualisation when it comes to wage-related benefits. However, similar backing is not given when it comes to means-tested benefits.

Means-tested or 'safety net' benefits are usually granted to breadwinners or families and form the main blockage in the social security system to the financial independence of women. Whenever they have a spouse or partner with an income, women cannot claim social security payments; they must turn to their spouses or partners for support. Nevertheless, the ideology of the welfare-state, culminating in the constitutional guarantee of the *right* to social assistance, has caused a change in perspective. Many people consider that they have a right to be supported by society whenever they cannot provide for their own subsistence. They no longer think that state benefits are a favour: it is felt to be a basic right, and, as all basic rights, an individual right. This contradicts the principle that social assistance is a measure of last resort. This latter principle underlies the view that people, and women in particular, should get their subsistence not from the state but should turn elsewhere, to lovers, friends or relatives. Under the pressure of economic crisis and a revision of assumptions among policy-makers, the support for this principle is rapidly growing.

Even though people have come to view social assistance as a right, the same liberal and right-wing critics of the state who favour an insurance-based ideology for wage-related schemes, believe that when it comes to social assistance people should not be treated as individuals, but should turn to their spouse or partner first. The notion of the retreating state (smaller bureaucracy, lesser expenditure) favours individualisation in wage-related schemes and opposes it in social assistance schemes. A clear reflection of this duality in the entire system of social security can be found in the government paper on the reform of the system.[2]

POLICY OF THE EUROPEAN COMMUNITY

Existing and proposed EC law on the equal treatment of men and women is enshrined in Article 119 of the Treaty of Rome. During the 1970s, Directives were adopted by the EC Council of Ministers, guaranteeing equal pay and equal treatment in access to employment, vocational training and promotion and working conditions, and equal treatment in statutory social security schemes. Despite the fact that the EC Action Programme on Equal Opportunities for Women (1982–5) refers to the need to individualise social security rights, an insurance-based assumption predominates in EC policy on the equal treatment of men and women. The Social Security Directive of July 1978, concerned with the equal treatment of men and women in matters of social security, defines equal treatment as a prohibition of all direct and indirect discrimination on the grounds of sex. But whether such a prohibition will bring about individualisation of social security rights is doubtful.

The Social Security Directive applies to the working population, retired or invalided workers and self-employed persons whose activity is interrupted by illness, accident or involuntary unemployment. The Directive applies to statutory schemes which insure against the following risks: illness, invalidity, old age, accidents at work, occupational diseases and unemployment. It also applies to social assistance benefits in so far as they are intended to supplement or replace insurance against these risks. The scope of the Directive is wide enough to incorporate nearly all statutory schemes. There are, however, certain exclusions, including survivors' benefits, some family benefits, and occupational schemes. The possibility exists to exclude, on a temporary basis, certain benefits or conditions from the scope of the directive. The Dutch government, however, will not make use of this possibility.

The Social Security Directive forbids discrimination on the grounds of sex, either directly or indirectly by reference in particular to marital or family status. The prohibition of direct discrimination is straightforward. It simply means that no reference may be made to sex in determining rights or duties. The notion of indirect discrimination, however, is a more complex one which was recently introduced in the Dutch legal system under the influence of international law and of United States jurisprudence.[3]

The prohibition in the Social Security Directive of indirect discrimination can be seen as an acknowledgement of the fact that women and men are in different positions regarding social security. Treating different situations similarly can be just as discriminatory as treating similar situations differently.[4] However, the notion of indirect discrimination is far more difficult to apply than the notion of direct discrimination.

The EC Commission has tried to formulate the interpretation and consequences of the prohibition of indirect discrimination under a Directive in its interim report.[5] The European Court has not yet had the opportunity to give its binding opinion on the interpretation of the Social Security Directive. The opinion of the Commission – being a close court-watcher – can be considered authoritative. The conclusion of the Interim Report, which is based on Court jurisprudence, is as follows:

> Indirect discrimination may be presumed where a measure which is apparently neutral in fact predominantly affects workers of one sex, without it being necessary to establish that discrimination was intended. On the contrary, it is for the person applying the measure presumed to be discriminatory to provide proof that it was objectively justified and did not involve any intention to discriminate.[6]

Although the Interim Report as a whole is vague and even contradictory, the above definition is an adequate summary of contemporary thought and jurisprudence on issues of discrimination. The main elements in this definition are determining the effects of a measure, and the possible justification of such effects, and shifting the burden of proof. The first element seems fairly clear, although the use of statistics to prove the negative effect is a recent innovation and raises a number of interesting questions.[7]

The concept of objective justification causes problems. No strict guidelines on what is and what is not 'objectively justified' have been identified. This lack of clarity is easily explained: the notion of objective justification may be presented as a weighing of the negative effect a measure produces for one of the sexes (usually women) against other interests in society. Inherent to the notion of objective justification is its specific character: each case can be different. Although the EC Commission in its Interim Report does not give strict guidelines on what is or is not objectively justified, it gives its view on one important question: increases in benefits for dependent spouses are allowed in order to guarantee a minimum income for the couple or the family.

THE DUTCH SOCIAL SECURITY SYSTEM

A brief outline of the Dutch system and the position of women in it must be given in order to see whether the principle of equal treatment (defined as a prohibition of direct and indirect discrimination) is likely to bring about individualisation of social security rights. The Dutch social security system is permeated by the traditional conception of the breadwinner. For a long time this reflected the ideas and behaviour of a considerable proportion of the Dutch population. Labour-force participation rates of women have always been, and still are, among the lowest in the EC. In 1960, 26.3 per cent of women worked in the labour force; the same as in 1900. In 1970 this figure rose to 30.6 per cent, at a time when the Irish participation rate of adult women was 34.3 per cent, and the EC average was 44.4 per cent. In 1980, 34.9 per cent of the Dutch women worked as compared with the EC average of 49.7 per cent. Throughout the last decade, the pattern has undergone a considerable change. The participation of women in the labour force is growing rapidly. Part-time work in particular is responsible for this growth: over 50 per cent of all working women work part-time as compared with 5 per cent of all working men.[8]

The economic crisis has prevented large numbers of women leaving their role as housewives to take up paid work. Unemployment rates of women are high relative to those of men and even higher when hidden unemployment is taken into consideration. Other problems include a striking lack of childcare facilities compared with some EC countries and a lack of provision for parental leave apart from a three-month maternity benefit.

Various factors tend to make working women more vulnerable to disincentives than men especially when they work part-time. As in other countries, most women are found in the lower strata of the working hierarchy. They have, relative to men, low pay, bad working conditions, fewer career possibilities and are more frequently found in part-time, temporary and other marginal jobs.

This has recently been illustrated by the impact of a revision of the tax system. Under the principle of 'equal treatment' the tax burden on couples where both spouses or unmarried partners have an income, was increased in order to eliminate a provision which directly discriminated against married women. As a consequence the position of the traditonal breadwinner underwent a considerable improvement. When the incomes of both partners influence the burden of tax on one another, it becomes highly unprofitable for women with small incomes, such as part-time workers, to do paid work. As a result over 10,000 women left their part-time jobs during the months after the new tax-system came into force. The same effect can be brought about by favouring breadwinners in social security.[9]

The Dutch social security system is said to be one of the most generous and complex ones in the world. This complexity together with the rising costs in a time of economic crisis and the EC Social Security Directive, encouraged the Dutch government to embark on a major process of reform. A number of changes, mainly the levelling-down of benefits, are in the process of taking place. A new system of unemployment and disablement benefits was voted on by the Dutch Parliament in May 1986 and approved. It came into force on 1st January 1987. Unfortunately, this new system is even more complex than the previous one. The women's movement is very dissatisfied with the application of the Social Security Directive contained in the new system and the only substantial result of the reform will probably be a cut in public expenditure.

Discrimination against women under the pre-1986 system may be compared with discrimination under the newly emerging system. The insurance-type benefits contained two main forms of discrimination against women. Unemployment schemes granted benefits for two and a half years to the unemployed, except married women whose benefit stopped after 6 months unless they could prove that they were the breadwinner. This form of direct discrimination was not abolished until May 1985, six months after the implementation period of the directive ended, and after vehement protests in parliament and the issuing of a writ by the trade unions against the government. The other main form of alleged discrimination arose from a built-in minimum guarantee for breadwinners in the schemes which protect against unemployment, disablement and illness. The level of the benefits for a breadwinner cannot fall below a certain minimum assumed to be sufficient for a family. This built-in guarantee will be eliminated and replaced by a new scheme envisaging increases in benefits. These increases are granted to breadwinners after a means test. Since the general level of benefits has been brought down, many long-term unemployed and disabled people will have to apply for these increases. If their spouse or partner has a part-time job, the same effect as brought about by the new tax system may be expected. It will become highly uneconomic for women part-time workers to remain at work, when their unemployed spouse or partner can get an increase in his benefit if she stays at home.

The view of the Commission, expressed in its Interim Report, does not consider such increases to be indirectly discriminating against women. They guarantee a minimum and therefore are objectively justified. The discouraging effect that these increases may have on the participation of women in the labour force is probably not taken into account.

The old-age pension scheme explicitly excluded married women. Married men were granted a flat-rate benefit, 70 per cent of which was granted to unmarried persons. This directly discriminatory system was changed in 1985, again after the expiry date of the Social Security Directive. Under the new system, married spouses each get 50 per cent of the former 100 per cent granted to married men. From 1986, unmarried partners, homosexuals as well as heterosexuals, are also treated as married couples. Their benefits will be brought down from 70 per cent to 50 per cent for each of the partners. Although direct discrimination of the old age pension scheme is now abolished, the position of working women has deteriorated (housewives do not pay contributions, they do receive a pension on the same level as other married persons): they must now pay contributions through an individualised system, whereas under the old system they often paid less than others. This increased cost is hardly offset by the formal 50–50 division of the family pension.

The system of social assistance benefits is the most important from the point of view of women. The majority of women have no paid job or wage-related benefit. If an unemployed woman is a single person living alone, she will receive social security payments up to the level of 70 per cent of the net minimum wage, and up to 90 per cent if she is a single parent. However, if she is married or cohabiting, the chance that she will be entitled to social assistance payments is very small. The means test takes the incomes of both spouses or partners into account. Since almost all men have paid work or wage-related benefits, their wives or partners receive nothing. If a married man, as a result of long-term unemployment, has to rely on social security, he receives the family payments (100 per cent of the net minimum wage). Unmarried partners each receive 50 per cent of the net minimum wage. Under the new system, the splitting of the family payments is also possible for married couples. This represents no material improvement for women. A certain deterioration has occurred: homosexual couples treated as individuals before 1986 are now treated as heterosexual couples. Again, this causes a rise in the number of people who will become financially dependent. The EC Commission's view on increases for dependent spouses (which it considers objectively justified when they guarantee a minimum income) makes it unlikely it will oppose the system embodied in the recent Dutch legislation, although this system is the main obstacle for women who want to be financially independent.

The guarantee of a minimum income, in particular the minimum for a family, plays a central role in the Dutch system. The rights of single persons, with or without children, are derived from family rights. Breadwinners are guaranteed – by different mechanisms – payments of at least the social minimum, the equivalent of the net minimum wage. Instead of this *family* minimum, a different minimum could also have been chosen to give a central role to an *individual* minimum. Granting individual minima, however, would assume that women, such as non-working wives of lower-paid men, are all capable of earning an income and therefore of receiving benefits. As the labour-force participation rates of women show, they cannot be expected to obtain jobs especially in a time of large-scale unemployment. Granting individual minima would amount to sheer poverty unless housewives, too, are granted benefits. As it stands, the system is permeated by advantages for breadwinners and traditional families. Those advantages have had, and might continue to have, an adverse impact on the economic independence of women. Women are not encouraged to take up paid work; and if they become unemployed, they not only lose their job, but, after a certain period, also their financial independence.

Changing the system based on family benefits into an individualised system is a costly operation. Individualisation would mean the abolition of all breadwinner-based benefits. Either dependent spouses or partners should also get benefits in their own right – which would imply a system of wages for housework – or the lower level of their husband's income would force them to make themselves available for paid jobs. An individualised system designed to promote equality would contain a right to unemployment benefits for married or cohabiting women who want to take up paid work. Both of these solutions are expensive, which makes them unpopular at a time when cutting expenditure plays a central role in the thinking of all major political parties.

Women's organisations have realised they lack the political power to change the contemporary breadwinner system into a wholly individualised system overnight. They are caught between the Scylla of poverty for traditional families when breadwinner-based benefits are abolished without the introduction of sufficiently high and individual benefits for women; and the Charybdis of a continuation of the breadwinner model with its financially dependent women and its disincentives for working women. The main opinion-leaders in the women's movement on these issues, the Emancipatieraad and the Breed Platform Vrouwen voor Economische Zelfstandigheid, stress the importance of transitional measures, reducing the number of breadwinner-based benefits where possible. In fact, an all-embracing plan should be developed to promote women's participation on the labour market, comprising reduction of working time, parental leave childcare facilities, individualisation (not just equal treatment) in the tax system, together with measures in the direction of a completely individualised social security system. The Emancipatieraad has proposed starting individualisation by abolishing all breadwinner-based benefits for the generation which was 18 years or younger in 1985.

The government has gone in the opposite direction and changed the social security system in a way that makes breadwinner-based benefits more important than ever. The levelling-down of benefits, together with a shortening of their duration especially for younger people, brings more people more quickly below the level of the social minimum. This enlarges the role of non-individual elements in social security and makes the guarantee of the family income, as opposed to the guarantee of an individual income, play an even more important role than before.

The effect of the Social Security Directive has been limited. A number of directly discriminating provisions have been abolished. The prohibition of indirect discrimination, although intended to acknowledge the negative effects that apparently neutral measures can have on the position of women, has not had any effect in the Dutch social security system. The government is introducing a new social security system which will prove to be even worse from the point of view of women than the previous system. Abolishing direct discriminatory provisions seems to be sufficient to avoid EC criticism, although the new measures will increase the number of women financially dependent upon their spouse or partner, and provide more incentives for women to leave part-time employment. The possibility of objective justification allows governments largely to ignore any charge of indirect discrimination. Unless the Court and the Commission are able to develop certain limiting conditions on the possibility of objective justification, the prohibition of indirect discrimination will be an empty formula. The same trends observed in the Netherlands can be discerned in other EC member states.[10]

In conclusion, the principle of equal treatment of women in EC law and policy is not sufficient to improve substantially the position of women in the Dutch social security system. An all-embracing EC policy aimed at individualisation of the social security system as part of a programme to promote the economic independence of women is needed. EC proposals for Directives exist on many components of such a policy.[11] It is, however, significant that the Council of Ministers has not yet adopted any other directives after the Social Security Directive of 1978.

Notes

1. A description of the demands of the Dutch women's movement relating to social security and economic independence can be found in publications of the Emancipatieraad and the Breed Platform Vrouwen voor Economische Zelfstandigheid. In particular, refer to: Emancipatiereaad, *Sociale Zekerheid en Emancipatie*, Emancipatieraad, The Hague, 1984; and Breed Platform Vrouwen voor Economische Zelfstandigeid, *Van vrouwen en de dingen die aan haar voorbijgaan*, The Hague, 1984.
2. The Dutch system is an example of a Beveridge-model with a strong emphasis on vertical redistribution. For further details, see E. James, *Social Protection in Europe*, Working paper 2, National Consumer Council, London, 1983. The emphasis on the difference between wage-related benefits and social assistance benefits can be found in the government paper on the revision of the social security system, Ministry of Social Affairs and Employment, The Hague, 1983.
3. The legal history of the notion of indirect discrimination dates back to the case-law of the Permanent Court of International Justice, The Hague; in particular, their decision in the case *Ecole Minoritaires en Albanie*, Avis 6

April 1935, Series A/B nr.64, p. 16. For the case-law of the United States Supreme Court, see 401 US 425 *Willie S. Griggs et al.* v. *Duke Power Company*, 8 March 1971.

4. *Italian Republic* v. *Commission of the European Communities*, 13/63, 17 July 1963, EC Court of Justice.

5. Commission of the European Communities, *Interim Report on the Application of Directive 79/7/EEC*, Commission of the European Communities, Brussels 1984.

6. The Court of Justice of the European Communities decided on a case of – presumed – indirect sex-discrimination in *Jenkins* v. *Kingsgate*, 96/80, 31 March 1981.

7. For further details, see C. M. Sjerps, 'Tellen en tellen is twee', in *Sociaal Maandblad Arbeid*, no. 5, 1985, pp. 362–73.

8. *Sociale Atlas van ve vrouw*, Sociaal Cultureel Planbureau, The Hague, 1983.

9. The number of 10,000 was mentioned in a press release of the Ministry of Finance, The Hague, 1985.

10. Eithne Fitzgerald, 'Towards equal social security in the Republic of Ireland', paper delivered at a meeting of the European Network of Women, Dublin 1983; Rada Gungaloo, 'Women and Marriage, two views on dependency and state policy', *Spare Rib*, November 1983, pp. 19–20; Mia de Vidts, 'De vrouw en de huidige crisispolitiek', in *Lilith*, nr. 35, 1984, Belgium, pp. 34–6.

11. Council of Ministers of the European Communities, *Action-programme on equal opportunities for women 1982–1985*, European Communities, Brussels, 1982.

7 The Women's Movement and Public Policy in Western Europe: Theory, Strategy, Practice and Politics

Joni Lovenduski

Since the mid nineteenth century, when its first organisations emerged, the women's movement has recognised the importance of public policy to women and has engaged in attempting to influence it. Such matters as power within marriage, the control of sexuality and fertility, family law, the rights and duties of mothers, the gender control of wealth and income, employment and education were all subject to legislation, regulation or other forms of state control. It was a desire to obtain influence over these areas which formed part of the motivation behind the struggle of many women for the vote. But votes for women did not lead to a significant feminine voice in the formulation of public policy. Newly enfranchised women brought their votes and influence to a political marketplace which had long been structured and fully occupied by men whose organisations and institutions were well entrenched. These were inhospitable to women whose organisations were regarded as insignificant by elites. Women thus were able to obtain only a minor presence in government and a minor influence over even those policies which most affected them.

A pattern of a division of organisational memberships resulting in a high degree of gender polarisation in public life has been found to be common to all of the European liberal democracies.[1] Whilst organisations in which women predominate do exist, and indeed are widespread, these, until the 1960s, had comparatively little political clout. But with the emergence of feminism in the late 1960s and early 1970s the organisational map of women's associations began to change. Women, with some success, renewed efforts to influence policy processes and outcomes. Often this was made possible by frequent collaboration within the women's movement between the new feminists and the traditional women's rights and voluntary sectors; a collaboration which led to changes in most parts of the movement as well as in some traditional political institutions.

The aim of this chapter is to identify, describe and assess the political strategies of the contemporary women's movement, suggesting some analytical categories whose use might facilitate further research. A discussion of how to define the women's movement is followed by an account of the strategic implications of feminist theory, after which the political practice of the women's movement is outlined and an assessment of its impact on public policy offered. The account shows that the diversity of the women's movement is an important political resource providing a flexibility which enables it to extract concessions from established political institutions.

THE CONTEMPORARY WOMEN'S MOVEMENT

Many of the analytical problems which arise when studying the contemporary women's movement are problems of definition. Normally commentators describe the contemporary women's movement as consisting of those who adhere to one of the various strands of feminist theory. In such an approach a place is virtually guaranteed to socialist and radical feminists; and liberal, or rights feminists, are usually included as well. However, little attention is paid to the large number of traditional women's associations whose goal often is to promote and enhance the status of women. But distinctions between those organised women who do and do not support policies aimed at improving the conditions of women are as important in an analysis of their impact on public policy as theoretical distinctions between feminists.

Who, then, is to be included in a definition of the contemporary women's movement? If we consider the movement simply to be one of women, then the sole criteria for membership will be that the organisation in question contains at least a majority of women or that the individual concerned is a woman activist of some kind. If, however, the women's movement is also to be regarded as being about issues, then membership criteria become more complicated. Difficulties arise about the nature of women's issues or of women's interests, and groups with different assessments of that nature may not be easy to classify. Arguably, most such problems may be overcome by stressing *permissive* policy goals. Accordingly those women who seek either individually or collectively to defend and expand women's economic, political, social and cultural rights may be considered to be part of the women's movement. This somewhat embracing definition has the benefit of including the range of organisations mentioned above whilst excluding groups which oppose women's emancipation.[2]

In such a formulation feminists are only part, albeit an important part, of a larger movement. They influence overall movement strategy and patterns of collaboration amongst organised women. Feminists are politically divided, however, and their differing theoretical preoccupations have different strategic consequences both within and outside the movement. These differences, although well described elsewhere, are sufficiently important that they ought briefly to be rehearsed here.

THEORY AND STRATEGY

There are feminist theories within a number of philosophical traditions and there are some common elements to the various theoretical strands. Notable amongst those common elements is the perception that women's issues are political issues (the personal is political) and that to be a feminist is to define those issues as the focus of one's political energies. Notions of sexism (unequal treatment simply on the basis of gender) and sisterhood (the solidarity of all women) are also common to all feminists. These concepts are shared by liberal, socialist and radical feminists each of whom brings a different theoretical and strategic perspective to a fundamentally feminist stance. In the discussion which follows I concentrate on the strategic implications of their thought. Liberal feminists,[3] often called rights feminists, hold that progressive reforms will lead ultimately to equality for women. They emphasise nurture-based views of women's oppression and regard socialisation rather than direct male obstruction as responsible for women's disadvantaged status. Liberal feminist goals have been characterised as emancipatory rather than liberatory, in keeping with the liberal tradition on which their theories are based.

Socialist feminism draws upon a history of concern by socialist theorists with the 'woman question'. In practice, socialist feminism shades into liberalism to its right and radical feminism to its left; but its distinguishing feature is the importance it ascribes to the politics of class division, although this is today more ambiguous than it was at the turn of the century when it was held that the exploitation of women by men was a product of capitalist economic arrangements, and would end when capitalism ended. Socialist feminists today are not convinced of this, regard women as dually oppressed by both capitalism and men, and believe that existing socialist groups have demonstrated a lack of interest in women's need to confront male as well as capitalist oppression. They thus find it necessary for women to have separate organisations, at least in the short term, whilst also working within traditional socialist organisations.

Radical feminism occupies some of the same terrain as socialist feminism and some radical feminists think of themselves as feminist socialists, a term which suggests similar views but different emphases. The tactics and preferred organisational forms of radical feminism are distinctive (consisting almost exclusively of separatist, non-hierarchical small groups) and it is the radical feminists who have kept the vision of a feminist utopia alive. Radical feminism is unambiguous in its location of the sources of women's oppression which it sees as first and foremost the fault of men. Not a fully developed or complete body of thought, radical feminism has been consistently innovative and its theories have evolved over time. They must be seen as grouped around the themes of patriarchy, the role of the family, sexuality and women's studies. Patriarchy refers to the cultural apparatus which ensures male dominance of women, whilst the family is regarded as the basic source of male power. It is there that the exploitation of women by men is institutionalised. Sexuality is possibly the most important preoccupation of radical feminism. It is sexuality which makes men the 'intimate' enemy. There are a range of radical views on this question. At a minimum, calls are made for an end to the double standard, to monogamy and to compulsory sex in marriage. In the late 1970s there was a swing away from advocating androgyny as a way to liberation, to a celebration of womanhood, paving the way for greater acceptance of the maximalist view that celibacy or lesbianism offer the only theoretically consistent sexual possibilities for committed feminists. Maximalist views are not widely held but their existence sites a parameter and points up certain contradictions in their position to those feminists who do not agree. Finally, radical feminists are committed to rescuing knowledge about women and are especially committed to historical excavations of the origins of patriarchy, a preoccupation expressed via a widespread and growing women's studies movement.

Liberal, socialist and radical tendencies are present in the second-wave feminist movements of most West European states, with the particular mix and form of each varying fairly predictably by national culture. All three strands of feminist thought are essentially radical in their assertion of women's equality and their challenge of the dominant evaluation of women as less than human and the definition of humanity itself as something which is essentially male. Feminism, it may be argued,[4] affirms a specific value framework which signifies a shift in women's political activism from a pressure group nature to a whole alternative politics. Groups and organisations which experience feminist politics will therefore be profoundly affected.

The early tactics of second-wave feminist politics involved radical activities, and new kinds of political action. Feminists pursued traditional political activities of all kinds but also established, for example, women's health centres and refuges, rape counselling services, abortion services, research and publishing co-operatives and most recently peace camps and their networks of support groups. In general, strategic choices have not paralleled divisions in the movement, and virtually all modes of political activism have been attempted. There has, however, been an implicit tactical division of labour between the tendencies. The main liberal strategies have been legal and legislative action, coalition-building with established political groups, single issue campaigns, service delivery, and influencing public opinion. Socialist feminists have participated in reform campaigns, practised labour movement entrism, developed critiques of capitalist culture, and produced theories of revolutionary change. Radical feminists have concentrated on the establishment of a small group-based counter-culture, set up consciousness-raising groups, and established alternative structures such as all-woman communes and business ventures. All of the tendencies have had some experience of most of the available activities, at least in the short term. Organisational separatism has attracted a considerable amount of male hostility in most countries. But drawing upon the experiences of the first-wave movement, feminists are convinced that, in the short term at least, women will only develop the skills required to fight their oppression in the absence of their oppressors. Whilst some radicals would extend their preference for separatism to all areas of life, most feminists regard separatism as a strategic and tactical expedient rather than a long-term goal. Hostility to men is not so total or so widespread as many of the women's liberation movement's critics suggest. And as David Bouchier points out,[5] critics of feminism's exclusion of men should recall that when the women's movement first re-emerged its early proponents began by asking over and over again for a dialogue with men which would simply treat women's issues with the same seriousness as they did issues affecting men.

Apart from separatism, the other important feature of new feminist organisation has been the widespread eschewing of organisational hierarchy and role specialisation. This has been combined with an avoidance of leaders and spokespersons and a preference for loosely organised umbrella or co-ordinating groups where a formal structure is unavoidable (e.g. for national campaigns). This pattern has its advantages, especially in the mobilisation of women new to political activism. Members do develop quickly and skills are shared by all. These small 'structureless' groups are, in their ideal form, what Rowbotham[6] calls prefigurative, in that they are a form of participatory egalitarian democracy keeping faith with liberatory goals. But as Freeman has argued,[7] such forms do not of themselves prevent the formation of elites who may in fact have particular advantages in a loosely structured and informal organisation. And even when elites do not emerge, the form is ill-suited to the pursuit of many goals, leading to duplication of effort, overload of key personnel and problems with maintaining continuity. Freeman refers also to what she calls the tyranny of structurelessness which may lead to a stifling conformity in which display of obvious and useful skill differences is regarded as competitive and even anti-feminist. This results in difficulties in making rapid responses to events. More important, in virtually every country under discussion the women's liberation movement is taken less seriously than it might be because of ineffective national co-ordination.

Vicky Randall[8] has suggested that perhaps feminism produces the structure it needs. But like all social movements feminism has multiple goals, and goals of self-realisation may require an organisation ill-suited to the goals of political change. Organisational contradictions are not particularly apparent for the long periods during which numerous small groups are working at their particular project in a congenial atmosphere, but they become important when the movement is under threat or when it wants to bring about a concrete and immediate change.

The variety and range of 'national' feminisms to be found in Europe is wide. Each movement is a distinctive one which, although influenced by women's liberation politics elsewhere (especially the USA), could have assumed its particular form only in its country of origin. Feminist movements of varying strengths emerged in many European countries during the early 1970s. In the new liberal democracies of Spain and Portugal feminism emerged later and developed more slowly, but both had identifiable feminist movements by the end of the 1970s. In almost all cases the first signs of new women's liberation movements appeared on the left where many of its early proponents had received their political training in the student politics of the 1960s. Their feminist activities signalled an interest in a cause which was to take them far from the socialist mainstream into new modes of thought and action. These, whilst often repeated in a number of countries, also reflected the political environments in which they were set.

Cultural, institutional, ideological and organisational factors, as well as differing emphases in feminist inputs, have produced variations in women's movement politics and organisational as well as theoretical distinctions have been important to its political strategies. In the women's movement as a whole, a distinction might be made between the rights organisations, the political organisations and the autonomous movement. The rights organisations may be regarded as consisting of traditional women's associations such as the British Townswomen's Guild or the Dutch Union for Women's Interests (*Verenigung voor Vrouwenbelangen*) and the voluntary sector. The various groups which operate within political parties and interest organisations to promote women and women's issues may be regarded as political organisations. Examples include the *Movimento di Liberazione Della Donna* (MLD) associated with the Italian Radical Party, the network of Labour Party women's groups in Britain, and the National Federation of Social Democratic Women in Sweden. Women's parties such as the *Parti Féministe Unifée Française*, associated with Gisele Halimi's *Choisir* group in the 1970s are also examples of political organisations. The autonomous movement consists of the vast array of small groups of radical feminists often organised around women's centres as well as the various national campaigning organisations. Examples include publishing concerns such as *Psych et Po's Editions des Femmes*, special interest groups such as the British Women's Reproductive Rights Campaign, the Dutch *Dolle Mina* and the Danish Redstockings.

Each type of group has at some time or another attempted to influence government policy and the movement as a whole has on occasion been united. But there have been important differences in their approaches to politics. Their preferred strategies have been greatly affected by the strength of the group's commitment to separatism, conditioned, that is, by what might be seen as a *separatism–integration* division. Tactics may be ordered on a parameter ranging from *ad hoc* activities and direct action, avoiding the contamination of conventional politics, to a full-scale use of lobbying and pressure group tactics and, where possible, electoral politics. There is a considerable overlap of groups and activities but, in general, the separatist autonomous feminists are highly, but not exclusively, concentrated at the separatist pole, whilst political organisations are more evenly distributed and rights organisations tend to cluster at the integrationist pole.

STRATEGY AND PRACTICE

Movement dynamics have not been the only influence on activity however. Political strategies have been developed in the context of a steady increase in support for the women's movement. A complex interaction between movement structures and the political system has taken place which might be seen as having effects which are both external and internal to the women's movement. The form and significance of each has varied considerably by nation. Briefly, external effects may be described as environmental – as a change in the political atmosphere as it affects women. This is most clearly seen in the politicisation of formerly 'private' matters such as domestic violence and reproductive rights and in changes in the public discourse on matters to do with women's emancipation. Data on attitudes of both men and women show a decline in sexism amongst both, although trends in the pattern of support for women's liberation appear to be more mixed.[9] Despite improvements, detailed scrutiny of the political environment indicates that important lags and gaps exist in the pattern of change. Amongst the employers, unions and, more surprisingly, the European judiciary and legal professions, knowledge of discrimination and of equality law is not widely held.[10] And impressions gained of enlightened attitudes in metropolitan centres or amongst national political elites often bear little resemblance to the thinking of the mass of the population or of local and regional elites.[11]

The receptivity of elites to new intellectual currents is itself an important variable here. Putnam has shown that national elites are often more receptive to new intellectual trends than non-elites or local elites.[12] This receptivity varies by national as well as local political culture. The issue of sexist language has, for example, been taken more seriously in France and in the Nordic states where the political culture is receptive to intellectual fashions than it has in Britain where it is not, despite perhaps greater efforts by British feminists to achieve policy status for the issue.

Internally, important effects have been the innovations which have occurred in women's movement organisations and practices as access to the policy process has been sought. At the outset, two important organisational concerns impeded effectiveness. Feminists wished to avoid hierarchy in their structures and they saw separatism as an essential precondition for women's activism. At different stages in the movement these preoccupations led to different results. Separatism was particularly important to all the types of feminism during the consciousness-raising phases when the nature of small group discussions required a great deal of trust between members. The small group structures which were suited to consciousness-raising served the movements anti-hierarchical goals as well, and for a time separatism and a small autonomous group form seemed to be the only compelling organisational requirements. Consciousness-raising was a particularly useful mobilising technique which greatly enhanced the self-esteem of those who practised it, enabling women to forge feminist political identities. However, problems came when the technique was exhausted and a transfer of energies to campaigns or other means of gaining concessions from political institutions was needed. At this stage inspiration was often taken from rights groups used to working with the political institutions who were influenced by the movement to seek feminist goals. During national campaigns the hierarchies which produce the official representatives, leaders and spokespersons favoured by the rights movement exhibit a better fit between structure and strategy. In general, the equation which states an equivalence between rights groups and policy effectiveness and small autonomous liberation groups and mobilisation is an appealing one, provided it is remembered that a characteristic of the women's movement is that both have been continuous processes. Whilst consciousness-raising groups are now less common, small groups continue to proliferate and are the preferred form for study groups, theory groups and various other projects which often enhanced the work of increasingly radicalised rights groups. The vitality of the small group structure has been convincingly demonstrated by autonomous feminism, which has proved capable of sustaining a leaderless, decentralised movement which avoided hierarchy and bureaucracy for a decade and a half.

Traditional women's organisations were much affected by second-wave feminism. Changes in the perspectives and practices of many rights and political groups became apparent by the end of the 1970s, as many European feminists transferred their activities to unions and political parties. Feminists infiltrated these established institutions rather than were co-opted by them. Processes of compromise and bargaining had taken place whereby traditional structures of representation altered their policies on women toward liberatory proposals, at the same time as feminists had to sacrifice some of their early unwillingness to work in male-dominated structures.

Early problems of strategic effectiveness have been overcome as much by innovation as compromise within the movement. In particular, five developments have been especially evident: *organisational transformation*; *the infiltration of institutions*; *institutional innovation*; *networking*; and *policy development*. These have enabled the women's movement to engage the political system whilst maintaining much of its organisational integrity, a happy situation made possible by the wide variety of organisations to be found within the movement and the possibilities for collaboration between them.

Support for this case may be found in a more detailed examination of the developments which have so far taken place. *Organisational transformation* refers to the political evolution of rights groups and voluntary organisations. Probably the most striking sustained example of organisational transformation is to be found in the voluntary sector of women's associations. Established for a century or more these organisations have by their nature come to assume a dual role. They have aimed to make 'a contribution to society and to enhance women's rights'.[13] Historically, the core of organised women has been the philanthropic voluntary associations which have been the setting for women's unpaid work outside the family. A recent comparative account of their political role indicates that their importance may be widely underestimated by students of women and politics. Helga Hernes[14] draws on data from the United Kingdom, Scandinavia, the Federal Republic of Germany, France, Austria and Italy to argue that the women's voluntary associations have transformed their function from one of private to public reproduction as traditional women's work has become professionalised and politicised. That same process has transferred women's dependence on male relatives to a dependence on the state. She identifies several uncompleted phases which characterise the change, of which the most important is the gradual sharing of humane responsibilities between the voluntary sector and the state, resulting in increased dependence on public authority. This generates organisational efforts by women reacting to state intervention enabling them to direct demands at public authorities. Two results of this process have been the increasing lobbying and negotiating responsibilities undertaken by traditional women's organisations (who are now regularly consulted over family, health and education policy), and the forms of local-level direct action observed by Barnes and Kaase.[15] Other phases involved the increased development of the tertiary sector such that work previously performed by women in homes has transferred to the paid labour market. The professionalisation of the caring professions has given rise to professional organisations comprised mainly of women, although these have tended to feature male-dominated hierarchies.

Gradually, women's associations have taken stands on women's rights. These were seen at first in terms of the human development made possible by increased educational opportunity and political participation, but, over time, rights at work have been included as have issues to do with sexuality. Thus in Britain, for example, the traditional women's sector has been active over issues of equal pay and opportunity legislation, and was also engaged in lobbying for the liberalisation of abortion statutes.[16] Under feminist influence organisational transformation has sometimes been of a more dramatic kind. Worth noting here is the 1983 assertion of independence from its sponsoring Communist and Socialist parties by the Union of Italian Women (UDI). This involved a severing of financial links and a deconstruction of its centralised hierarchy as feminist ideas took hold in the UDI. More usually, however, an apparent alliance between the voluntary women's sector and new feminists has developed, whereby the former often gains admission to political fora, to give evidence, for example, whilst the latter acts as a watchdog.

The *infiltration of institutions* has taken various forms including the movement of feminist activists into existing party and trade-union and other interest organisations. Often this has involved making use of pre-existing women's sections. Alternatively women members have organised themselves into internal caucuses and have then worked together for women to be promoted within the institution and for women's issues to be given agenda status. Usually the two strategies are integrated, and as women gain experience of promoting issues they find themselves in a position to be promoted within interest organisations, as well as to conduct further internal campaigns. In Britain, experience gained in battles over equal pay in the unions left residual networks of women with the skills and confidence to tackle the abortion issues in the Labour movement. The National Abortion Campaign was able to mobilise this network[17] and achieve active and valuable union support at local and national level for the protection of abortion provision. As a result of the campaign the union women's organisations were strengthened and were able to win support for policies against sexual harassment at work and an expansion of union efforts to promote women. The National Abortion Campaign also changed, as members gained skills at parliamentary lobbying and the organisation evolved into an effective watchdog. A more prosaic example has been Women in the Civil Service, a rights organisation which has operated to promote women and sex equality policy both in the British civil service itself and in the various civil service unions.

In Italy, too, the unions were infiltrated by feminists who brought questions about the traditional sexual division of labour and formed themselves into important internal groups including '*Intercategoriale*' groups which bridged union political divisions. Making use of the new democratic instruments generated by the egalitarian anti-institutional push of the 1969 'Hot Autumn', feminists were able to use the 150 Hours scheme as an organisational base.[18]

Partly because of a realisation of their political potential and partly because women are often less well-established in other posts there was an immediate influx of feminists into teaching the 150 Hours. Although tension between feminists and unions over feminist inputs soon became apparent there was strong union support for the increased attendance of courses on themes of interest to women. Union leaders wanted the growth in women's awareness to be translated into campaigning around union issues and into political activity. The '150 Hours' were another post-'Hot Autumn' opportunity to instil a feminist presence in the unions and they became a forum for arguing a series of connections between feminism and the unions in general. Officially unions have been obliged to be accommodating.

Italian feminists themselves have described their activities in the trade unions in *L'Acqua in gabbia*,[19] an account which reveals a considerable ambivalence in the unions' response to feminist entrism. Many of the women who became union activists in the 1970s were disillusioned new-left members, some were full-time trade-union officials, some were 150 Hours teachers and some were factory committee delegates. These relatively emancipated women often had women's-movement experience. They decided to work in the trades unions as a result of a perception that it was important both to confront the problems of work and to relate to a mass movement. They began with intentionally informal meetings for women (*Coordinamenti*), held after branch or regional union meetings. As these gatherings were open to any woman, membership tended to fluctuate, leading to accusations of unrepresentativeness. Local housewives, homeworkers and unemployed women were included by some groups – a practice which was perceived by the unions as separatism and led to criticism and hostility from male unionists. However, *Coordinamenti* proliferated in all the major towns and proved a powerful draw for women.[20] Related to this development was the emergence of 'women only' 150 Hours courses which often became consciousness-raising groups which continued beyond term. In short, the early to mid-1970s saw the formation of a feminist sub-culture within the Italian unions. Despite numerous setbacks a network of experienced feminist union activists is in place.

Institutional innovation has consisted of the establishment of alternative institutions and of women-only or women-directed elements within institutions. Thus there is a close relationship between strategies of institutional infiltration and institutional innovation. Examples include self-help groups, local government women's committees and women's rights offices as well as such spectacular innovations as full-scale ministries for women's rights. These have not always been feminist or even women's-movement initiatives but have sometimes subsequently been colonised by movement activists. These illustrate well the division of labour within the movement. The GLC women's committee, for example, provides the opportunity for separatist radical feminists to meet, raise and discuss issues which then find their way onto policy agendas where they are taken up by the more integration-minded political sectors of the movement. Women's committees have been set up in a number of British local authorities and have proved their worth both in raising specific women's issues and in getting the gender implications of other policies considered by local elites. Initiated by integrationists (socialist feminists who had 'infiltrated' the Labour Party) they are now being colonised by separatists and are an example of an institution capable of bridging movement differences. Other examples include Yvette Roudy's Women's Rights Ministry in France and the Dutch Emancipation Council. Both attempt to provide an overview of how a range of government policies affect women. In addition, they bring specific women's issues before the legislature and fund a range of movement activities.

Networking by women in strategic positions for the purposes of both mutual support and policy advocacy has been a feature of women's-movement strategy since its inception. Examples may be found in the various civil services, government agencies (especially between women's-movement supporters in equality and other agencies), political parties, professional organisations, unions and other interest groups. Such networks characterise the institutions of most European states but become very thin near the top, reflecting the absence of women in powerful positions. Relatively little research has been undertaken on women's networks in Europe and almost no published work is available on their operation or articulation in the individual states. Attempts to establish a network at EEC level are, however, better documented.[21]

Policy formulation and development has engaged all the sections of the women's movement in one manner or another. The voluntary sector has for some time been called on regularly to provide evidence for official inquiries and investigations and rights. Political feminists have worked on particular policies within their organisations. They have made considerable use of the findings of research and scholarship undertaken by the women's studies movement. The theories and insights of radical feminism have been a steady source of ideas, as has the practical experience gained in alternative institutions (separatist and self-help organisations). The Equality agencies have funded feminist research to assist their policy development, as has the EC and the Nordic Council. Numerous examples of specific proposals that have been generated by such research might be cited: the NCCL proposals on the reform of rape law and sex-equality legislation, Inner London Education Authority guidelines on sexism in schools, and the EEC recommendations on positive action are but a few of these.

STRATEGY AND POLICY

The developments described above have now characterised most of the European women's movements for some time. But to what effect? How, if at all, has women's-movement intervention affected public policy? There is no unambiguous answer to such questions. Policy towards women is in many respects shaped by the same forces which affect it in other areas. The process of policy formulation and implementation is determined by a social fabric in which hierarchies based on class, gender, religion, region, race and ideology are intertwined. Its analysis requires understanding of the environment in which it is enacted, its visibility, degree of controversiality and scope as well as the type of policy under consideration.

Those who wish to reform the status of women via the political system face a prestructured policy process in which gaining agenda status for issues is the first of many difficult steps. At this and later stages, the environmental variables of social, economic and political climate will have an important bearing on whether issues gain consideration. For example, the changes in the social climate of the 1960s, which generated the emergence of the new left and the student movement, included greater educational access, greater economic prosperity and freedom-enhancing technological change which contributed to the development of anti-discrimination policies in the 1970s. The economic expansion and growth of the early 1970s was also important. Both of these factors influenced the organisation of women themselves, which in turn influenced the political climate in the sense that attitudes toward women and views of the appropriate role of the state altered. In some states important women's policy networks began to develop which would become able to exercise a significant leverage on political elites. An indicator of the extent of these changes is to be found in the ways in which issues came to be posed. Such phrases as 'a woman's right to choose' were not part of the discourse in the early 1970s, but by the end of the decade described part of the legislative agenda in some states.

The possibilities for influencing policy will also depend upon systemic variables as the degree of centralisation of government and the scope for different kinds of policy processes. European governments tend to be extremely centralised, which reduces but does not eliminate the opportunities for incremental policy-making. But incremental policy-making opportunities are provided for women in the member states of the European Communities. Equality provisions in the Treaty of Rome have been successfully extended via a series of directives and recommendations. Equality agencies in the member states have made use of the European Court to extend the coverage of national legislation.[22] Thus a nation's membership or non-membership in particular international organisations may have a bearing on strategies to alter policy. Political variables such as the lobbying strength of women are also important, as are political coalitions – in particular the alliances between women's movement organisations and unions and/or political parties. Leadership considerations are rather less important in the area of women's policy, although the benefit to be gained from more women leaders prepared to take up relevant issues is illustrated by the degree of overload suffered by those few already in position. In many respects women's policies are no different from policies in other areas. If a policy has a low visibility, fits in with prevailing values and involves narrow concerns, its chances of adoption are greater than if it is controversial, wide-ranging and conspicuous. Low-visibility goals such as the removal of formal quotas from educational access have been accomplished with apparent ease by women's rights campaigners, whilst high-visibility issues such as the radical amendment of rape and abortion statutes have proved much more difficult to resolve.

The type of policy which is under consideration is also held to be important. Lowi argued that the amount of controversy and resistance a policy generates is predictable from its type: distributive policies are likely to meet little resistance whilst regulatory policies can expect to meet moderate but not insurmountable levels of resistance. Redistributive policies, on the other hand, will be highly controversial and will face high levels of resistance.

The various policy areas which are important to organised women are numerous, including most areas of public and family life. The contemporary women's movement has highlighted certain issues which have come to be regarded as of particular importance, notably abortion, equal rights, rape, domestic violence and equal opportunity. In Lowi's terms, equal rights and opportunity policies are mainly redistributive whilst the others are regulatory. Arguably all have redistributive implications. Between the late 1960s and 1986 most West European states have adopted policies in these areas. Change was not always made in response to women's-movement pressure but representatives were normally involved at some stage over each issue. Key women's issues have successfully obtained agenda status. But this access is by no means guaranteed. And the experience of the Italian and West German movements over policy on rape and abortion has shown that the politically important capacity to define issues continues to elude the women's movement.

CONCLUSIONS AND PERSPECTIVES

The point has already been made that European feminists differ in the degree to which they have been willing to be integrated into formal political institutions which are, concomitantly, known to vary in their receptivity to women. But everywhere some progress has been made and some women's movement objectives have been met. Nevertheless, important male strongholds remain intact.

It was because women are marginal to the political system and women's causes were seen as ·peripheral that feminists found it necessary to opt for social movement forms of organisation. These proved strong enough to help women gain access at particular points of the political system. Access, once achieved, raised problems of incorporation or co-option for many feminists who were loathe to accept the values of the hierarchical political system. At this point the experiences and skills of the rights movement and the established networks of the voluntary sector became important as modes of collaboration within the movement were devised. Today a range of women's movement organisations conduct a range of policy-directed activities involving varying levels of engagement with the political system. Negotiation and compromise are frequently features of that engagement. As gains are made, the movement becomes more demanding. This places strains on the political system which, as it is presently constructed, will be unable to cope with the non-negotiable nature of many feminist goals. Thus the ultimate point of women's-movement politics must be change in the way politics and the role of the state are conceptualised. This is a qualitative change which should not be confused with the more limited incremental changes states have so far been willing to make. The capacity of any system to make such accommodation will depend upon a variety of historical, economic and cultural factors; hence states will vary considerably in their ability to absorb women's politics. Indeed, it is widely argued by feminists that such capacities are everywhere insufficient.

There is, however, no convincing evidence that West European states are nearing the limits of their ability to accommodate elements of women's-movement programmes. Women pursuing integrationist strategies will be able to point to improvements and advances of various kinds for some years to come. Thus the strategies and institutions discussed above will remain central to women's-movement politics for the foreseeable future and ought therefore to comprise an important focus of research on women and politics over the next several years.

Notes

1. Helga Hernes, 'The role of women in voluntary associations and organisations', in Council of Europe report on *The Situation of Women in the Political Process in Europe*, Strasbourg, 1984. *European Women and Men in 1983*, Commission of the European Communities, Brussels. Joni Lovenduski, *Women and European Politics: Contemporary Feminism and Public Policy*, Wheatsheaf, Brighton, 1986, chs 3 and 5.
2. Difficulties remain over organisations which advocate a mixture of restrictive and emancipatory policies: for example, Catholic women's groups which may oppose abortion rights but support anti-discrimination policies. Such groups are relatively few in number, however, and are perhaps best dealt with on a case-by-case basis.
3. See David Bouchier, *The Feminist Challenge*, Macmillan, London, 1983, for a full discussion of these distinctions in Britain. See also Anna Coote and Beatrix Campbell, *Sweet Freedom: The Struggle for Women's Liberation*, Picador, London, 1982.
4. Angela Miles, 'The Integrative Principle in North American Feminist Radicalism: Value Basis of a New Feminism', *Women's Studies International Quarterly*, vol. 4, no. 4, 1981.
5. Bouchier, *The Feminist Challenge*, p. 153.
6. Sheila Rowbotham, in Rowbotham, L. Segal and H. Wainwright, *Beyond The Fragments*, Merlin Press, London, 1979.
7. Jo Freeman, *The Politics of Women's Liberation*, Longman, London, 1975.
8. Vicky Randall, *Women and Politics*, Macmillan, London, 1982.
9. Lovenduski, *Women and European Politics*, ch. 4; see also *European Men and Women in 1983*.
10. Jennifer Corcoran and Elaine R. Donnelly, *Report of a Comparative Analysis of the Provision for Legal Redress in Member States of the European Economic Community in Respect of Article 119 of the Treaty of Rome and the Equal Pay, Equal Treatment and Social Security Directives*, prepared on behalf of the Equal Opportunities Commission and the Emancipatieraad for the EEC Advisory Committee on Equal Opportunities for Men and Women, February 1984.
11. Hernes, 'The Role of Women'.
12. R. Putnam, *The Comparative Study of Political Elites*, Prentice-Hall, Englewood Cliffs, New Jersey, 1976.
13. Hernes, 'The Role of Women'.
14. Ibid.
15. Samuel H. Barnes and Max Kaase, *Political Action: Mass Participation in Five Western Democracies*, Sage Publications, Beverley Hills and London, 1979.
16. See Elizabeth Meehan, *Women's Rights at Work*, Macmillan, London, 1985 and Keith Hindell and Madeline Simms, *Abortion Law Reformed*, Peter Owen, London, 1971.
17. Joyce Outshoorn and Joni Lovenduski, *The New Politics of Abortion*, Sage, London, 1986.

18. The '150 Hours' is a scheme of paid educational leave negotiated by the metal-workers union as part of their work contract in 1973 and afterwards extended to many other categories of worker. The scheme gives 150 hours per year of paid leave to up to 2 per cent of workers from any particular firm, to be used attending classes in order to gain the basic middle school diploma awarded at the end of the period of compulsory schooling. Classes are held during the working day and at first were held in the factory itself. Lesley Caldwell emphasises the significance of such a scheme in a country with an elitist school system and no tradition of adult education. It is a popular innovation with some 320 courses having been organised in Milan and its surrounding province alone in 1982. Significantly the courses have had a certain political ambiance due to having first been won by a militant union. See Lesley Caldwell, 'Courses for Women: The Example of the 150 Hours in Italy', *Feminist Review*, 14, summer 1983.

19. F. Bocchio and A. Torchi, *L'Acqua in gabbia' voci di donne dentro il sindicato*, La Salamandra, Milan, 1979.

20. Lynn Froggett, 'Feminism and the Italian Trade Unions: *L'Acqua in Gabbia:* a Summary and Discussion', *Feminist Review*, 8, summer 1981.

21. See Catherine Hoskyns, 'Women's Equality and the European Community', *Feminist Review*, 20, summer 1985.

22. Lovenduski, *Women and European Politics*, chapter 7.

8 Do Women Make a Difference? The Impact of Women MEPs on Community Equality Policy

Elizabeth Vallance

The object of this chapter is to discuss the impact of women MEPs on community equality policy. If women MEPs are indeed instrumental in the pursuit of women's interests and in keeping these to the fore politically, they could be an important lever in the political process which itself results in policy changes. Yet the connection between more women in the policy-making process and greater emphasis on women's issues is neither direct nor unambiguous. To begin with, when people question, or assume, an identifiable 'female' impact on politics, they can, and often do, mean a number of things. They may, first of all, be talking about the behaviour of women as voters (such as whether they are less likely to vote, or be more conservative). Second, they may be talking about the impact of women voters on political issues (whether women are more interested in moral issues; whether there is indeed a 'gender gap' which politicians ignore at their peril). And third, they may be looking at the impact of women not as voters but as legislators, and investigating both the types of issue in which they are involved (are they preoccupied with 'social welfare' issues?) and their influence specifically on equality policy (do women tend to support the rights and interests of other women?).

Evidence on the questions relating to women as voters, on how they vote and the issues they find important, is beginnng to build up into a fairly consistent body of knowledge which challenges convincingly the entrenched assumptions of past political science.[1] Evidence on the impact of political women operating in legislatures is, however, less available and what does exist is somewhat equivocal. Some people suspect that political women are politicians first and women only very much second, so that any belief that they will particularly support the interests of women or change the central preoccupations of politics is unfounded. A recent survey of European political attitudes, for example, found that the majority of respondents (60 per cent of men and 53 per cent of women) believed more women in office would not make any real difference to the course of political events.[2]

Indeed, it does seem clear that very few women go into politics with the primary intention of representing women and their interests.[3] Women candidates who make a point of raising their femininst beliefs during their campaigns are apparently liable to frighten the electorate, and those who do not mention women's interests at all do better than those who do.[4] Again, it has been shown that, in an election, a male defender of equal rights will defeat a male opposer, but a female defender will lose to a man who says nothing about such issues.[5]

Once in office, too, there is some evidence that women representatives are unlikely to take up exclusively 'female' interests. In both the House of Commons and the House of Lords, for example, research shows that women's interventions in debates and questions are much wider than this, and, especially in the case of the Lords, there is little difference between their contribution and that of the men.[6]

In another context, a survey of the attitudes of both male and female politicians in Hawaii to women and women's interests showed similarly little significant difference between the sexes.[7] As an argument for getting more women into public office, then, the claim that women really make a difference in politics seems weak and it is hard not to agree that 'simple grounds of justice' rather than a shift in political preoccupations must remain the most compelling reason for their greater representation.[8]

And yet this is not the end of the argument, for there is also evidence that tells another story. Quite apart from the fact that some feminists want to believe that women have a 'special contribution' to make to public life, the electorate also seems to think that women's political interests and competence are different from men's. A 1972 American study, for example, showed that those questioned believed women representatives were interested in and better than men at dealing with issues related to poverty, health, education and peace (whereas men were believed to be stronger on diplomacy, the economy and defence).[9] Some studies of representatives themselves, too, seem to show that female MPs have done more to advance women's interests than their male colleagues. A Finnish report, for example, shows that women representatives rather than men 'have made a definite contribution to politicising the wants, needs and demands of women'.[10] In America, studies show that women in Congress, regardless of party, are much more supportive than men of women's rights and significantly more likely than men to sponsor legislation in the traditional 'women's interest' areas of health and welfare and consumerism.[11]

In the separate but related sphere of the judiciary, too, Beverley Cook suggests that female judges 'make a difference' and live up to their expressed feminist views much more consistently than their male colleagues.[12] Many of the researchers who suggest that women seem not to be very different from men in their political views and concerns, concede that they are frequently sympathetic to women's issues, and tend to become to some extent involved in them once they are in office. And all agree that when women's concerns are raised in Parliament, it is very largely the women who do the time-consuming work of lobbying, sitting on committees and getting up petitions, while the men will contribute, at most, sympathetic attitudes.[13]

Although one more enquiry into women's political interests is unlikely to produce an entirely unequivocal answer to the question of whether women make a difference, the European Parliament does offer special conditions which highlight the issues involved here. To begin with, since direct elections in 1979, every member state has sent proportionately more women to the European assembly than to its national parliament.[14] At the high end of the national scale, Denmark, with 25 per cent women in the Folketing, has 37 per cent women in the European Parliament: at the low end, Britain with 3 per cent in the House of Commons, sends 15 per cent to Europe. In between, some of the differentials are not so great; Greece with 4 per cent nationally has 8 per cent in Europe, Ireland with 8 per cent nationally has 13 per cent in Europe, but the pattern still holds and overall the national average of 10 per cent is well below the 17 per cent at Strasbourg.[15] This was not always the case, for when the members of the European Parliament were (before 1979) simply delegates from national parliaments, with their overwhelming male majorities, the number of women MEPs was very small. Immediately before the first direct elections, for example, only 11 of the 198 delegates were women (5.5 per cent). It is possible, therefore, to compare the performances of the earlier assemblies with the later, more female-dominated, ones.

The argument that larger numbers of women in an assembly will make a difference to their self-confidence and therefore performance, has often been made. For example, Sinkkonen and Haavio-Mannila, in the Finnish research already referred to, find that the more women there are proportionately in parliament, the more they are liable to press for women's equality and to introduce and support legislation to this end.[16] The theoretical case here was put by Viola Klein, who talks about the 'in-group' (in this case the majority male culture of parliaments) taking over the 'out-group' (the minority female one).[17] The fewer the number of women in an assembly, the more likely they are to become a part of the prevailing male ethos, to reinforce its values and preoccupations and be unwilling to raise too often the interests of the 'minority'. Where they are proportionately better represented, it is argued, women will more confidently put their own case. What that case is and whether it is significantly different from men's, it is one of the purposes of this chapter to assess.

The other reason why it may be helpful to investigate the European Parliament in this context, is that there has been a fair amount of recent legislation there specifically directed at women. Article 119 of the Treaty of Rome asserts 'the principle of equal remuneration for the same work as between male and female workers'. While this statement of principle did not itself ensure equal pay, it opened the way for much secondary legislation going far beyond the purely economic sphere. The Social Action Programme and the Directives on Equal Pay, Equal Treatment and Social Security have considerably extended the scope of the EEC's concern with equality policy, and beyond this, the Parliament and its women members may have been instrumental in still further developments.[18] Although the stage was set for this before women came into Europe in large numbers in 1979, it is mostly since then that 'equality at work' has been extended into related but separate spheres like education, training, promotion, job segregation and the highly complicated areas of 'equal value' and indirect discrimination. Again, this chapter will try to assess the extent of the women MEPs' influence in this process.

Almost immediately the elected Parliament met in 1979, an *ad hoc* Women's Committee was established which finally produced, in 1981, the enormous Maij-Weggen report.[19] In response to this, the Parliament set up the Committee of Enquiry into the Situation of Women in Europe which published eighteen separate reports covering, *inter alia*, the implications for women of taxation laws, information policy, parental leave, vocational training and the new technologies.[20] After the 1984 European elections, a new Women's Committee, the first to be established as an official committee of the Parliament, was set up. There has been, therefore, over the past five or six years, a continuing focus for pressure by women MEPs, more confidently asserting the importance of women's concerns.

As has been said, there are, in a parliamentary context, two main areas that can be defined as women's interests, and they ought to be distinguished: first, those areas which directly affect women as women – for example, equal pay; second, areas in which women have involved themselves as an extension of their traditional role as homemakers and carers of children and men – issues such as education, consumer protection and health and welfare. These subjects are sometimes seen as 'soft', although they probably require no less skill and ability to manage than foreign policy, the economy or defence. Both nationally and in the European context, women politicians have often been unwilling to become involved in these areas, not wanting to be seen in women's traditional role, and thus run the risk of being professionally undervalued.[21] However, party leaders have tended to appoint women in those areas rather than others and there is no point in refusing Education and insisting on Defence if you want promotion. Group Chairs, in the European Parliament, appoint their Group's committee members and women predominate in the health and welfare type of committees. This involvement in social issues is common too among women in national politics. For example, in Britain, four of them have at one time or another been Secretary of State for Education (indeed this was Mrs Thatcher's only Cabinet experience before becoming Prime Minister). Even Barbara Castle, who did break out of this mould as Minister of Transport and Secretary of State for Employment, was back heading Social Services in 1974–6.[22]

The same picture emerges in the European Parliament when committee membership is considered. In a Parliament where women in 1979 made up 16 per cent of the total membership, the committee on Social Affairs and Employment had 27 members, 9 of whom were women (i.e. 33 per cent). Environment, Public Health and Consumer Protection also had 27 members, 11 of whom were women (41 per cent). The Committee on Youth, Culture, Education, Information and Sport had 8 women among its 25 members (32 per cent). At the same time, however, the committee on Transport had 25 members, all of whom were men, and the committee on Economic and Monetary Affairs had 37 members, only one of whom was a woman. After the 1984 election, although the balance of women's representation was still predominantly social, they were now represented on all committees of the Parliament. Their proportion on the 'social' committees too, has gone down, while on some of the 'harder' ones, it has gone up. For example, Social Affairs is now 23 per cent female, Environment and Public Health 26 per cent, and Youth, Culture and Education 16 per cent. Transport, on the other hand, has gone up to 12 per cent and Economic and Monetary Affairs is now 14 per cent female.

More women too have become Committee Chairs. By 1984, six out of seventeen committees were chaired by women – one of those, of course, being the committee on Women's Rights, now led by Marlene Lenz. Of the other five, two of them are in traditional 'female' areas: Environment, Public Health and Consumer Protection is now chaired by Beate Weber, and Youth, Culture, Education, Information and Sport by Winnie Ewing. The remaining three are in more technical areas: Shelagh Roberts is chair of the Committee on External Economic Relations (having previously been chair of Transport), Marie-Claude Vayssade heads the Committee on Legal Affairs, and Katharine Focke that on Development and Cooperation. These women are, however, still the exceptions, and women continued to predominate on the same committees: yet there seems no reason, apart from tradition, why this should be so. The only committee where women actually outnumber men is that on Women's Rights, where they make up some 70 per cent of the membership. Here, it is at least arguable that they, rather than the men, have a greater understanding of the nature of the discrimination against them and possess also the interest and commitment to try and change it. But there is no obvious reason why women should be thought, because of their sex, to have a better understanding of other areas.

Membership of committees is, however, only one indicator of women's interests and specialisms. Another is the areas in which they intervene in Parliament itself. In order to find out the position here, all interventions by women MEPs during 1979–80, as recorded in the index of the *Official Journal* of the European Parliament, were analysed. These show that women tend to be preoccupied not so much by 'women's issues' or a specifically 'feminist' approach, as by their own specialisms, on which they may be spokespersons for their Groups. Speaking-time in the plenary sessions is so scarce that it is unusual for anyone other than a group leader to be called unless s/he is selected as spokesperson on a particular issue. An examination of the *Official Journal* shows that MEPs' specialisms tend to relate to their committee membership, and a high proportion of women therefore specialise in consumer and welfare issues. For example, Maria Luisa

Cassanmagnago Cerretti, who in 1979 was a member of the Social Affairs and Employment committee, the Environment, Public Health and Consumer Protection committee and the EEC–ACP Consultative Assembly, intervened very largely on questions relating to those three issues[23] (only 6 of her 42 interventions were on other questions). Similarly, Barbara Castle, with no consumer or welfare background, but on the Agriculture Committee, intervened most on agriculture (39 per cent), and Mrs Wieczorek-Zeul made 40 per cent of her interventions on her committee specialism, External Economic Relations. Group discipline is such that when women speak in this context, they tend to put forward the political policy of their group rather than any more personal or specifically 'female' point of view. In the 1979–80 session studied, Hanna Walz, for example, made 36 per cent of all her interventions on Group policy issues.

Again, even in the 1981 women's debate, in which Group discipline was noticeably lax because of the controversy over abortion, Shelagh Roberts on behalf of the European Democratic Group (largely the British Conservatives) criticised the report on women for 'overstating the case' and suggested that 'we should limit our aspirations'. This was probably her own personal view, but more importantly it was the position of her Group and in accordance with Conservative philosophy.

Parliament does not, of course, only debate internal Community policy, but spends much of its time examining current international issues. The shooting-down by the USSR in 1983 of the South Korean plane was such an occasion. In spite of its formal powerlessness in the context, Parliament was burning to discuss this most controversial international incident of the season. On such issues, too, women make their contributions, whether speaking in a debate or merely signing a resolution. Again, however, their interventions are normally, and were in this case, predictably political, putting their Group lines rather than any specifically and identifiably feminist position. MEPs sometimes intervene too on constituency issues. The level of interventions here tends to depend on individual MEPs' interests and on specific circumstances. For example, in 1982, Italy suffered an earthquake and France heavy flooding, both of which were sufficiently serious events to encourage a number of French and Italian MEPs, both male and female, to raise them in Parliament. Many constituency problems are too limited in scope, or too detailed, to bring up on the floor of the chamber, and are most appropriately dealt with by lobbying for grants or putting questions to the Commission, rather than by discussion in Parliament. Some MEPs, however, specialise in issues which are wider but which specifically affect their constituencies. For example, Joyce Quin's speciality is now shipbuilding, although she had no particular knowledge of this before 1979, simply because she represents Tyne and Wear which still depends heavily on that industry. Beata Brooks often brings the problems of Wales before the Chamber and, perhaps most outstanding among the British MEPs in this context, Winnie Ewing, who made 30 per cent of all her interventions in 1979–80 on constituency matters, continually raises in the Parliament the issue of Scottish independence. While it is clear, then, that women tend to intervene proportionately more than men in social welfare 'women's' areas, these tend also to be just the areas in which women are given special responsibility within their Groups: the areas, therefore, in which they might be expected to feel competent and be given the time to contribute. Overall, MEPs, both male and female, tend to put the Group line, intervening mostly in such terms and occasionally on constituency interests.

At another level, there is the view of 'women's issues' not as social welfare issues but as those areas which exclusively or largely affect women and their treatment in society. As has been mentioned, many women MEPs worry that, if they are thought to be stressing the women's view much of the time, men will simply leave them to discuss discrimination among themselves. This concern about the possible 'marginalisation' of equality issues lay behind the rejection by many members, some of them women, of the whole idea of a Women's Committee of the Parliament. It was feared that if a formal structure existed for the discussion of 'women's concerns', these would simply be hived off and lost, rather than taken seriously by all MEPs. Some women are also afraid that if they continually raise women's issues they will be labelled as 'women politicians' who have no real expertise or technical competence. And while it is common for politicians to have special knowledge of and support for all sorts of social groups, somehow for a woman to specialise in the interests of women is seen as less important than, say, a knowledge of the interests of fishermen or miners. While this view prevails, it is perhaps surprising, not that so few, but that so many, ambitious women are willing to put their own credibility at risk, particularly with their male colleagues, by pursuing the interests and rights of their sex.

Not all the women, however, feel it is incumbent upon them to support women's rights. Elaine Kellett-Bowman, for example, does not believe women need special support or legislative programmes.

She did not approve of the women's *ad hoc* committee or the Committee of Enquiry and was opposed to the establishment of an official women's committee in 1984. Barbara Castle's attitude towards women is rather ambivalent. She claims, 'I've always thought of myself as an MP, not as a *female* MP. Being a woman here is something I'm not ever conscious of. I never had any conscious determination not to take up women's issues in the European Parliament – I have just not been particularly interested in them.'[24] Yet in national politics, her position was rather different. She wanted to take on the men's specialisms and beat them at their own game. 'I refused the maternity benefits committee and stuck out for sewers and drains', she says. These citadels had to be taken and she knew she could take them. She was always vaguely contemptuous of 'women's concerns' or of any suggestion that she might not be a match for the men in their own terms. In Europe, too, she has never approved of women merely taking on women's issues, fearing not only that the 'serious' areas then get left for the men; but that women, as she puts it, 'get enclosed in the antechambers of power [instead of] going for the centre, going for the top'. She admits that she is still not interested in the Women's Committee, because, as she believes, 'Power lies where the money is . . . so if you want to follow the money, you have to get on a technical committee like Agriculture.' (Mrs Castle is on the Agriculture Committee.)

Shelagh Roberts (UK European Democratic Group) is realistic about the difficult and conflicting pressures on women MEPs: 'Women don't want to be forced into women's issues – they have other interests and their electorate is larger than just the female. But if women don't press those issues they tend to get overshadowed. Men have other priorities.' The figures on intervention on women's issues confirm this. In the early 1970s, when there were only 5 per cent or so women MPs, interventions on women's issues were always below 1 per cent in the case of both questions and resolutions. In 1979, when 66 women were suddenly elected where there had been only 11 before, the proportion of questions on women rose from zero to over 2 per cent of the whole, and of resolutions, from 0.6 per cent to 6 per cent.[25] This higher level of activity has continued since 1979, and since 1980 seems to have been co-ordinated firstly by the *ad hoc* committee on women's rights and then by the Committee of Enquiry into the Situation of Women in Europe. Most prominent in continually raising women's issues in the Parliament have been some of the best-known members of these women's committees – among them Anne Marie Lizin of Belgium,

Maria Luisa Cassanmagnago Cerretti of Italy, and Yvette Roudy (who became the French Minister for Women). Question Time is probably most productive as far as the women are concerned, because it is easier to table questions than to instigate debates and resolutions. In 1979, 52 questions were asked concerning women and this level of activity was maintained in 1980 and 1981. Since 1981, the various reports of the Committee of Enquiry into the Situation of Women have provided ready-made resolutions which have produced around 5 per cent of the total resolutions before Parliament. It was probably largely as a result of this pressure (and Ivor Richard, past Commissioner on Social Affairs, has suggested as much) that the Commission introduced its Action Programme for Women in 1982.

But, as has already been shown, even these women who are prominent in this area, in fact spend only a small proportion of their time on women's issues. When their total personal interventions are analysed, it emerges that Anne Marie Lizin, for example, made most of her contributions in Parliament not on women, but on her speciality – energy. Similarly, Marie Luisa Cassanmagnago Cerretti contributed most on Social Affairs and Employment, her committee concerns, and Yvette Roudy, on Group political issues. Even Johanna Maij-Weggen, who was seen as the great champion of women's rights in the Parliament after her huge report in 1981, spent five times as much time on environment, public health and consumer protection as on sex equality. Yet these women have the reputation of continually raising questions affecting women, to the exclusion of any other political interests they may have. This illustrates how women are 'labelled', in exactly the way so many of them fear, for showing even a modicum of sustained interest in the rights and concerns of their own sex. Although this shows that women are not in any sense exclusively concerned with the interests of women and, as has been said, there is little evidence of a specifically 'feminist' view on political issues such as defence or economic policy, yet there is strong evidence of a much greater involvement of women than of men in the whole area of sex equality. For example, only 15 per cent of the women but 92 per cent of the men (in 1979–80) made no interventions at all here. Of the 28 men who did intervene, 19 did so only once (none more than twice) and of these, 17 were merely signing a motion.[26] To this extent, women have made a difference by keeping equality issues before Parliament, and this pressure, largely by the women, has meant the encouragement of a mass of secondary legislation on sex equality by the EEC.

To ask if women legislators have had an impact on community policy here is, of course, not the same as asking if they are actually successful in changing the life chances and conditions of other women. It can be argued that the three Directives have not been spectacularly successful so far in ensuring equal treatment to women in all member states of the Community.[27] Indeed, in several cases, women's conditions have improved for reasons quite unconnected with Community policy. For example, the Italians' relatively good record on equal pay (women's earnings were 87 per cent of men's by 1982, compared with, for example, Britain's 73 per cent)[28] is largely the result of successive government's attempts to tackle low pay by compressing differentials. As women figure heavily among the lowest paid, they have benefited accordingly by this policy. Yet it has nothing to do with EEC legislation *per se*. Again, it is a constant source of irritation to the Commission that Denmark maintains its good results on equal pay and equal treatment without the *individual* legislation on which the Community's policy here is based. (Denmark favours *collective* agreements, mostly made at the national level.) Such examples, however, although they may cast doubt on the effectiveness of the Community legislation in this area, do not invalidate the claim that women are influential in having such legislation considered and even passed. It may well be that 'legislating for equality' is itself an activity of dubious value,[29] but this is to raise a rather different question from the issue of women's contribution within the existing legislative arrangements, and one which would have to be the subject of quite another paper.

What difference, then, have women made to European social policy? As we have seen, they certainly do not, in the European case, either devote themselves exclusively to social concerns or raise only equality issues in the Parliament. Indeed, it would be surprising if they did, when they all represent constituents whose interests they have to support before they can expect to be re-elected. They are, in this respect, politicians first and women only incidentally. Again, as we have seen, they are proportionally over-represented on the 'social' Committees of the Parliament, those on so-called 'women's concerns', and their involvement in these areas is therefore much greater than in spheres like defence or industry. Women do not, however, seem to move the central focus of politics here from the 'male' ones of foreign policy or the economy, which remain the prestigious specialisms. Their ability therefore to change traditional political priorities and preoccupations appears to be minimal. Yet their concerted perception of themselves as women, with particular experience and concerns, has greatly affected the emphasis of European politics and it is in the area specifically of equality policy that women have had their greatest impact. As is clearly apparent from the analysis of the women's interventions, they are just as concerned, if not more so, with constituency issues or their specialist interests, as with specifically women's issues, but the increased concern with women and equality since the elected Parliament of 1979, with its large influx of female MEPs, is striking. For example, the number of written questions relating to women went up from 12 in 1978 to 45 in 1979.

Women have probably had an impact, too, on the level and extent of equality legislation passed by the Commission during the 1980s. True, the three Directives were already on the statute books before 1979, but it is very likely that there would have been little or no follow-up in the form of the Action programme or further draft Directives if the Women's Committee, in its various manifestations, has not been the focus of concerted effort for the extension of the original legislation.

It is also probable that, without the discussion engendered, in particular by the Committee of Enquiry into the Situation of Women in Europe, the whole question of sex equality and its achievement would not have been taken forward in the way it was. From the Enquiry came the realisation that equality was not to be achieved simply by fiat: that the real impediment to it was no longer (if indeed it ever had been) direct discrimination against women, but the much more complex and 'indirect' forms often written into the structure of social institutions and working patterns. This realisation, largely as a result of the work of the Enquiry and its supporting committees, helped change the whole nature of the debate and may have moved it significantly forward.

This is not at all to say that other factors were not significant in the legislative activity of the late 1970s and early 1980s. The time, for example, was propitious: there was still a hangover from the 1970s fashion for women's rights, briefly 'flavour of the month' with many European politicians, while the recession had not yet begun to cut into expenditure programmes. Again, it is arguable that committed individuals in DGV (the Social Affairs Directorate) and in the Women's Bureau were at least as important to the equality programme as the Women's Committee. Ivor Richard himself and several members of his cabinet were continuously supportive of the Action Programme and the draft directives, and it is probable that without the efforts of Odile Quintin and her staff in the Women's Bureau, agitation from the Parliament would have been in vain. At the least, however, having that constant pressure applied to the Commission by the women in Parliament was undoubtedly politically helpful to DGV, which was able to point to this as evidence of the strong and enduring feeling in the Parliament about women's affairs.

Just as the commitment of some individuals was important to the European equality programme so, too, was the desire of some governments to improve the position of their women nationals, and this, it could be claimed, had more influence on the legislation than any agitation in the European Parliament itself. However, without the framework provided by the Community, it is likely that governments like the Greek or the Irish would at least have taken very much longer to introduce legislation. People agitating for change in those societies could, as it was, point to the European initiatives and use them as a focus in their own campaigns.

Finally, too, it is sometimes said that the women in the Parliament have not been so important to developments in the field of equality as has the sustained pressure and expertise of national equality agencies (like the EOC) and the specialist advisory committees and networks. Indeed, equality agencies have done what they can to publicise women's rights and, where they are allowed to, to help individual women pursue their claims through the courts. But they are not strong in most member states and their resources are desperately inadequate. The advisory committees, although they too are important in monitoring legislation and providing expert experience, are of limited value unless they have political support. Without this, their engine is idling and all that intellectual horse-power will be unable to move things alone.

It is clearly not the case, then, that women on their own make a difference. All sorts of factors affect the seriousness of the attempt to make equality a reality: the time, the economic conditions, the political will, the individual actors among governments and their advisers – and the women in politics. More women there are certainly not a sufficient condition of women's interests being taken more seriously politically: yet perhaps they are a necessary one. For, in politics, nobody fights other people's battles; nothing is an issue until it has been shown to be electorally significant. If women do not fight for the rights of other women, more than one female MEP has asked, who will? To have more women in such positions of power is to have more chances of keeping the whole area of sex equality in the foreground politically, in good times and in bad. Perhaps, ironically, it is even more important to have women there in significant numbers when there is less chance of success, when recession and slump spell the end of governmental generosity in equality programmes; when such concerns are easily dismissable as frivolous in comparison to, say, unemployment. In the halcyon days of the 1970s, when resources were plentiful, equality seemed easy and women had many friends. At that time the women in Parliament could be looked on as just another area of support for a well-subscribed cause. In the darker times ahead, it may be that the support becomes the central prop in maintaining interest in what are now much less popular policies. It would seem, then, in the European context at least, that women in Parliament have played a significant part in the development of the community's equality policy. Not that they are by any means the only factor in the equation: as has been said, economic conditions, social attitudes, timing, political will and individual actors have all contributed here. But the existence of the Women's Committee in one form or another has facilitated the continuous discussion of sex equality so that the debate has been moved on from a worthy but simplistic concern with, for example, 'equal pay' and 'equal treatment', to a realisation of the intricacies of 'equal value' and 'indirect discrimination'. And, perhaps most important of all, the women in the Parliament have provided a focus for the equality campaign: they could be pointed to by those in the Commission who wanted action as indicative of an enduring political commitment to women within the Parliament, and they have been a rallying point for lobbying by those outside the institutions of the EEC. They might do worse in the future than maintain and extend those roles.

Notes

1. See M. Goot and E. Reid, *Women and Voting Studies*, Sage Professional Papers in Contemporary Sociology, 1975; and S. Bourquet and J. Grossholtz, 'Politics an Unnatural Practice', *Politics and Society*, Vol. 4, no. 2, 1974, pp. 225–66. On the 'Gender Gap', see E. Klein, *Gender Politics: From Consciousness to Mass Politics*, Harvard University Press, Cambridge, Massachusetts, 1984.
2. *Women and Men of Europe in 1983*, Supplement No. 16 to *Women of Europe*, Commission of the European Communities, 1984, p. 38.
3. See, for example, E. Vallance, *Women in the House*, Athlone Press, London, 1979, p. 90.

4. See S. Carroll, 'Women Candidates and Support for Women's Issues', quoted in V. Sapiro, 'When Are Interests Interesting?', *American Political Science Review*, vol. 75, no. 3, 1981, p. 711.
5. J. Perkins and D. Fowlkes, 'Opinion Representation Versus Social Representation: or Why Women Can't Run As Women and Win', *American Political Science Review*, vol. 74, no. 1, 1980, pp. 92–103.
6. See E. Vallance, 'Women in the House of Commons', *Political Studies*, vol. 29, no. 3, 1981, pp. 409–14; and G. Drewry and J. Brock, *The Impact of Women on the House of Lords* (Studies in Public Policy no. 112), Centre for the Study of Public Policy, University of Strathclyde, 1983.
7. S. Mezey, 'Women and Representation', *Journal of Politics*, vol. 40, no. 2, 1978, pp. 369–70.
8. J. Evans, 'The Good Society? Implications of a Greater Participation by Women in Public Life', *Political Studies*, vol. 32, no. 4, 1984, p. 626.
9. Louis Harris Poll 1972 quoted in V. Sapiro, *The Political Integration of Women*, University of Illinois Press, Urbana, 1983, pp. 144–5.
10. S. Sinkkonen and E. Haavio-Mannila, in M. Rendel, ed., *Women, Power and Political Systems*, Croom Helm, London, 1981, pp. 195–215.
11. F. Gehlen, 'Women Members of Congress', in M. Githens and J. Prestage, eds, *A Portrait of Marginality*, Longman, London, 1977, p. 315; and P. Norris, 'Women in Congress: A Policy Difference?', *Politics*, vol. 6, no. 1, 1986, pp. 34–40.
12. B. Cook, 'Will Women Judges Make a Difference in Women's Legal Rights?', in Rendel, *Women, Power and Political Systems*, pp. 216–37.
13. In this context, see E. Vallance, *Women in the House*, pp. 88–9, on the example of the proposed abortion law reforms in Britain in the 1970s.
14. Spain and Portugal, although members of the Community since January 1986, are not included in this survey. Their MEPs are not yet elected but are simply delegates from their national assemblies.
15. For an outline of the reason for this greater female representation, see, for example, W. Kohn, 'Women in the European Parliament', *Parliamentary Affairs*, vol. 34, no. 2, 1981, pp. 210–20. See also J. Lovenduski, *Women and European Politics: Contemporary Feminism and Public Policy*, Wheatsheaf, Brighton, 1986.
16. See note 10 above.
17. Viola Klein, *The Feminine Character: History of an Ideology*, Routledge & Kegan Paul, London, 1946.
18. For an account of the Action Programme and the three Directives, see V. Hall-Smith *et al.*, 'Women's Rights and the EEC', in *Rights of Women in Europe*, 1983, chs 3 and 5–7.
19. So-called after its rapporteur, Johanna Maij-Weggen of the Netherlands.
20. Reports of the Enquiry, *European Parliament Working Documents*, 1–1229/83/C, January 1984.
21. For a more detailed account of the backgrounds and involvements of women MEPs, see E. Vallance and E. Davies, *Women of Europe*, Cambridge University Press, 1986, pp. 58–72.
22. See E. Vallance, *Women in the House*, Appendix 3, p. 186.

23. All details on interventions derived from the *Official Journal*, Annex, Debates of the European Parliament 1979–80 Sessional Index Edition.
24. All quotations are from interviews with the author.
25. Figures from the *Official Journal*, compiled by June Neilson. I am grateful to June Neilson for permission to use these findings.
26. *Official Journal*, 1979–80, Sessional Index Edition.
27. See E. Vallance, *Community Equality Policy and its effects on the situation of women in the member states*, Report to the Commission of the EEC, 1984.
28. Figures from the Equal Opportunities Commission.
29. See for example, R. Cotterrell, 'The Impact of Sex Discrimination Legislation', *Public Law*, Winter, 1981, pp. 469–76; and R. Abel, 'Redirecting Social Studies of Law', *Law and Society Review*, vol. 14, no. 3, 1980, pp. 805–27.

9 The Impact of Parties on Economic Equality

Pippa Norris

In the countries of Western Europe there has been a wide range of policy initiatives over the last decades to tackle the economic problems facing women, including policies on equal pay in the labour market, sex discrimination in recruitment and promotions, and equal opportunities in education, training and social security schemes. Although changes have been implemented by all administrations, socialist governments have claimed a large share of the credit. It was Mitterrand who initiated the Ministry for Women's Rights in France, Papandreaou, leader of PASOK, who created the Greek Council for Sexual Equality, the British Labour party which set up the Equal Opportunities Commission to monitor equal pay, and the Socialists under Gonzales who introduced recent divorce and abortion reforms in Spain. Feminists who work within left-wing parliamentary parties claim that this can be one of the most effective routes to improving the position of women. Yet many other feminists are sceptical about how far political parties, seen as part of the patriarchal power structure, can have any fundamental impact on the position of women. Instead it can be argued that the economic position of women is more strongly affected by secular trends common to all post-industrial societies, such as the growth of the service sector, the decreasing size of modern families and the increasing participation of women in the paid labour force.

In the light of this debate the aim of this chapter is to analyse how far socialist parties have had a significant impact on the economic position of women in Western Europe. The context of this study is the extensive literature which has developed in political science concerning the effect of party governments on social equality, using local, national and cross-national comparisons. There has been considerable research to analyse policy outputs, especially the influence of left-wing parties on the growth of the welfare state, although there is little agreement about the results of this work. In particular, academic controversy has centred around the rival claims of political and socio-economic explanatory frameworks, as illustrated in the systems model in Figure 9.1.[1]

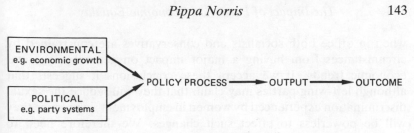

Figure 9.1   Systems model of the policy process

THE INFLUENCE OF ENVIRONMENTAL RESOURCES

On the one hand many writers emphasise the role of environmental factors on policy outcomes. In the United States, early studies by Dawson and Robinson, generally confirmed later by others,[2] suggest that socio-economic factors (per capita income, urbanisation and industrialisation) had more effect on state expenditure on welfare policies than political variables (party controls, turnout, inter-party competition). These studies suggest that we can predict policy output more accurately by a knowledge of the state's economic and social structure then by its politics.

Many comparative studies of industrialised societies support these general conclusions. Cutright, Parkin, Wilensky and other writers have tried to determine the correlates of social policy in a large number of countries.[3] They found that the best predictors of levels of social welfare expenditure were not political but environmental, including levels of socio-economic development, the structure of the population and the age of the social services programme. As Wilensky concluded:

> Economic growth and its demographic and bureaucratic outcomes are the root cause of the general emergence of the welfare state. As for the political system and ideological factors, these categories are almost useless in explaining the origins and general development of the welfare state.[4]

In other words, there were general pressures in all industrial societies for a common set of programmes which were independent of whether the political system was capitalist or communist, liberal democratic or authoritarian. Countries which are industrialised, affluent and urbanised have welfare state policies irrespective of party political factors. In the long run, political factors mattered, if at all, only in influencing the timing of the introduction of new social programmes. Parties claim to have different goals which they will implement, but when in office both socialists and conservatives are constrained by circumstances from having a major impact on general social and economic trends. If we accept these conclusions it suggests that although left-wing parties may claim that they will reduce the sexual discrimination experienced by women in employment, in practice they will be powerless to effect such changes. We therefore need to distinguish between the rhetoric and reality of sexual equality, what parties promise and what parties do.

Writers have come to these conclusions from diverse intellectual backgrounds, derived from the theories of functionalism, the 'end of ideology' debate, neo-Marxism and radical feminism.[5] The *functionalist* view argues that the needs of modern technology inherently lead to a certain type of social structure, irrespective of governmental aims to change society.[6] It can be suggested, for example, that the expansion of the service sector and developments in new technology created greater demand for women workers, which in turn led to an expansion of public childcare services to facilitate the entry of married women into the labour market. In this view the provision of childcare would be influenced more strongly by general economic trends than by specific political factors such as the strength of the women's movement or the role of left-wing parties.

The second theoretical perspective takes up Bell's thesis that there has been an end *of ideologically based politics* since the Second World War.[7] Given the development of 'catch-all' parties, who try to win votes across all social groups, the partisan composition of governments will have little impact on social inequalities. If policies like equal pay legislation attract widespread public support and votes, with the parties largely indistinguishable ideologically, we would not expect social democratic parties to have a stronger impact on inequalities than others. In this view, political pluralism serves to make significant redistributive efforts extremely difficult; any moves designed to benefit one disadvantaged group will be confronted by multiple groups strongly opposing any threats to their established position. Positive quota systems to benefit women, for example, may be difficult to introduce given the opposition this would provoke amongst other groups such as trade unionists and business organisations. In pluralistic parliamentary systems, therefore, left-wing governments are constrained from radical moves to change the economic situation of women.

In addition there is the *neo-Marxist* school, which includes a variety of arguments concerning the relative autonomy of the state, but which tends to emphasise that in contemporary capitalist societies the mode of production predetermines to a large extent the outcome of social conflicts. For many neo-Marxists political parties are marginal to the process of social change, compared with the underlying economic forces of social inequality.[8] In this view, left-wing parties working within parliaments in capitalist societies do not have the power to effect a radical shift of economic resources through social policy. Socialist governments may pass legislation on equal pay or sex discrimination, but this will prove to have little substantive impact if it seriously threatens the interests of capital.

Lastly there is the *radical feminist* view, a diverse body of thought which tends to emphasise that left-wing parties are as patriarchal as any others, run predominantly by men and for men. Socialist parties may pay lip-service to the need to take account of women 'and other minorities', but their primary concerns are with the politics of class. In Simone de Beauvoir's words, the Left have proved themselves both the chosen friends and the worst enemies of the women's movement. Rather than attempting to influence the traditional political system, in a broad coalition with left-wing parties and organised labour, many radical feminists contend that women need to work in autonomous self-help groups to improve their position. In an intense debate within feminism many radicals argue that we cannot look to social democratic parties to change the system, as they are themselves part of the system.[9]

All of these theorists, for different reasons, agree that party politics does not have a major influence on policy outcomcs. If we accept these general conclusions, we are left with the proposition that social democratic governments can have little impact on the economic position of women. They might claim to be more sympathetic towards women's issues, their rhetoric might be more feminist, but in practice they will be constrained from having a major impact on sexual inequalities. Instead, socio-economic forces, including the demand for women in the labour market, the level of industrialisation, educational trends, patterns of family life, cultural expectations and economic growth, will be the primary variables determining such factors as the number of women in the workforce, their occupational pay and status, as well as child support services and welfare benefits. If this prespective is valid, social democratic governments cannot play a major role in increasing sexual equality, nor can we look primarily to the formal political process for social change.

Previous studies have focused upon the effects of welfare

expenditure on social stratification. Social policy concerning sexual equality, however, has been less concerned with spending programmes than with measures to create equal opportunities for women in employment. It is therefore appropriate to use alternative indicators of policy outcomes, including female labour force participation, pay and occupational segregation. We can test the effects of environmental variables on these indicators by using covariance structure analysis (Lisrel) within the model illustrated in Figure 9.2 on page 155. Lisrel allows us to estimate the reciprocal effects of economic, political and social factors on the dependent variables of economic equality in a single causal model.[10] Lisrel was selected as it has the advantage over alternative methods, such as multiple regression, of testing the goodness of fit of the overall model. The resulting model can be accepted since it plausibly explains a high degree of variance in the dependent variables. Although the Lisrel procedure is fairly complex, the results are straightforward to interpret and only statistically significant relationships are reported.

Amongst economic factors which would be expected to affect the *demand* for female workers are the level of development and growth in the economy. That women's labour force participation is largely a consequence of economic development has been emphasised by a number of previous studies.[11] In this view, industrialisation brings women to the workplace through changes in the occupational structure, especially the growth in service and white-collar work, coupled with increased educational opportunities. On these grounds we would expect the number of women in employment to be positively affected by the level of economic development and economic growth, measured as per capita GNP (1981) and growth over the last decades in per capita GNP.

In addition some suggest that social factors may influence the *supply* of women in the workforce, since the declining size of families will give women more opportunities to participate. Trends towards increased divorce and marital instability may also have an effect, since more women will be forced into employment to support themselves and their children.[12] Lastly, as women gain more formal educational qualifications this should expand their employment opportunities and career prospects. Therefore female rates of fertility, marriage and college education should influence female labour force participation.

In turn these socio-economic factors would be expected to affect female pay and occupational segregation. According to neo-classical economics, the supply and demand for women in the job market is one of the primary explanations for their economic rewards.[13] If economic development leads to increased demands for the skills and experience which women bring to the labour market, for example by the growth of the service sector, then it is argued that in a situation of perfect competition the wage rates for women will rise to attract them into the labour force. Neo-classical economists assume that the decision to enter the workforce is one aspect of consumer choice. Women are faced with the choice between leisure, work and the consumption of goods and services. This choice is made in the context of intervening variables, including *facilitating* conditions such as the woman's education and experience, *enabling* conditions such as the number and age of any children in the household, and *precipitating* conditions including the financial circumstances of the household.[14] According to this perspective, women will enter the workforce if wage rates are sufficiently attractive to make work preferable to leisure, and employers will offer sufficient wage rates to meet the demand for labour.[15] If there is stronger demand for labour than present employees can meet, for example substantial growth in middle management in insurance and banking, then due to market forces qualified women should move into these areas, leading to a gradual decrease in occupational segregation by sex. On this basis we would expect the primary factors affecting the economic position of women to be general social and economic trends, including growth in the economy, levels of economic development, rates of fertility and marriage, and rates of female education.

THE INFLUENCE OF POLITICAL PARTIES

These conclusions are controversial, however, and not fully supported by the literature in political science or feminist theory. An alternative school of thought disagrees with the emphasis on environmental variables, suggesting that political explanations of policy outputs are more appropriate, including the influence of political parties, interest groups and elite leadership.[16] For those who stress the influence of political factors the role of parties is seen as central, which has led to extensive research at the local, state and national levels of government concerning the policy effects of left-wing and right-wing parties. Many recent writers suggest that within the context of democratic governments it can matter a good deal which party is in power.

Comparative studies of the expenditure patterns at the level of local authorities have found that there are variations in services according to party control in Britain and the United States.[17] Cross-national comparisons have also found that political variables were significant in explaining policy outputs.[18] Studies of Western nations by Hibbs and Schmidt have found that socialist governments tend to pursue policies leading to high inflation and low unemployment, contrary to conservative governments.[19] Others have found a consistently positive association between left-wing party dominance and egalitarian policies in twenty-five Western countries, reflected in the redistribution of incomes and access to higher education.[20] According to this array of studies, the control of government by different parties significantly affects policy outputs and outcomes.

If we accept these conclusions we would expect that social democratic governments could have an impact on public policies concerning sexual equality. Some studies suggest this more specifically. In a comparison of abortion policies in democratic societies, Field found that liberal policies were more frequently adopted by socialists than by other parties.[21] Lastly, Brooks, in his comparison of the impact of left-wing mobilisation in nineteen capitalist democracies, included a measure of sexual equality, defined as the ratio of males to females in terms of income and white-collar occupations.[22] This measure can be questioned, but on this basis the study found that between 1950 and 1970 sexual equality increased in fourteen of the nineteen nations compared, with the largest gains in Japan, Sweden and Norway, and an actual decline in Canada, the USA, Ireland, France and Switzerland. Brooks concluded that there was therefore a modest relationship between left-wing mobilisation and sexual equality.

It might be expected that political parties would have a significant influence on the economic position of women in Western Europe through a range of direct and indirect public policies. This includes policies concerning the availability of childcare facilities, maternity/paternity leave, the tax structure, social security schemes, in addition to specific legislation on equal pay, equal worth, affirmative action, sex discrimination and protective restrictions. To promote equal opportunities governments can create administrative bodies to advise on women's rights, and use public information campaigns and positive quota systems to stimulate female access to jobs traditionally held by men.[23] Governments within the European Community have introduced a range of policies designed to improve female pay and employment opportunities.[24] In part this has been a response to the main EC initiatives, including Article 119 on Equal Pay in the 1962 Treaty of Rome, the Social Action programme in 1972, and the subsequent Directives on equal pay for work of equal value and equal treatment in terms of recruitment, promotion and training.[25] The chapter by Catherine Hoskyns in this volume gives examples of the policies adopted in the Federal Republic of Germany and the Republic of Ireland.

Governments have the potential to affect women in the labour force through a range of more indirect measures, such as regulations on minimum wages, policies on migration, the provision of social services, and – of growing importance – training schemes to alleviate unemployment. These are indirect instruments, as the intention is not necessarily to benefit women as such – for example, minimum wage standards in Italy are designed for all workers – but since women are amongst the lowest paid, they are the main beneficiaries. Again the expansion or contraction of social services has an impact on all employees in these fields, but as a result this mostly affects women as social workers, nurses and teachers.[26] Through both direct and indirect measures we would therefore expect governments to have a substantive as well as symbolic impact on sexual equality, with left-wing governments improving the position of European women in accordance with their more egalitarian ideology.

Parties are classified into left-wing and right-wing categories to assess partisan strength. All major parties who are self-designated as socialist, social democratic, labour or communist are classified as left-wing, in accordance with previous studies. It is more difficult to establish criteria for the right-wing classification, especially with liberal parties ranging from 'extreme free market' to 'centre-reformist' in orientation. This study, however, can use the right-wing classification developed by Castles.[27] For all groups, partisan strength is measured by the annual average proportion of seats in the national legislature held by major parties from 1960 to 1981, which takes into account the cumulative impact of these parties in opposition as well as in government. This is preferable, therefore, to alternative measures of partisan support, including their electoral support or Cabinet seats. Only major parties are included, that is those with over 5 per cent of legislative seats, since others could not be expected to have a significant influence on policy. To analyse the impact of parties we first need to establish some systematic comparative measures of economic equality.

MEASURES OF ECONOMIC EQUALITY

Before proceeding with the substantive analysis we should mention that there a number of problems associated with the availability and reliability of comparative statistical data on women. Often standardised data are not available: for example, there is no reliable comparative source on the sex-segregation of specific occupations beyond major (one-digit) International Standard Classification of Occupation (ISCO) groups. Accuracy is a problem, since sex-based stereotypes continue to affect the design of censuses and surveys.[28] Conventional statistics can often be misleading, such as women's participation in the rural economy which is frequently under-reported because of their status as unpaid family workers. Much female economic activity is simply ignored as a contribution to the economy, including women's work as homemakers. Statistical concepts can be problematic – for example, the category of 'unemployed worker', since this rarely includes discouraged job-seekers and the under-employed, such as part-time workers who would like to work full-time. Official statistical sources are far from ideal for these reasons, but within these limitations they provide a broad indication of the comparative position of women.

Bearing in mind these qualifications, five indicators have been selected for this analysis, including differences between the sexes in terms of (i) how many women are in paid employment (*Labour Force Participation*), (ii) what sorts of income they receive in all sectors and in manufacturing alone (*Equal Pay*), (iii) how far they are restricted to distinct categories of 'women's work' (*Horizontal Occupational Segregation*), (iv) how far women are in the most prestigious sorts of careers (*Vertical Segregation*), and (v) how far they feel their work is rewarding (*Subjective Satisfaction*). The selected measures focus on a range of significant indicators of economic equality as the basis for a comparative analysis of sexual stratification.

Given the problems of statistical concepts in this field we should briefly discuss the major operational definitions. When we refer to changes in labour force participation the proviso should be included that of course women have always worked, in the care of children and the elderly, the production of food and the maintenance of the household, but unpaid labour is invisible in official statistics. Trends in labour force participation mean that increasing numbers of women are entering the *paid* workforce, either full or part-time, as defined by the ILO.[29] On the basis of these data we can analyse where there have been the strongest trends in female employment and where women continue in traditional roles within the home and family.

Equal pay can be compared using alternative measures, including monthly, weekly or hourly wages; gross pay or take-home pay after tax deductions, with or without overtime and bonus payments. As the most straightforward measure, comparison will be made of full-time hourly pay in all sectors except agriculture which excludes national differences in the length of the working week and the problems of defining part-time work and payments in kind. On the basis of these measures, we can see where there are the strongest pay differentials between women and men and how far there have been significant moves towards equal pay over the last decades.

With horizontal segregation, women are limited to certain *types* of jobs: in factories as sewing-machinists not welders, in schools as nursery not secondary-school teachers. With vertical segregation, women are limited to certain *levels* of jobs: as lecturers not professors, or as general physicians not neuro-surgeons. Occupational segregation is significant since the labour market is divided into segments which are largely self-contained, with little mobility for workers to transfer to different sectors. The sectors in which women are concentrated tend to be disadvantaged in terms of skills, status, security and earnings, to form a 'secondary labour market'. In Europe, women predominate in certain occupations: they are 90 per cent of all secretaries and typists, 80 per cent of nurses and midwives, 92 per cent of housekeepers and maids, and 80 per cent of charworkers and cleaners.[30] To analyse this more systematically we can define the degree of horizontal segregation as the relationship between the proportion of women in the occupational sector and the proportion in the labour force as a whole.[31] Using these coefficients allows comparison between countries, separating segregation from other factors such as growth in the female labour force. Vertical segregation can be defined as the proportion of women in the most prestigious occupations, as administrators and managers, engineers and architects, university teachers, physical and life scientists, and medical practitioners. With these measures we can analyse where women are breaking through into traditionally male careers, and how far horizontal and vertical segregation is changing over the years.

In addition to the objective conditions of pay and conditions there is also the question of subjective satisfaction, and how far women and men feel that their jobs are interesting and rewarding. Although difficult to assess, we can use the 1983 EuroBarometer survey

(N.9790) to construct an Occupational Satisfaction Index for the countries of the European Community.[32] Respondents were asked a series of questions about their employment, including items concerning whether their work was interesting, whether their abilities were put to good use, and whether they have a chance of promotion. From these items we can create an index of average male and female satisfaction for each country. (See Table 9.1.)

Table 9.1   Occupational satisfaction index

Q: 'For each of the following statements would you tell me if it applies or not to your work: "The work is interesting", "My abilities are put to good use", "I have a chance of promotion".'

	Interest			Abilities			Prospects		
	M	W	Diff	M	W	Diff	M	W	Diff
Belgium	0.77	0.76	−0.01	0.81	0.73	−0.08	0.45	0.28	−0.17
Denmark	0.96	0.90	−0.06	0.89	0.84	−0.05	0.21	0.15	−0.06
France	0.89	0.79	−0.10	0.71	0.69	−0.02	0.50	0.38	−0.12
Germany	0.91	0.84	−0.07	0.84	0.77	−0.07	0.36	0.16	−0.20
Greece	0.67	0.67	0.00	0.55	0.52	−0.03	0.28	0.50	0.22
Ireland	0.83	0.73	−0.10	0.85	0.80	−0.05	0.45	0.42	−0.03
Italy	0.69	0.71	0.02	0.67	0.71	0.04	0.30	0.18	−0.12
Luxembourg	0.85	0.80	−0.05	0.75	0.88	0.13	0.61	0.48	−0.13
Netherlands	0.80	0.78	−0.02	0.82	0.80	−0.02	0.42	0.16	−0.26
UK	0.85	0.78	−0.07	0.82	0.75	−0.07	0.50	0.28	−0.22

Source: EuroBarometer 1983.
Note: Percentage satisfied N.4346.

The study focuses upon the nineteen countries of Western Europe to allow the comparison of party governments within relatively similar economic and political systems. This includes all members of the European Community, and countries affiliated to the Council of Europe. To provide a wider perspective, however, selective comparisons are made with other developed democratic states, including those in North America (United States and Canada) and the Pacific region (Australia, New Zealand and Japan). Given the range of initiatives within the European Community this allows us to see whether member states have progressed at a faster rate towards economic equality than other societies, or whether over the last decades changes have been fairly uniform cross-culturally.

CONCLUSIONS

The results of these measures of sexual stratification, as shown in Table 9.2, show that economic inequalities by sex persist everywhere. There are, however, substantial contrasts between the countries of Western Europe, as certain societies are considerably more egalitarian than others in terms of labour force participation, equal pay, horizontal and vertical segregation, as well as occupational satisfaction. Whilst there has been a general trend towards more women entering paid employment in Western Europe, this has not affected all societies to the same extent. As a result, in recent years, while almost half the work force is female in Denmark and Sweden, only a quarter are women in the Netherlands and Ireland. The contrast

Table 9.2 Comparative economic equality, 1981

	LabForce	Equal Pay	H.Seg	V.Seg	OSI
Austria	38.6	0.74	0.37	0.21	—
Belgium	29.6	0.73	0.44	0.22	−0.27
Denmark	45.4	0.80	0.39	0.23	−0.17
Germany	38.5	0.72	0.42	0.20	−0.34
Greece	31.4	0.70	0.41	0.31	0.02
Finland	46.6	0.61	0.41	0.16	—
France	38.8	0.80	—	0.22	−0.24
Iceland	41.5	0.80	—	—	—
Ireland	27.8	0.62	0.45	0.16	−0.19
Italy	33.2	—	—	0.20	−0.06
Luxembourg	33.3	0.63	0.16	—	−0.05
Netherlands	26.1	0.77	0.24	0.17	−0.31
Norway	41.3	0.80	0.38	0.19	—
Sweden	46.6	0.87	0.41	0.18	—
Switzerland	36.1	0.66	0.27	0.15	—
UK	36.5	0.69	0.35	0.16	−0.36
Average:					
W Europe	37.0	0.73	0.36	0.20	−0.20
N America	42.0	0.59	0.57	0.19	—
D Pacific	36.9	0.69	0.42	—	—

Notes: See text for details. All are male:female ratio measures.

North American Region includes Canada and the United States; Developed Pacific Region includes Australia, New Zealand and Japan.
Sources: ILO Yearbooks (ILO Geneva); EuroBarometer, *European Women and Men* 1983; *The Economic Rule of Women in the EEC Region* (UN, New York, 1980).

between societies is even more marked if we look at labour force participation rates by age. In nearly all Western societies about two-thirds of women are in paid jobs in their early twenties but in their later years there is a divergent pattern. In certain societies such as Denmark and Finland, women continue in paid work in middle age, while in countries like Germany and Britain there is a gradual decline over the years as women leave the workforce to have children, although they often return in later years (the 'M' curve), but in some nations including Luxembourg and the Netherlands, there is a steady decline as women leave the labour force. The net result of these trends is that amongst married women there are twice as many full-time housewives in the Netherlands and Ireland as in Denmark and the UK.

Similar striking cross-national variations are clear in terms of pay differentials. There have been general trends in most Western countries towards improving female pay; according to ILO data in the countries under comparison, average hourly pay for women increased from 63 per cent of male wages in 1961 to 77 per cent in 1983. These increases, however, were far from uniform, so that in recent years whilst women receive 87 per cent of the average hourly male wage (all sectors) in Sweden and 80 per cent in France and Denmark, they are paid only about 60 per cent in Finland, Ireland and Luxembourg.

Countries also show marked variation in terms of horizontal segregation in the major sectors where women are under-represented, in production and administration. The greatest sex differentials are apparent in Luxembourg, the Netherlands and Switzerland. These countries are also characterised by significant vertical segregation, although women are under-represented in the selection professions in all Western societies, as engineers and architects (12 per cent), physical and life scientists (37 per cent), university teachers (36 per cent) and medical practitioners (35 per cent). Lastly, as we might expect, these differences between women and men in objective working conditions are reflected in subjective attitudes. Men expressed greater satisfaction with working conditions in all EC states except Greece, with the greatest sex differentials in Britain and the Netherlands. In general, women felt that they had few opportunities for promotion, accurately reflecting the conditions of occupational segregation. As we might expect, women were least satisfied in those societies where vertical segregation was strongest.

To explain these cross-national differences we can use covariance structure analysis (Lisrel) to examine the effect of political and socio-economic factors on measure of economic equality. Lisrel has the advantage over other methods of allowing the reciprocal effect of all variables to be estimated in a causal model which can be tested as a whole.[33] The results of this model, including only significant relationships ($p = 0.05$), are summarised in Figure 9.2.

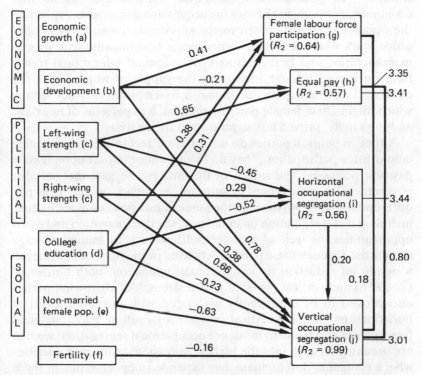

Figure 9.2   Causal model of economic equality

Notes and Sources: The estimates are based on Lisrel Maximum Likelihood coefficients. Only statistically significant relationships are reported ($p = 0.05$). (a) Growth in GNP per capita 1960–81 (*World Bank Tables II*, Johns Hopkins Press, 1983); (b) GNP per capita 1981 (World Bank, ibid., 1983); (c) average percentage seats held by parties 1960–81 (T. T. Mackie and R. Rose, *International Almanack of Electoral History*, Macmillan, 1984); (d) percentage male to female students in third-level education 1981 (UNESCO, 1984); (e) percentage working age female pop., single, widowed, divorced or never married, 1981 (*UN Demographic Yearbook*, 1984); (f) fertility rate 1981 (*UN Demographic Yearbook*, 1984); (g) ratio of male:female labour force participation 1981 (*ILO Yearbook of Labour Statistics*, 1960–84); (h) ratio of male:female full-time hourly pay *c.* 1981 (ILO Yearbooks); (i) males:females selected sectors, 1981, see text for details (ILO Yearbooks); (j) males:females in selected professions 1979, see text for details (UN, 1980).

This analysis suggests political parties have little impact on female labour force participation which was affected primarily by levels of economic development and female education. Together these factors explained 64 per cent of variance, confirming the results of previous studies.[34] In post-industrial societies, therefore, it seems that economic development changes the occupational structure, expanding the opportunities for women in the service sector and white-collar office work whilst leading to a decline in traditionally male jobs in manufacturing and heavy industry. In addition, educational trends have an impact through increasing the supply of women with the qualifications and experience required by employers. Other factors which might affect female participation, such as patterns of marriage and the family, proved less significant in the analysis.

Although political parties do not have a direct influence on female labour force participation, they do have a major impact upon female pay and positions. The results of this analysis suggest that socialist governments have achieved a substantive impact on reducing pay differentials ($=-0.56$) through the range of measures outlined earlier, including direct legislation on equal pay, sex discrimination and equal opportunities, as well as indirect policies such as minimum wage standards. Through these policies left-wing parties have also achieved a significant reduction in occupational segregation, both horizontal ($=-0.56$) and vertical ($=-0.38$). The strength of right-wing parties also proved to be significantly associated with increased levels of horizontal ($=0.45$) and vertical ($=0.65$) segregation. Environmental factors were also found to influence occupational segregation; women are breaking through into the higher professional careers in societies where economic development has expanded opportunities in these occupational sectors and where there is a high proportion of non-married and well-educated women, which is to be expected, given that entry into the higher professions is largely restricted to college graduates.

This research needs to be extended by looking in depth at contrasts between particular countries to evaluate which policies have proved most effective. It remains to be seen whether left-wing governments have an impact primarily through *direct* measures specifically designed to increase female equality (such as equal pay legislation), or through *indirect* policies which have a major effect on the employment of women (such as the provision of social services). Within the limitations of this analysis, however, we can conclude that politics *does* matter. Socio-economic trends have a strong influence on economic equality but within this context parties can have a significant impact on the position of women. Socialist parties have reduced the pay differential and occupational segregation facing women, although still not as far as many activists in the women's movement would desire. Before socialist activists indulge in self-congratulation, however, it should be noted that in Western Europe although differences between male and female pay have decreased over the last decades, in 1983 women in full-time work are still taking home only three-quarters of the average male pay packet. Any improvements in the economic position of women should be judged in this light.

Notes

1. D. Kavanagh, *Political Science and Political Behaviour*, Allen & Unwin, London, 1986; 'What do Elections Decide?', in H. R. Penniman and A. Ranney (eds), *Democracy at the Polls*, American Enterprise Institute, 1981.
2. R. Dawson and J. Robinson, 'Interparty competition, economic variables and welfare policies in the American States', *Journal of Politics*, vol. 25, no. 2, 1963, pp. 265–89; T. Dye, *Politics, Economics and the Public: Policy Outcomes in the American States*, Rand McNally, Chicago, 1966; I. Sharkansky and R. Hofferbert, 'Dimensions of state politics, economics and public policy', *American Political Science Review*, vol. 63, no. 2, 1969, pp. 867–80; R. I. Hofferbert, 'The relationship between public policy and some structural and environmental variables in the American states', *American Political Science Review*, vol. 60, no. 1, 1966, pp. 73–82.
3. P. Cutright, 'Political structures economic development and national security programmes', *American Journal of Sociology*, vol. 70, no. 3, 1965, pp. 537–50; F. Parkin, *Class Inequality and Political Order*, MacGibbon & Kee, London, 1971; H. L. Wilensky, *The Welfare State and Equality*, University of California Press, Berkeley, 1975; R. Rose, *Do Parties Make a Difference?*, Macmillan, London, 1984; A. King, 'What do Elections Decide?'.
4. Wilensky, *The Welfare State*, p. xiii.
5. J. E. Brooks, 'Left Wing Mobilisation and Socio-Economic Equality', *Comparative Political Studies*, vol. 16, no. 3, 1983, pp. 393–416.
6. K. Davis, *Human Society*, Macmillan, New York, 1949; T. Parsons, 'Equality and Inequality in Modern Society', *Social Inquiry*, vol. 40, spring 1970, pp. 13–72.
7. D. Bell, *The End of Ideology*, Free Press, Glencoe, 1960; R. M. Christenson *et al.*, *Ideologies in Modern Politics*, Nelson, London, 1971.
8. I. Gough, *The Political Economy of the Welfare State*, Macmillan, London, 1979.

9. Simone de Beauvoir, 'France: Feminism – Alive, Well and in Constant Danger', in R. Morgan (ed.), *Sisterhood is Global*, Anchor Press, New York, 1984; S. Rowbotham, L. Segal and H. Wainwright, *Beyond the Fragments: Feminism and the Making of Socialism*, Merlin, London, 1979.

10. Within this model it is assumed that the economic equality factors are the effects of the economic, political and social causal variables. Unlike multiple regression, Lisrel allows us to test how well the reciprocal effects fit the overall model.

11. *Women and Employment*, OECD, Paris, 1980; A. Collver and E. Langlois, 'The Female Labour Force in Metropolitan Areas: an International Comparison', *Economic Development and Cultural Change*, vol. 10, 1962, pp. 367–85; H. L. Wilensky, 'Women's Work, Economic Growth, Ideology and Structure', *Industrial Relations*, May 1968, vol. 17, no. 3; R. Klein, 'Industrialisation and the Changing Role of Women', *Current Sociology*, 1963, vol. 12, pp. 24–34; M. Semyovonov, 'The Social Context of Women's Labour Force Participation: A Comparative Analysis', *American Journal of Sociology*, vol. 86, no. 3, 1980, pp. 534–49; L. Pambert, 'Personal Preference, Social Change or Economic Necessity? Why Women Work', *Labour and Society*, ILO, Geneva, 1982.

12. Collver and Langlois, 'The Female Labour Force'; Pambert, 'Personal Preference'.

13. B. Berch, *The Endless Day: The Political Economy of Women and Work*, Harcourt Brace Jovanovich, New York, 1982.

14. That is, the choice between leisure, work and the consumption of goods and services takes place within the context of social factors affecting employers and employees in the labour market.

15. Berch, *The Endless Day*.

16. S. Huntington, *Political Order in Changing Societies*, Yale University Press, New Haven, Conn., 1968; S. Erikson, 'The relationship between public opinion and state policy', *American Journal of Political Science*, vol. 20, part 1, 1976, pp. 25–36; G. Almond and J. Coleman, *The Politics of Developing Areas*, Princeton University Press, 1960.

17. J. Alt, *The Politics of Economic Decline*, Cambridge University Press, 1971; N. Boaden, *Urban Policy Making*, Cambridge University Press, 1971; L. J. Sharpe, 'Does Politics Matter?', in K. Newton (ed.), *Urban Political Economy*, Pinter, London, 1981; Sharkansky and Hofferbert, 'Dimensions of State Politics'; R. Fry and R. Winters, 'The Politics of Redistribution', *American Political Science Review*, vol. 64, no. 2, 1970, pp. 5–22.

18. F. G. Castles and R. McKinlay, 'Does Politics Matter?', *European Journal of Political Research*, vol. 7, no. 2, 1978, pp. 169–86; J. Dryzek, 'Politics, Economics and Inequality: A Cross-National Analysis', *European Journal of Political Research*, vol. 6, no. 4, Dec. 1978, pp. 399–410.

19. D. A. Hibbs, 'Political Parties and Macroeconomic Policy', *American Political Science Review*, vol. 71, no. 4, 1977, pp. 1467–87; M. Schmidt, 'The Politics of International Labour Markets', *International Political Science Association Conference*, Paris, 1985.

20. C. Hewitt, 'The Effect of Political Democracy and Social Democracy on Equality in Industrial Societies: A Cross-National Comparison', *American Sociological Review*, vol. 42, 1977, pp. 450–64.
21. M. J. Field, 'Determinants of Abortion Policy in the Developed Nations', *Policy Studies Journal*, vol. 7, 1979, pp. 771–81.
22. Brooks, 'Left Wing Mobilisation'.
23. *The Integration of Women into the Economy*, OECD, Paris, 1985; *Yearbook of Labour Statistics*, ILO, Geneva, 1984.
24. European Commission, *Community Law and Women*, European Commission, Brussels, 1983.
25. H. Warner, 'EC Social Policy in Practice: Community Action on behalf of women and its impact in the Member States', *Journal of Common Market Studies*, vol. 23, no. 2, 1984, pp. 141–67; C. Rodano, *Report on the Situation of Women in Europe*, European Parliament Working Documents, Strasbourg, 1984.
26. M. Rein, 'Social Policy and Labour Markets', *International Political Science Association Conference*, Paris 1985.
27. Castles and McKinlay, 'Does Politics Matter?'.
28. A. Oakley and R. Oakley, 'Sexism in Official Statistics', in J. Irvine (ed.), *De-mystifying Social Statistics*, Pluto Press, London, 1979; *Improving Concepts and Methods for Statistics and Indicators on the Status of Women*, UN, New York, 1984.
29. ILO, *Yearbook*, 1984.
30. United Nations, *Improving Concepts and Methods*.
31. OECD, *Women and Employment*, p. 40.
32. The survey for the EuroBarometer 19, *European Women and Men*, 1983, was originally designed by Jaques René Rabier and Ronald Inglehart. The author would like to thank the European Commission, BASS and the ESRC at Essex for making the data available.
33. K. G. Joreskog and D. Sorbom, *Lisrel VI: Analysis of Linear Structural Relationships by the Method of Maximum Likelihood: User Guide*, University of Uppsala Press, 1984; W. Saris and H. Stronkhorst, *Causal Modelling in NonExperimental Research*, Sociometric Research Foundation, Amsterdam, 1984.
34. Collver and Lenglois, 'The Female Labour Force'; Wilensky, 'Women's Work, Economic Growth, Ideology and Structure', *Industrial Relations*, vol. 7, no. 3, May 1968; Klein, 'Industrialisation and the Changing Role of Women'.

10 Women in Decision-Making Arenas: Italy[1]

Giovanna Zincone

THE CAREER OF POLITICS

I argue in this chapter that modern political systems represent political groups and not social groups. Social groups are defined as those sets of individuals which, because of a shared characteristic such as race, language, religion and sex, do not have free access to all social roles. Political groups refer to those sets of individuals, characterised by low internal competition and high external competition, who aim to influence or change the decision-making process in order to achieve certain ends. In other words, present-day political institutions do not represent bodies, states or conditions, but interests.[2]

Changes in social structure have led to the dominance of interests; social groups are gradually disappearing, hence the increasing difficulty of distinguishing between them. In this respect, women have the 'advantage' of being a group which is easy to identify. Although in general there is far more freedom to choose social roles than in the past, women remain one of the most notable exceptions. Women still tend to have a more limited real choice, being automatically assigned the family role as mother and housewife, with access to many other roles frequently barred or extremely difficult to perform. Despite the fact that women constitute an easily identifiable social group, there is no assurance that they will be represented in a system where representation is organised by political groups. In fact, I do not personally consider that direct form of representation of women would necessarily be desirable. I do not support the view that women have the right to 51 per cent of posts in decision arenas simply because they make up 51 per cent of the population.

This chapter explores why there are so few women involved in making political decisions and considers how their number could be increased. In doing this I shall look at the most important decision-making arenas and at the obstacles which prevent women in Italy from gaining access to them. A definition of political careers are those careers which lead to the arenas in which key decisions are made, decisions which are most likely to prevail over others. This definition

160

allows us to consider representative institutions, already the subject of many studies, and also the higher ranks of public administration and the magistrature.[3] This definition also helps to identify the great difference in the powers possessed by the various arenas of decision-making. So when we look at the representative capacity of a group we must consider not only its chance of being present in an arena but the nature of that arena. There are questions about now influential the institutions are on which women are represented. The hierarchical position and the jurisdiction of an institution must be taken into account to avoid a false impression of the extent to which a group is effectively represented.

An analysis of differences in the distribution of power in hierarchies, or the relationship between institutions and their individual members, is, however, outside the scope of this work. Although it would be methodologically more correct to take systematically these factors into account, this would render the analysis excessively complex. However, we should bear these factors in mind when evaluating the relevance of the presence of women in the various arenas examined, but exclude them from consideration when assessing the opportunities offered by the procedures for recruitment of women and their chances of making a career.

Certain authors have claimed that there is an inverse relationship between the importance of the arena and the presence of women. This is, however, a claim which is not always borne out by the evidence. In Italy, for example, there are more women in Parliament than in regional or local government.[4] (See Tables 10.1, 10.2 and 10.3.) Therefore, although it may be true that in general we find fewer women in the crucial arenas than in the secondary or marginal ones, this is the consequence of a series of factors conditioning recruitment and career progress and it is not an universal rule.

Table 10.1 Parliament: percentage of women deputies in each legislature

Legislature	I	II	III	IV	V	VI	VII	VIII	IX
Dates	1948–1953	1953–1958	1958–1963	1963–1968	1968–1972	1972–1976	1976–1979	1979–1983	1983–
% Women	7.8	5.7	4.1	4.6	2.8	4.1	8.5	8.2	7.9
Total of MPs	574	590	596	630	630	630	630	630	630

Source: Chamber of Deputies, *Le Legislature repubblicane nelle statistiche parlamentar*, January 1977. Data from *La Navicella*, Rome, 1979, and 'Risultati delle elezioni per la Camera dei Deputati, 26/6/1983'.

Table 10.2   Percentage of women senators in each legislature

Legislature	I	II	III	IV	V	VI	VII	VIII	IX
Dates	1948–	1953–	1958–	1963–	1968–	1972–	1976–	1979–	1983–
	1953	1958	1963	1968	1972	1976	1979	1983	
% Women	0.9	0.4	0.8	1.9	3.4	1.8	3.4	3.4	4.9
Total of senators	242	243	249	321	322	322	322	322	322

Source: Data from *La Navicella*, Rome, various years, and 'IX legislatura. Elenco provvisorio dei senatori, 13/8/83, Bozza', Senate, Rome, 1983.

Table 10.3   Number of women regional councillors according to legislature and region

	1980 No. of women	1985 No. of women	Total of RC
Piemont	6	9	60
Valle D'Aosta	1	1	35
Lombardia	5	3	80
Trentino	6	6	70
Veneto	4	6	60
Friuli	2	3	62
Liguria	2	5	40
Em Romagna	4	7	50
Toscana	5	4	50
Umbria	1	1	30
Marche	4	5	40
Lazio	4	6	60
Abruzzi	3	2	40
Molise	—	—	30
Campania	3	2	60
Puglia	1	2	50
Bascilicata	1	1	30
Calabria	2	2	40
Sicilia	4	3	90
Sardegna	2	4	80
Totals	60	72	

Sources and Notes
Research of CNR 83/0123.03.09 Data gathered by Antonia Melis. Dates of election in regions with special autonomy rights are the following: Val D'Aosta 26.06.83; Sicilia 21.06.81; Trentino 20.11.83; Sardegna 24.06.84; Fruili 20.06.83

The model that I have constructed (Figure 10.1) should help to explain the nature of the difficulty women have in the recruitment procedures and in reaching the top decision-making arenas. It should assist in identifying the factors which influence the opportunities for a social group or for a single individual to gain access to arenas in different political systems. We are clearly concerned with a set of factors which occur in quite different combinations from one arena to another and from one political system to another.

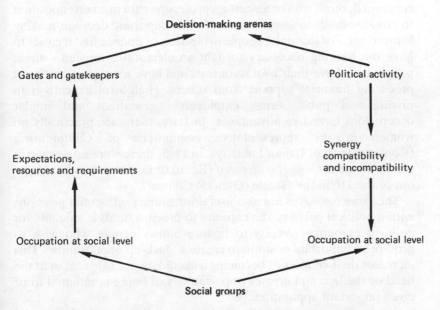

Figure 10.1   Social groups and decision-making arenas

SOCIAL GROUPS: REQUIREMENTS, RESOURCES AND EXPECTATIONS

In the model illustrated in Figure 10.1 the starting-point is the social group. Belonging to a given social group can affect the ease with which a person pursues a certain occupation. This membership of a social group influences the acquisition of professional qualities and abilities useful in a political career. For example, when proficiency in public speaking is essential, teachers, lawyers and actors are at an advantage. If a degree in law is advantageous, the gender, or regional or ethnic groups which most frequently have legal training, are clearly favoured.

Similarly those groups which for any reason cannot obtain these will necessarily suffer discrimination. In Italy, there is a steady increase in the percentage of women law graduates, but they have not yet achieved parity with men: the percentage of women rose from 19.2 per cent in 1972 to 39.3 per cent in 1982.

The kind of occupations people have can facilitate or require the acquisition of certain qualifications necessary and the resources useful for entering political organisations. As far as financial resources are concerned, those who enter certain professions are in a better position to raise the funds to assist their election to important decision-making institutions. For example, people in business or finance find it easier to have the backing necessary to fight an electoral campaign – these people both have their own resources, and have more possibilities of procuring financial support from others. High-level executives in private and public firms, employers' associations and similar occupations have like advantages. In Italy, there are practically no women in the representative committees of *Confindustria* (Confederation of Italian Industry); in 1985, there were no women in the 26-member *Consiglio direttivo* (Board of Directors) and only one out of the 116 in the *Giunta* (General Council).

The same resources are also useful for gaining influential positions within political parties. The capacity to procure funds is valuable for political exchange. Access to finance allows people who wish to acquire an important position to create a 'back-up organisation'. This increases their chances of becoming a candidate in a safe seat or at the head of the list, and creates opportunities of being nominated to or given important appointments.

Some professions provide both 'informal' assets and financial resources. Top executives and bureaucrats, because of their position, are able to acquire the professional qualities necessary for a political career as well as useful financial support. Established professional figures have the advantage of being well known, which makes it possible to reduce campaign costs for their parties because their names will attract votes. Many lawyers, businessmen, university professors and journalists have skills which are useful for a political career and this results in 'over-representation' of these professions in elective offices.[5]

In Italy, parliamentarians are the only part of the political class who have been comprehensively studied.[6] Women MPs have less often followed the traditional professions than their male colleagues. (See Table 10.4.) As far as career patterns are concerned, for women, as for men, membership of associations carries less weight than in the past.

Table 10.4   Professional composition of the Chamber of Deputies: IX
Legislature

	Females	% total females	Males	% total males	Total	% Total
Leaders of political organisations and unions	5	10	101	17.4	106	16.8
Journalists	2	4	71	12.2	73	11.6
Lawyers			92	15.8	92	14.6
Engineers	7	14	65	11.3	72	11.4
University lecturers	2	4	59	10.2	61	9.7
Teachers	16	32	36	6.2	52	8.3
Doctors	1	2	15	2.6	16	2.5
Factory or agricultural workers	3	6	23	3.9	26	4.2
Others	1	2	76	13.2	77	12.2
Missing values	13	26	42	7.2	55	8.7
	50	100	580	100	630	100

Source: M. Guadagnini, 'Tra Famiglia e Parlamento', *Rinascita*, 11 May 1985,
pp. 13–14.

There has been a sharp fall, for example, in the number of communist
MPs coming from the UDI (Italian Union of Women),[7] a women's
association which once gave important support to the PCI (Italian
Communist Party). Women in Parliament are distinguished today by
the relative unimportance in their political careers of the intermediary
step of election to local councils, which seems to be almost obligatory
for men in politics.[8]

Belonging to a social group also means sharing subcultural values. A
good example of the relevance of cultural characteristics is the classic,
although partially obsolete, apathy 'syndrome', which unfortunately
seems to linger more in Italy than in other European countries.
Discriminatory and limited access to social occupations can reinforce
the subcultural values of the group. Because a housewife is not
expected to make a political career she is less likely to aspire to one
than, for example, a top manager.

GATES AND GATEKEEPERS

We can apply the model illustrated in Figure 10.1 to any decision arena
and at any stage of a career. The model can be applied in modular form
up to the most important arenas. At each stage we find, as has already

been emphasised, the need for aspirations, resources and qualifications, but we also find a 'gate' screen, or filter. For example, the gate to membership for a union or a party may consist of an admission procedure. Representative institutions, too, have their gates which consist of nomination procedures and electoral laws.

The requirements and resources needed to open these different gates vary according to the nature of the gate. Which are the easiest gates to open for groups which lack social resources? More specifically, which are the easiest for women? Duverger maintained in his report for UNESCO that women's representation would benefit from a proportional system.[9] The evidence of Duverger's preference for the proportional system may be questioned. For instance, although in Italy there have always been more women members in the Chamber of Deputies (elected with a proportional system with preference voting) than in Senate (elected with a form of majoritarian system with one candidate per party for each constituency), in recent elections, due to the backing of left-wing parties, the increase in the number of women in the Senate was greater than in the Chamber. But Duverger made the important point of linking the electoral system with resources. He argues that, 'in a small constituency the electoral costs are lower than in a larger one. Without wishing to appear too optimistic, we can say that candidates without party support can get elected here. In a large constituency they have no chance. Only parties or party-like organisations can bear the campaign costs.'[10] In large constituencies the backing of either a party or a trade union is almost essential, but the support of pressure groups with financial resources and/or the support of the mass media may help to compensate when this is lacking.

In Italy, for election to the European parliament, there are only five large constituencies, which perhaps explains the particular difficulty Italian women had in reaching this decision-making area. Women are absent from or have little influence either in economic interest groups or among editorial staffs of the larger newspapers. As a consequence there are now only 8 women out of 89 Italian representatives in the European Parliament. This is a reduction from the 10 out of 71 after the 1979 elections. Only Greece had proportionately fewer.

The effects of resources, gates and gatekeepers must be considered together. For elections to the main representative bodies, the gatekeepers are the parties. Depending on their relationship with social groups we can identify two kinds of attitudes on the part of the parties:

(a) 'receptive' parties, i.e. those which receive electoral support from the social group in question;
(b) 'promoting' parties, i.e. those which promote the interests of particular groups and attempt to place their members in prestige positions.

These two kinds of attitudes do not generally coexist in the same party and they are often mutually exclusive. In Italy, as far as women are concerned, the Christian Democrats (DC) are traditionally a receptive party and Communists (PCI) a promoting party. The increase in the number of women senators in the last elections was due, as we have already mentioned, primarily to the action of the Communist Party. Even though the situation is now changing, it cannot be said that the PCI is especially receptive or the DC particularly promotional.

The following hypothesis can be formulated. When consensus and social support are weak and promoting parties are strong, 'controlled' electoral systems are preferable – that is, systems in which a party can determine which candidate will be elected (e.g. single-member constituencies and party-list systems of proportional representation).[11] Where, on the other hand, consensus and social support is strong (with widespread feminism, the backing of pressure groups and/or the mass media) and there is an absence of promoting parties, then 'free choice' systems are preferable – that is, proportional systems with preference votes, transferable votes, and *panachages* which promote the ability of the electors to choose.

In the 1985 Italian local and regional elections, female candidates benefited from a readiness to include women on lists of left-wing parties and from a relatively pro-feminist feeling on the part of the left-wing electorate. For this reason the percentage of women elected for the PCI and small left-wing parties increased, despite the overall loss of votes on the left in these elections.

In the same elections, the Commission for Equal Opportunities (set up in June 1984 as a consultative body for the Prime Minister) sent a letter to all Party secretaries, asking them to put women at the top of lists in the elections in which a system of preference voting was used and give them safe constituencies in the single-member constituency elections. The letter produced little change – only twelve more women councillors. But some, although relatively few, of the women elected, subsequently obtained prestigious posts – for example, those of provincial president and mayor.

The political culture of feminist groups and their readiness to enter existing party structures, to set up permanent organisations of their own and to communicate their values to traditional women's associations and to women already active in parties, are all variables which can affect the chance of turning existing parties into promoting parties and influence the probability of drawing advantages from bodies set up to deal with other more general problems (such as civil rights bodies in the United States). These, in turn, affect the likelihood of fair representation on representative bodies. Italian feminist groups, since they grew up within the new Marxist groups and the student movement, have been reluctant to accept the 'rules' of politics in respect of representation, leadership, permanent organisation, and existing parties. Women belonging to feminist groups have only recently agreed to be candidates in the Communist Party. We can say that, in general, women who have embarked on a political career in Italy are not feminists (particularly in their attitude to the male political elite), and with few exceptions active feminists have not had political careers. This is one of the main reasons for the under-representation of women on elective bodies.

Similar observations may be made about decision-making arenas that in Italy (as in other countries) are not elective, such as the magistrature and the civil service. The resources required in these cases are primarily the level and kind of education. In Italy, the 'gate' for both civil service and magistracy initially is an examination; the gatekeepers are senior magistrates and civil servants, who are in turn influenced to a greater or a lesser degree by 'shadow' gatekeepers such as political parties. Entry to top positions is, officially or unofficially, influenced by political considerations and it appears that this is one of the most difficult types of 'gate' for women to pass through.[12] This may appear to contradict what has previously been said about systems of controlled recruitment, but it is a sad fact that even promoting parties, when they have to make a public nomination, tend to be less willing to choose women than men. This confirms the thesis of Maurizio Cotta, who claimed that even progressive parties will accept women *only* when it serves to improve their image and *only* where there is stiff electoral competition from moderate parties with a high level of female support.[13] Although apparently convincing, this ignores one important element: parties have a differing propensity to promote women due to their very different cultural roots.[14] The likelihood of a party promoting a woman increases when the female electorate makes its presence felt (either through active feminist groups outside the party or through female lobbies within the party) and decreases when nominations are not influenced by women's groups. The appointment procedure may also be weighted against women when the level of resources and requirements asked for is high, since the number of potential women candidates will then be very much lower than the number of potential men candidates. For example, until January 1986, there was not a single woman in the Constitutional Court, whose members are chosen from judges, university professors of law and lawyers with at least twenty years' practising experience. Women who fulfil the requirement for senior magistrates are necessarily few, since the career of judge was opened to women only in 1963.

The changes currently being made in the structure of the Italian public administration are likely to be unfavourable to women. There is a tendency to set up within and alongside the regular civil service new bodies and agencies composed of members appointed by the parties, by unions and by employers' associations. This is probably to the increasing detriment of women. As already mentioned, parties, when they are away from the public eye, seem reluctant to assign positions of responsibility to women. The same is true of unions and, even more so, employers' associations. Neither of these two organisations (especially the latter) gives much importance to women's representation.

In general, the influence of the gates varies according to the resources of women and the attitudes of the gatekeepers. The hypothesis, applied to the representative bodies reformulated in the following way, can be applied to all arenas.

Systems controlled by gatekeepers (i.e. procedures such as designation, nomination, co-option and electoral systems in which successful candidates can be predicted) are preferable when the gatekeepers are favourable to the group or anxious to appear so.

Systems in which the resources and characteristics of the candidate are important (i.e. preference votes, where there is election rather than co-option, examination entry, etc.) are preferable when the group is well endowed with the necessary resources (i.e. public support, professional qualifications, and the right level and kind of education).

SYNERGIES, COMPATIBILITIES AND INCOMPATIBILITIES OF SOCIAL AND POLITICAL ACTIVITIES

The opportunity for members of a social group to enter and make a career in political arenas does not depend only on the factors already considered but also on the possibility of reconciling a political role and their normal occupations.

The link between a social group and the range of occupations to which it has access can be either strong or weak. For example, the opportunity for West Indians in Britain to obtain well-paid jobs is lower than for white Britons. A similar generalisation applies to women. Occupational segregation takes two forms – one which obstructs the path of women to the top of a career ladder (vertical segregation), and the other which hinders access to many specific jobs (horizontal segregation). There is also segregation in relation to the size of firm, the length and continuity of professional activity and other factors. These forms of segregation mean that the scope of work opportunities for women is far more limited than for men. This limitation in social activity is also a handicap in a political career, because women less often have the type of occupation which may lead to a political career (first part of the model), and because the kind of activities 'assigned' to women are less often 'synergetic' or compatible with politics (second part of the model).

It has been emphasised that some professions and some social roles aid and others prohibit entry into politics. This point can be made more strongly: a political career is compatible with or even advantageous to the exercise of professions and social occupations. Lawyers, for instance, who invest time in politics may risk losing a few clients but they acquire the sort of prestige and influence which may assist them in their profession. The same is true for university staff and probably also for most business people. Another important relationship between professional and political occupations is the degree of compatibility between the two occupations in terms of timetable and mobility. Those who have a professional activity which can be transferred entirely or partly to the capital city, where parliament is located, will find themselves is less practical difficulty than others if they decide to embark on a political career. The most difficult situation is faced by an employee with fixed working hours who will have to face the choice between an insecure political office and a secure job.

One of the main divisions which can be distinguished in the world of work is that between 'private income jobs' and piece-work occupations. In the first, earnings do not depend directly on the quality and quantity of performance, and there is a guaranteed income and relative job security (examples are jobs with public authorities and certain large firms); the second is the kind of job where earnings are proportionally related to the quantity and quality of work produced –

there is generally little security of income or of employment (examples are cottage industries and small firms). There is a continuum with the pure type of private income work at one extreme and piece-work at the other. Most employees are in a mixed situation somewhere in the middle of the continuum. Working women tend to be concentrated at the two poles of the continuum.

Women in 'private income jobs' have the possibility of reconciling social and political activity with relative ease. In Italy, women make up 37.5 per cent of the civil service staff, and as much as 64.6 per cent among teachers (1980). These data should be compared with the percentage of women on the total employment: 32.2 per cent (1985). In Italy, public administration and other state bodies facilitate the involvement of their employees in political activity, by arrangements for taking time off and for leave of absence. By contrast a political career is relatively incompatible with 'piece-work' – and 80 per cent of workers involved in the Italian informal economy are women.[15]

Women are distinguished by occupational polarisation and by one other important general factor – the burden of family and household responsibilities. There are few cases where the link between social group and social occupation is so strong and leaves so little choice for those who belong to the group. An overwhelming majority of women carry out family duties without significant male help. This unequal distribution of family work between husband and wife is especially the case in Italy. Only 15 per cent of husbands claim to help their wives regularly (compared with the EC mean of 33 per cent).[16] The responsibilities and time involved in looking after a family are incompatible with the duties and time necessary for political activity or a political career. The greater the political commitment the less compatible this becomes with family life. Family life is the most demanding when children are young,[17] which is why there are so few young mothers in politics.

If family and political responsibilities are incompatible, changes in both are necessary. One way of redistributing the work involved in bringing up a family is by obtaining assistance from outside, which means improving and extending private and social services available to families. In Italy, there are problems of finance and availability. Home-helps now receive wages similar to those of industrial workers. Many qualified people such as nurses and nannies receive more than the average industrial wage. Creches and kindergartens for the very young are adequate in the North but much less so in the South of the country. Services for the elderly and chronically ill are inadequate everywhere, so the transfer of domestic work to services outside the family is impractical.

Redistribution can be achieved within the family, with men taking over family responsibilities and adopting a more active paternal role.[18] This has been made easier in Italy by granting parental leave – both to mothers and to fathers,[19] with admittedly limited results. Better results would probably not be achieved by granting men a flexible working week. In Italy, as elsewhere, men who work flexible hours tend to use their free time on a second job and not on family work. For men, 'moonlighting' is particularly common when they have small children,[20] because it is the time in the family life cycle when there is the greatest need for more money. It is also the time when there is more work to do at home, and women generally cope with it alone, whether or not they are working. At the age at which one should be investing most in a career, and in politics, women are overwhelmed by housework and family commitments. This is particularly true in Italy, where 'moonlighting' by men is widespread.

POLITICAL ELITES AND DECISION-MAKING ARENAS

The relationships between different political elites and between different decision-making arenas can influence the possibility that a woman can pursue a political career.

Lack of material resources reduces the opportunities for less favoured groups to obtain even the least important and least valuable political resources. Part-time, seasonal and temporary work are areas which traditionally employ women in economies with low unemployment. But in certain countries, like Italy, the job shortage is so great that men too take this kind of work.[21] It can be hypothesised that women in Italy are infrequently represented at the local political level because local party elites are even more reluctant than national elites to share power with women and because, given the larger size of the class of political activists in Italy compared with other countries,[22] this excess 'political working force' implies that even the less attractive posts tend to be monopolised by men. An increase in the number of political posts would probably not improve the situation because women would only obtain the marginal posts, and also, in the present economic climate, such an increase is out of the question.

The number of political posts available is also reduced when a pluralism in the holding of offices is allowed. Incompatibility rules can be used to prevent a reduction in the number of political spoils. In Italy, a double mandate, in European and national Parliament, is permitted. But it is not possible to be both a member of Parliament and regional councillor or a member of Parliament and a mayor of a town with more than 20,000 inhabitants. MPs can, however, hold the post of town or provincial councillor. These dual mandates discriminate against women.

Excessive mobility between social and political elites can also act in a negative way. Lateral entry into politics is of no value to women if they are weak in the social elites; public administration and business, for example, which often provide the means to effect a lateral entry into politics, are elites in which there are very few women. The lack of women in the American and Japanese legislatures may be due to an excessive mobility between elites in those countries.

The chances of women making successful careers in politics are higher through direct rather than lateral recruitment. It is therefore essential for a women to take up a political career while young if she aims to reach the top. A 'direct recruitment' career, however, is slower; and even here men progress relatively more rapidly. This is a deterrent to attempting a political career. A woman who wishes to enter political life knows she will have to make a higher investment and gain a lower professional reward than a man, and face the problems of incompatibility with family life. As long as this remains the situation, the propensity of women to enter politics will remain lower than for men. Italy is a middle-ranking country in this respect – it is neither particularly favourable nor particularly unfavourable to women making a career in politics.[23]

Notes

1. The present study would not have been possible without the previous research undertaken on women and politics. The report of Mossuz-Lavau and Sineau, the work done by Hernes at the Council of Europe, and the book of Lovenduski and Hills, have proved extremely valuable. Equally valuable was the experience of working with Corcoran, Lovenduski, Moreau-Bourles and Sineau in our research on the access of women to decision-making arenas for the EEC Commission for Employment, Social Affairs and Education. This research, directed by the author, was conducted under the auspices of the Centro di ricerca e documentazione

'Luigi Einaudi', Turin. New data have been provided by another research project under the auspices of the Consiglio Nazionale della Ricerche (83/0123.03.09) directed by the author and reported in *La partecipazione politica femminile in Italia*. I should like to thank Joan Scott and Sara Hanley for their constructive remarks.

2. For the evolution of theory and of representative institutions, see: G. Sartori, 'Democrazia e definizioni', Il Mulino, 1965, in particular the second chapter and appendix to the third edition; the chapter 'Representation' by A. De Grazia ('Theory'), G. Sartori ('Representational Systems') and K. Janda ('Representational Behaviour') in D. L. Sills (ed.), *The International Encyclopaedia of Social Sciences*, vol. 12, Macmillan Free Press, New York, 1968; the sections by F. W. Coker and C. C. Rodee, 'Representation' in the above work; the chapter by M. Cotta, 'Rappresentazione Politica', in N. Bobbio, N. Matteucci and G. Pasquino (eds), *Dizionario di politica*, UTET, Torino, 1983; F. Mura, 'Rappresentazione Politica', in P. Farneti (ed.), *Politica e societa*, vol. 11, La Nuova Italia, Firenze, 193; H. F. Pitkin, *The Concept of Representation*, University of California Press, Berkeley, 1967; J. R. Pennock and J. W. Chapman (ed.), chapter 8; *Political Representation: An Overview*, Alberton Press, New York, 1968; D. Fisichella (ed.), *La rappresentanza politica*, Giuffre, Milano, 1983.

3. This extension does not complete my definition of politics which includes illegal, hidden and invisible powers. On this theme, see the works of D. Wise and T. B. Ross, *The Invisible Government*, Random House, New York, 1964; G. Galli, *La crisi italiana e la destra internazionale*, Mondadori, Milano, 1974, and *L'Italia sotterranea*, Laterza, Bari, 1983; the papers presented by G. Galli, M. Stoppino and Arlacchi to the study group on *Hidden forms of power* as part of the conference 'Political Science in Italy' organised by the Centre for political science studies of the Feltrinelli Foundation, Milan, 17–19 May, 1984.

4. G. De Santis and G. Zincone, *Women at Work in Italy: an Institutional Approach*, Italian section of the research on *Decision-Making Arenas Affecting Women at Work in Four European Countries*, EEC Commission for Employment, Social Affairs and Education, 1983. In Belgium, France and Greece there are more women in the Cabinet than in Parliament: J. Mossuz-Lavau and M. Sineau, *Les femmes dans le personnel politique en Europe*, p. 34, Report of the Council of Europe, Rights of Man Division.

5. For a comparative study of the political elite which focuses on social composition, see M. M. Czudnowski (ed.), *Does Who Governs Matter?*, Northern Illinois University Press, Dekalb, 1982.

6. Cf. M. Cotta, 'Classe politica e Parlamento in Italia', Il Mulino, 1979, and 'Mutamento e stabilita', in 'Identikit della classe politica', *Biblioteca della Liberta*, Torino, vol. 17, no. 79, 1980.

7. Cf. M. Guadagnini, 'Tra famiglia et Parlamento', *Rinascita*, 11 May 1985, pp. 13–14.

8. Ibid.

9. M. Duverger, *La participation des femmes a la vie politique*, Unesco, Paris, 1955, p. 87.

10. Ibid., p. 88.
11. In certain circumstances a single-member constituency can be considered a controlled system. However, this kind of system tends to produce a personal consensus around the elected MP, which emancipates him or her from the party. Cf. Mossuz-Lavau and Sineau, *Les femmes dans le personnel politique*, p. 78.
12. As far as the influence of political preferences on careers in the magistrature in Italy is concerned, a turning-point (1968) has been the election on competitive lists (politically orientated lists) of the members of *Consiglio Superiore della Magistratura* (Upper Council of the Magistrature), which takes decisions on the promotion and transfers of magistrates. In the public administration, with a law of 1969, it became possible for a candidate with any kind of university degree to take the examination for admittance to training courses, which in practice amounts to appointment, as very few are failed at the end of course examinations. This gave an advantage to women, who less frequently have degrees in the subjects previously most frequently requested, such as law, political science and economics. For a more detailed study of access to non-elective decision-making bodies in Italy, see De Santis and Zincone, *Women at Work*.
13. Cotta, *Classe politica e Parlamento in Italia*.
14. On the attitude to women in the Marxist culture and Catholic culture, I refer the reader to my article 'Costruzione e costrizione', in Un mondo di donne, *Biblioteca della Liberta*, vol. 16, no. 69–70, 1978 in particular the section 'Matrici e radici'.
15. L. Frey, R. Livraghi, G. Mottura and M. Salvati, *Occupazione e sottoccupazione femminile in Italia*, Angeli, Milano, 1976.
16. See J. Norderial Means, 'Political Recruitment of Women in Norway', *Western Political Quarterly*, vol. 25, 1972, pp. 491–505; J. Lovenduski and J. Corcoran, *Women in Decision-Making Arenas in the United Kingdom*, British section of the research group *Decision-Making Arenas Affecting Women at Work in Four European Countries*; J. Hills, 'Candidates: The Impact of Gender', *Parliamentary Affairs*, vol. 34, 1981, pp. 221–8; I. Hellevik, 'Do Norwegian Voters Discriminate Against Women Candidates? A Rejoinder', *European Journal of Political Research*, vol. 9, 1975, pp. 285–300.
17. Cf. M. Weber, 'La culture politique des femmes', in Mossuz-Lavau and Sineau, *Les Femmes dans le personnel politique*. It is clear that there is a strong link between having children and mobility: children of pre-school age permit an involvement in local politics but not at national level.
18. Looking after children would appear to be one of the domestic jobs least disliked by Italian men. Cf. C. Saraceno, *Il lavoro mal diviso*, De Donato, Bari, 1980, p. 205, Manchester, Equal Opportunities Commission (EOC), 1983.
19. Cf. Equal Opportunity Law (n. 903, 9 December 1977).
20. G. Ragone, 'Le motivazioni al secondo lavoro', in L. Gallino (ed.), *Il lavoro e il suo doppio*, Il Mulino, 1985.
21. Cf. M. Martini, 'E la donna italiana e piu diversa', *Quale impresa*, vol. 5, July 1978, pp. 34–44.

22. Cf. G. Galli and A. Prandi, *Patterns of Political Participation in Italy*, Yale University Press, New Haven and London, 1970.
23. 'Un mondo di donne'. This emerges also from comparative studies which include Italy. See note 1 and 'Un mondo di donne'.

11 The Achievements of the French Ministry of Women's Rights: 1981–6
Michelle Coquillat

The creation of the Ministry of Women's Rights in 1981 marked the political recognition of a new and important philosophy. This philosophy emanated from the feminist tradition and laid the social and cultural basis of a policy for women. The new conception was founded on the idea of rights; that is to say, on a recognition and an assumption of equal citizenship and not on traditional notions of protection for and assistance of women.

The French Revolution of the late eighteenth century did not secure for women a proper autonomous status. Despite the efforts of the female revolutionary Olympe de Gouges, the Declaration of Rights remained that of men, and excluded women who remained juridically in a state of inferiority and dependence. This lack of autonomy was confirmed by the Napoleonic Civil Code. During the nineteenth century women became instruments of the Industrial Revolution and were the least of its beneficiaries. Progress in establishing women's rights was slow.

It was not until late in the twentieth century in 1974 that the right of abortion – the liberty to dispose of one's own person, body and procreative power – was granted to women. This measure provoked violent reactions on the part of some conservatives and revealed a mentality of considering women as objects belonging to those who hold power in society. Procreation is a power, and in a society which denies women participation in power, the right of autonomous decisions over procreation is also denied to them. The new conception of women's rights, above all of individual women's rights, allows women to participate fully in a system where their identity is properly recognised. This includes a cultural identity which has been formed during a long period of subordination and dependence. The Ministry established in 1981 had a budget ten times larger than that of the preceding administration dealing with the condition of women, and thus had the resources necessary to engage in the search for a new cultural and social balance between men and women.

On 14 July 1983, the National Assembly, on the initiative of the Ministry of Women's Rights, passed 'The Law on Equality in Professional Matters'. This important law incorporated the principle of equal pay for equal work and forbade all discrimination against women in hiring, promotion and training. The law thus recognised the need for training to help women to catch up, because there can be no equality in work when there is inequality in training. Hence equality programmes have been introduced into firms. Sofinco, a nationalised bank, has been working on training with the objective of having 30 per cent female management by 1987. At Moulinex, women were promoted to higher positions after 18 months' training. The law also forbids sexual discrimination in the civil service. Recruitment must be undertaken on an equal basis: this is very important because of the numerical significance of women civil servants in France.

This law is part of a sustained movement in favour of the training of women. In 1984, the Ministry of Women's Rights launched a major television campaign on the theme 'Jobs do not have gender: schools train all of us for all types of job'. People were shown the picture of a small boy and a small girl exchanging their toys, and followed by an assertion that this sort of equality was not enough: it was also necessary to have equality in training in a country where jobs are sexually segregated to a serious degree – girls make up only 16 per cent of pupils in engineering schools, and less than 1 per cent of the famous Ecole Polytechnique.

An agreement was reached with the Ministry of National Education to rectify the position. This agreement is concerned mainly with:

- the training of teaching personnel, in particular with sessions concerned with the analysis of prejudice linked to gender and the ways of overcoming these prejudices at the level of the primary school;
- the physical layout of facilities and premises to assist the integration of young women into scientific and technical milieux;
- increasing by 30 per cent the number of women in scientific and technical streams by a voluntary policy of equal recruitment, by creating new classes, and by introducing conversion classes facilitating a move from literary or tertiary streams towards scientific or technical subjects.

In each institution someone was put in charge of monitoring the implementation of this policy.

Much progress has also been achieved in the area of autonomy and personal rights. The Ministry of Women's Rights endeavoured to offer to all women of all social levels information on contraception. In addition to publishing a brochure *Contraception is a Fundamental Right*, in November 1981 it launched a national campaign on television about contraception – 'Today every woman should be able to choose'. On 1 December 1982, a law on financial aid for the voluntary termination of pregnancy was passed by Parliament. The laws of 1975 and 1979 had authorised voluntary termination, but women who did not have sufficient financial resources often had to make use of clandestine facilities. Financial benefit for voluntary termination greatly improved the situation and brought more dignity and justice for all women. The number of public hospitals undertaking voluntary termination greatly increased. The number of family planning centres and contraception information centres increased from 150 in 1981 to 374 in 1984.

Some women have been demanding a statute allowing them to take their place in society in accordance with their own capacities and not in a way purely dictated by their marital or family status. There are some achievements in this direction. The partners of artisans and shopkeepers saw their legal position improved. Their professional and social rights were protected by a law of 10 July 1982 setting out these different situations which they may choose: partner and associate or salaried employee or head of the enterprise. Thus, the partner and the associate as well as the wife who is head of an artisan or commercial enterprise, benefit financially in the event of maternity. This arrangement applies to women in the liberal professions as well as to a female associate of a member of a liberal profession. Of course, if a woman is a salaried employee of her partner, she benefits from the rights applying to all salaried employees. This radical text, adopted unanimously by Parliament, was necessary to remedy the deficiencies of earlier legislation. The laws of 1973 and 1975 on subsidy for foodstuffs represented some progress, but was inadequate. The change brought about by the new law provided a system of family payments to parents whether they were single or not. The law introduced for the benefit of single parents a method of advanced payment in the form of sums of money called 'family support'. To make sure the information was available to those concerned, the

Ministry of Women's Rights conducted a publicity campaign through brochures with diagrams and annexes.

In the area of fiscal equality, progress has been attained in two ways: first, the elimination of the legal concept of head of family: two signatures are now obligatory in the declaration of income (finance law of 1983) for tax purposes; second, taking into account the work of married women: deduction from taxable income of the costs of looking after children under five has been extended to married couples (Finance Law of 1982).

The law of 4 January 1984 has improved the position regarding parental leave and has granted it to the father as well as to the mother. Under previous arrangements, the father could only exercise his right if the mother explicitly gave up hers. Those concerned were given the choice between giving up employment completely or reducing work to half-time. This choice is available for adopted as well as natural children.

The law of 1965 maintained the principle according to which the husband alone administered the property of the family and property of children. A bill was presented to the Council of Ministers on 14 March 1985 to end such inequalities between married people. The new law gave women, like their husbands, responsibility for day-to-day running of family life. In property matters, the spouses must undertake jointly those acts which seriously affect the family patrimony. Women showed, during consultations on the law organised by the Ministry of Women's Rights on 8 March 1985, that they felt the most deeply about the requirement of dignity.

On 28 January 1985, the Ministry of Women's Rights launched a series of regional discussions which continued throughout 1985 on the theme of women, violence and security. These seminars carried on discussions already begun and included sessions for police personnel to improve the sensitivity towards women who have been victims of rape and battering. New proposals were also put forward to promote security for women. This initiative was part of a general policy which led *inter alia* to the opening of numerous reception centres and shelters for battered women. Action against violence to women is closely linked to the cultural policy undertaken by the Ministry of Women's Rights. In fact, the cultural factor is without doubt the common denominator of the whole cluster of initiatives undertaken by the Ministry. All the important policy measures undertaken between 1981 and 1986 were the outcome of critical analysis and of a challenging of certain cultural perceptions of the role of women and their image as part of a couple in society.

During the 1970s, feminist movements were in revolt against a dominant culture which limited women to specific, marginal activities and which thus promoted an image which was restrictive and devaluing. To give women dignity and autonomy, the Ministry of Women's Rights was determined to attack stereotypes and to promote the emergence of a new image of women, as vital partners in progress and modernisation. This was an unprecedented task for it called into question a whole patriarchal cultural tradition. Moreover, in the cultural domain, the difference between the sexes seemed to be one of segregation. Women were isolated in a status which may have been complementary but which was nevertheless inferior. The thrust and originality of the Ministry was to integrate all the legitimate aspirations of women into a coherent policy. Each woman was able to recognise herself in this policy, finding an antagonism between the rights of women and the rights of the family.

The challenging of sexual stereotypes has been carried especially into the realm of school books. School books often portrayed a nineteenth-century social structure where the separation of men's and women's roles remained very marked by patriarchal stereotypes. Such conditioning was even more effective because the segregation of roles corresponded to a differentiated education of the two sexes right from the initial entry at six years old through secondary schooling. The Ministry of Women's Rights undertook, with the help of the Ministry of National Education, a policy to correct this situation. Four posts of Women's Studies in the universities were created. An action programme on the theme 'Women and Research' under the aegis of the National Centre for Scientific Research (CNRS) was set in motion.

The Ministry also took a close look at language use. This is not a marginal matter in advancing the place of women in modern society. Language ought to reflect the evolution of ideas. The setting-up of a Commission on terminology in February 1984, composed of experts whose job it was to study the feminisation of professional names, is not just about language, but part of a global affirmation of the feminine identity and part of the reduction of inequality between men and women. The Commission concluded its work at the end of 1985.

Since 1981, the Ministry of Women's Rights has also made a significant effort to promote creative work and cultural training of women. Whether we refer to theatre, music, plastic arts, poetry or literature, very few women have had their work recognised and promoted by public authorities. Their creative effort has often been marginalised. They were viewed as consumers of culture rather than as participants in the creation of culture. A task of the Ministry was to support the creative capacity of women and to secure its proper place and legitimacy. This is why the Ministry has developed, along with other ministerial departments, several original activities: exhibitions of the plastic arts inside the ministry buildings themselves; financial help to cultural associations and to reviews; and the creation of two literary prizes – the Georges Sand prize and the Alice prize awarded on 8 March each year. The Georges Sand prize is awarded in recognition of a work concentrating on new egalitarian symbolism, written by a woman; the Alice prize is given for a non-sexist, lively work for children written by a woman. The existence of these prizes helps to correct a situation in which literary prizes are rarely awarded to women. In the musical area, until the decision of the Ministry to sponsor six works a year by women composers, there had been only one woman beneficiary out of forty sponsorships by the state.

In the plastic arts, an active policy concentrating on the national and international promotion of women's works was very important. To promote this, the Ministry created the Camille Foundation which acts by means of a purchasing fund. The works acquired by the Foundation are for exhibition and also for loan and distribution to provincial museums. National and international exhibitions were planned for each year. A panel of seven experts, artists, art critics and writers direct the activities of the Foundation. This Foundation was made possible through financial collaboration between the Ministry, the Cultural Ministry and numerous patrons.

In addition, the Ministry has worked through a broad network of voluntary associations which it tried to shape and to develop. Financial aid has been given to women's associations, and the Ministry has contributed to the creation of some 350 new jobs. The Minister has taken a close personal concern to make sure that the imaginative and creative potential of the associations is used to the full. In the near future, a bill will be introduced by the government allowing the associations to act as prosecutor in cases involving discriminatory attitudes which women encounter in various daily situations. Again, the Ministry is concerned to ensure the recognition of women's associations at the highest level – the National Council of Associations – as well as the participation of women's associations in public discussion and debate.

Much progress was made from 1981 to 1986 but the profoundly sexist character of society had the effect of limiting political and administrative success. It is clear that the demand for liberty and women's rights is in complete contradiction with the conservatives who only want to 'help'. Just as one gives help and assistance to a child, this denies women the status of responsible adults endowed with equal rights. Some people would like to maintain protective legislation towards women. One of the biggest surprises has been to see the progressive Trade Union Confederation, the CGT, come out against the opening-up of night work to women, which would provide women with the possibility of attaining all technical posts in various undertakings. This constitutes an example of how protective legislation excludes women from the world of work and from certain posts of responsibility.

The battle over part-time work is also beginning. Conservatives see in this the possibility of marginalising women's work. Confined to part-time labour, women never reach positions of serious responsibility in a firm. One cannot belong to junior managerial grades and also be a half-time worker. The Socialist government considered the expansion of part-time work as a remedy for the employment crisis and set out to establish coherent policies on it. The Ministry of Women's Rights had to make sure that there was real equality in the choice of part-time work and not a ghettoisation of women as has happened in Sweden. Choice of working-time for all is defensible; condemning the great majority of women to part-time work is not.

Just as the Ministry of Women's Rights achieved a great deal, so too it encountered setbacks. The Ministry had intended to use its influence alongside other departmental Ministries, but administrative problems occurred. The whole thrust of government policy was in favour of autonomy for women. However, ministerial departments with their own particular interests presented great difficulties getting new points of view accepted. Some circulars remained dead letters and certain initiatives failed. As already mentioned, in 1984 the Ministry of Women's Rights was able to create, with the help of the Ministry of National Education, four posts in women's studies in the Universities. The recognition of feminism as an object of university study is of major importance, since the creation of these posts is part of a long-term objective for the training of secondary-school teachers to deal with the problem of sexism. Thus nothing should have hindered the functioning of these first posts. But outstanding candidates were rejected by selection committees in law, history, and political science because they refused to acknowledge the feminist specialism of the candidate. Thus two of these posts are held by teachers who have themselves conducted no research into feminist matters. Therefore a very good initiative was thwarted.

Why has this happened? Precisely for the reasons which make essential a Ministry of Women's Rights: <u>because the social and cultural structures of France are profoundly misogynist and macho</u>. <u>This has been understood by certain men of the left, and, as a result, some legislative advances have been possible: the abortion law</u> and the law of equality in professions. But when we approach the central core of political, economic and cultural power, we get back to the old latin certitudes: those of the superiority of men over women. The political Left, nevertheless, can play a part in promoting a general policy of reducing inequalities. A return to conservatism, stopping all possibility of political action in favour of ensuring women their autonomy, is unfortunately a regression. It is no accident that it was a Frenchman, Stendhal, who wrote in 1817: 'The admission of women to perfect equality would be the surest sign of civilisation.' We have a very great deal yet to do.

12 Women's Equal Right to Equal Education

Margherita Rendel

The right to education has appeared in many human rights documents since the end of the Second World War, and is usually defined in terms of access to educational institutions rather than in terms of the content of what is taught, although broad humanistic phrases often appear. All instruments state the principles of equality and non-discrimination irrespective of sex, race and so on. The United Kingdom has signed and ratified most of them.[1] Nearly all are enforceable, if that is the right word, by a system by which governments report to a committee of experts named and elected by governments – a kind of peer-review. The exceptions in Europe are the Treaty of Rome and the legislation of the European Economic Community (EEC), and the European Convention on Human Rights and Fundamental Freedoms and its Protocols (ECHR).[2] Both these sets of instruments establish principles of non-discrimination and provide for enforcement through binding decisions of Courts. These two sets of provisions are related in that all members of the EEC have ratified the ECHR, although not all adherents of the Convention are members of the EEC. The possibility of the accession of the EEC to the ECHR has been discussed since 1972. Since 1974, the European Court of Justice (ECJ) has increasingly recognised at least the persuasive force of the ECHR and in 1977 the Council of Ministers recognised the Convention.

In this chapter I examine how far women in Britain have equal access to equal education and what help and assistance can be found in Europe, should remedies in Britain prove inadequate. I argue that the ECHR, its Protocols and its jurisprudence may offer more scope for challenging unequal opportunity, unequal provision of education, unequal treatment and stereotyping in texts and in the content of education than English or Scottish law or than the law of the EEC. It is necessary to begin the examination in Britain because remedies from the EEC and the ECHR are not normally available in the first instance. In particular, applications under the ECHR are inadmissible unless the applicant can show that domestic remedies have been exhausted.

185

It is also necessary to consider a little what is meant by an equal right to an equal education. To do this, I have formulated the following questions: Is there a right to education? If so, what sort of right? And what sort of education? Can the right, if it exists, be enforced? Is the right the same for females and for males? If not, in what ways does it differ? Why does it differ? Does any difference matter? If so, what can be done about it? It is not practicable to answer each of the questions in turn, but they are my guides through complex data. Also, I am leaving aside such philosophical questions as the peculiarity of education as a compulsory right.

We shall see that there is no right to education in England. Furthermore, the feminist research of the last fifteen years has demonstrated how the ideological content of the official curriculum and the hidden curriculum and of what is taught has disadvantaged girls and women. Bias has also been found in relation to race, class, and other characteristics. How many disabled or handicapped individuals appear in children's readers? What help can we hope for from Europe?

A RIGHT TO EDUCATION IN BRITAIN?

In English law, there is no right to education. There are a number of duties in relation to education. The legal, political and administrative structure of education in Scotland is similar to that in England and Wales, but the organisation of schools, examinations (and consequently curriculum) and of the teaching profession differs. These differences are not significant for the discussion that follows. Section 1 of the 1944 Education Act lays a duty on the Secretary of State to promote the education of the people of England and Wales, the progressive development of institutions for this purpose, and to secure the effective execution of their duties by local authorities under the Secretary of State's control and direction. Section 36 lays a duty on the parents to cause their children of compulsory school age to receive efficient full-time education suitable to their age, ability and aptitude, either by regular attendance at school or otherwise.

The content of these duties is set out in institutional and administrative terms. Local Education Authorities (LEAs) must provide sufficient schools for primary and for secondary education, and these schools must be sufficient in number, character and equipment to afford all pupils opportunities for such variety of instruction and training as may be desirable in view of their different ages, abilities and aptitudes; primary and secondary education must be carried out in separate schools; provision must be made for handicapped pupils. LEAs must provide free transport for children who live more than a specified distance from school; schools must keep registers of attendance; LEAs must arrange for cleansing children from vermin. LEAs must also provide adequate facilities for full-time and part-time further education and give scholarships for undergraduate and some similar courses. The duty to provide nursery education was abolished by the 1980 Education Act.[3] There are also a number of permissive powers.

As regards the content of education, the one compulsory subject in the curriculum is religious education; and there must be an assembly of the school for a daily act of worship.[4] Section 53 requires LEAs to provide adequate facilities at all levels of education for recreation, and for social and physical training.

The Secretary of State has a duty to inspect educational establishments, except universities, and to ensure provision for an adequate supply of trained teachers.[5]

These duties tend to fall into one of two categories. Some are phrased in general terms which are not easily susceptible of precise legal definition. What precisely is efficient education suitable to a child's age, ability and aptitude? What is sufficient equipment to afford all pupils opportunities? and so on. Other duties which are precise, like the provision of free transport, keeping registers and cleansing children from vermin, are ancillary to education.

The provisions for enforcement in the Act itself are extremely limited. Section 40 sets out the penalties to which parents are liable if they do not ensure that the children receive an education. Parents do, however, have a right to challenge, by appealing to a special tribunal, the decisions of LEAs allocating their children to schools and determining that their children should go to special schools, i.e. schools for handicapped children.[6] This right of parents is clearly important. Some students have successfully challenged the refusal of an LEA to award a grant for higher education. Apart from these opportunities, enforcement of the Act depends almost entirely on those with complaints appealing to the Secretary of State who may settle disputes, give directions to an LEA to prevent an unreasonable exercise of its functions and act where an LEA is in default in respect of a duty.[7] These powers are within the discretion of the Secretary of State and may be, and have been, challenged in the courts by LEAs (for example, *Secretary of State for Education and Science* v. *Metropolitan Borough of Tameside*, 1977).[8] In principle, there are two legal remedies available to the dissatisfied individual: action for breach of statutory duty and application for judicial review seeking an order of mandamus. However, these are discretionary remedies and not granted if other remedies are available. Since the Act expressly provides for complaints to be made to the Secretary of State, it seems most unlikely that a successful case could be brought. There are, however, further difficulties. For a statutory duty to be enforceable, it has to be precise, but, as the phrases quoted earlier show, the duties of LEAs are far from precise. Furthermore, in order to sue, plaintiffs would have to show that they had a direct and personal interest going well beyond that of the public at large.[9]

The problem of securing an adequate educational system has arisen in a particularly sharp form since 1979. Government cuts imposed on local authorities have resulted in a number of authorities being unable to provide a service commensurate with their statutory obligations. The HMI, attached to but independent of the DES, have reported in increasingly strong terms on the adverse effects of expenditure cuts on the quality of education. By May 1984, the HMI stated that the circumstances and lack of resources were 'such as to make worthwhile learning well-nigh impossible', and in the following year they stated that 'the needs of adult unemployed, ethnic minorities, and girls and women' were not well provided for. The HMI have repeatedly stressed the adverse consequences of the decline in resources for in-service training and for books and materials for improving and developing the curriculum.[10]

Some groups of parents are contemplating legal action, but their chances of success are thought to be very low. The real difficulty is that although the local authority would be the defendant in any legal action, it is the central government which is responsible for the failure of the LEA to carry out its duties. However, even if legal action were successful, the government would be able to pass legislation nullifying the effect of the court decision.[11] This means that a political rather than a legal remedy must be sought. However, the government would fail in such legislation only if its own supporters refused to support the measure. It is by no means certain that such a revolt by government backbenchers would take place over the deprivation enforced on state schools and colleges, and adult education.[12] There may therefore be no political means of ensuring that the claim to effective education for the people of England and Wales, apparently promised by Section 1 of the Education Act 1944, is made good without a change of government (or a change in government policy).

GIRLS AND BOYS, WOMEN AND MEN

Differences in the treatment of girls and boys, women and men and their achievement in education have been abundantly demonstrated. The statistical evidence shows that girls tend to take fewer examination subjects; that these tend to be concentrated in the arts subjects and biology, but that the girls have a higher success rate than the boys, a result perhaps of fewer girls than boys being entered for the examinations. The higher the level in the education system, the smaller the proportion of girls or of women students; and the more scientific or technological, the more 'masculine' the subject, the less likely that there will be girls or women studying or teaching it. It is the same with posts in educational establishments or in educational administration: the more senior the post the less likely that it will be held by a woman.[13]

These results are the more curious in that the evidence shows that girls before the age of puberty are better at their school-work than boys and that they are in general more likely to be quiet and conscientious students.[14] One traditional explanation is that at the age of puberty, girls recognise their feminine role as future wives and mothers and prefer it to other work. Feminists have offered rather different and more convincing explanations. They have shown the emphasis in schools, as well as outside them, that is put on women's feminine role to the exclusion of other roles, an emphasis which goes so far as to render women invisible throughout most of the curriculum.[15] Furthermore, the way in which girls and women students are treated makes clear to them that they should not seek for themselves other major roles.[16] This type of indoctrination of girls – and boys – in the schools has a long history.[17] It is sometimes justified on the grounds that it corresponds to the interests of the two sexes. But this is a circular argument since girls and boys have been brought up to have different interests.[18]

Another justification is that education should prepare children for 'the world outside', 'the world of work', 'adult life' and so on. This argument, which is particularly prominent at present, is not irrelevant to the purposes of education. It does, however, subordinate the purpose of developing the full potential of the individual – a concept which commonly occurs in UN instruments – to the existing social structure and to the short-term and assumed demands of the labour-market. The existing social structure accords women a subordinate role in political, economic, cultural and social life, and stresses (but does not reward) their role in the family where they service the male labour-force, and produce and socialise the future labour-force.[19] The labour-market treats women as marginal, low-paid, unskilled workers for use when required – a reserve army of labour.[20] Education has been used to reinforce women's subordinate position both in the family and in the labour-market,[21] thereby upholding the patriarchal order.

Education therefore is not neutral in the values it inculcates in both girls and boys. It is one of the ideological structures[22] which maintain a gender-segregated, hierarchical and, for women and other disadvantaged groups, oppressive society at variance with the values expressed in human rights instruments. Yet human rights instruments and equal opportunities legislation are ostensibly intended to counteract these injustices and to offer remedies to individuals.

In principle, in Britain, girls' opportunities for education should no longer be less than those of boys. This is because s.22 of the Sex Discrimination Act 1975 (SDA)[23] makes it unlawful to treat girls less favourably than boys in access to any educational establishment or in the way in which they are treated in it. The SDA permits single-sex establishments but requires LEAs to provide their educational facilities without discrimination. The broad definition of discrimination covers both direct discrimination and indirect discrimination.[24] One immediate effect of the SDA was to render unlawful the *numerus clausus* operated by some university departments and medical schools, thus enlarging the right to education of a few women.

Very few educational cases have been brought under the SDA so far. *Whitfield* v. *London Borough of Croydon & Woodcote High School*, 1979, was one case which concerned both access to courses and equal treatment. As a result of her mother's protests, Helen Whitfield and other girls were admitted to the craft, design and technology classes at the school only if they opted in, whereas the boys were assigned to these classes automatically. The judge held that although the sexes were treated differently, since boys had to opt in to Home Economics there was no discrimination (a curious concept of non-discrimination). He further noted that at the girls' and boys' senior high schools which most of the girls and boys subsequently attended, only home economics or craft subjects respectively were offered, and therefore the pupils at Woodcote High School were not disadvantaged. This is tantamount to saying that because B discriminates, it is all right for A to discriminate. Although this case was lost, the Equal Opportunities Commission (EOC), the statutory body set up to enforce the SDA, claims to have persuaded LEAs and the overwhelming majority of schools that they must allow girls access to scientific, technical and craft subjects and boys access to domestic and childcare subjects on equal terms.[25] As part of its functions of promoting greater equality between men and women, the EOC has produced many publicity and information materials concerned with equal access, and with assisting teachers, schools, careers officers and others to encourage girls to take science and technology.

Debell, Sevket and Teh v. *London Borough of Bromley*, settled out of court before the hearing, concerned the allocation of boys and girls to classes in a primary school. When there were too many pupils for the top class, the Head kept down the eight youngest girls instead of the eight youngest pupils of whom four were boys and four were girls. Following the initiation of proceedings in the County Court, the LEA paid compensation into court and admitted in an open letter that there had been breaches of the SDA. Both these cases were primarily concerned with access.

Since a right to equal access does not give girls access to equal education, we must consider who controls the content of education: of courses, of teaching materials and the hidden curriculum. Section 23 of the 1944 Education Act places control of the *content* of education in the hands of LEAs. In fact, this control is shared by teachers, LEA inspectors, HMI, examining bodies and, in principle, by governing bodies of schools. In practice, there has been no central government *control* over the curriculum,[26] although there has been much influence through HMI, advice from advisory bodies, and recommendations for the design of school buildings – for example, fewer science laboratories in girls' schools.[27] Official advice, recommendations, the syllabuses of examining bodies, the texts and materials published have reinforced traditional gender stereotypes and sex-roles and ensured the invisibility of women. The treatment of girls by teachers, and fellow-students also, may be such as to make it more difficult for girls to make the best use of the education to which they have access. Furthermore, even where girls have access to the same education as boys, its content and the way in which it is presented favours boys at the expense of girls. Equality of access does not necessarily mean equality of outcome. The content of education denies the substance of a right to equal education, although access offers the form of such a right.

Since it is so difficult to enforce the claim to an educational service commensurate with statutory requirements, the possibility of obtaining control over the curriculum and the content of education such as to ensure that the education of girls and boys is both equal and equal in its outcomes, is even more remote. In any case, practical difficulties have to be overcome. There is as yet relatively little expertise on how to achieve such ends although this expertise is steadily and rapidly growing.[28] Also, existing texts and materials cannot simply be scrapped and replaced, both because of limited resources and because of a shortage of materials. Expertise has been developed by an advisory body, the Schools Council now abolished,[29] and continues to be developed by some LEAs with important equal opportunities programmes, for example the Inner London Education Authority and the London Borough of Brent and by groups of women teachers. The paradox here is that the lack of central government control which makes the difficulties in changing the curriculum also provides opportunities for others to carry out this function. The present policy of cuts in education services, discussed earlier, has especially adverse effects on girls and women, in hindering the provision of new non-sexist materials, in obstructing the retraining of teachers and in restricting the access of women to education which they, more than the males of their age-cohort, did not receive at school.

Thus, in Britain, not only is there no right to education, but such education as is available, in principle equally to females and to males, is not in fact equal for females and for males. The difference does matter, since the lesser education which females receive reduces their access to further training, jobs, salaries, to independence, and ultimately to power and prestige in society.

THE RIGHT TO EDUCATION IN EEC LEGISLATION

As is well known, the Treaty of Rome does not mention education; nor does the Equal Treatment Directive (ETD). The Treaty deals with vocational training and retraining in Articles 118, 125 and 128, and the ETD aims to assist not only vocational training, but access to such training.[30] Article 4 specifies the meaning of training: 'Access to all types and to all levels, of vocational guidance, vocational training, advanced vocational training and retraining.' Access to vocational training, especially when training is defined broadly, has clear implications at least for secondary schooling, since the qualifications required for access to vocational training are obtained usually at school.

Notwithstanding the absence of education from the Treaty, both the European Parliament and the Education Ministers and the Education and Training Section of the EEC have substantially expanded the EEC's work on education, and the EEC has prepared a number of programmes on equality for girls in education, but little progress is being made in implementing them.[31] At its meeting on 3 June 1985, the Committee of Education Ministers formally agreed on a programme of positive action for schoolgirls to encourage women to enter non-traditional studies and careers, especially information technologies and bio-technologies. Whether realistic funds will be allocated to implement the programme remains to be seen.[32] Keiner and Wickham[33] stress the scope given by the teleological interpretation of the Treaty of Rome for developing policies with wide implications. Since the obligations of member-states are ultimately enforceable by the ECJ, it may be that British women's human right to equal education will be obtained eventually through the EEC rather than through national legislation.

THE EUROPEAN CONVENTION ON HUMAN RIGHTS

Education was not originally included in the ECHR because it was not possible to secure agreement on the form any provision should take. The provision finally agreed reads:

> No person shall be denied the right to education. In the exercise of any functions which it assumes in relation to education and to teaching, the State shall respect the right of parents to ensure such education and teaching is in conformity with their own religious and philosophical convictions.[34]

There were several reasons for the difficulties. First, while the governments expected to provide a universal education service, they did not wish to commit themselves to provide additional services, for example for adult illiterates or for children in remote areas with no reasonable access to schools. Second, with the exception of the Netherlands, they wished to avoid having to subsidise denominational schools. Third, considerable anxiety was expressed, particularly by Christian Democrats, about the recognition of parents' philosophical convictions; there was a fear that the provision would open the way for children to be educated as Marxists or Communists. The Consultative Assembly of the Council of Europe answered the latter objection by pointing to Article 17 of the Convention which prohibits any one from engaging in activities which might destroy or limit rights set out in the Convention.[35] Furthermore, some States, for example Sweden, legally required some form of religious education in schools. It is clear that the values or ideology and, to this extent, the content of education, was very much a concern of the politicians, lawyers and government experts drafting the Article.

Article 2 of the Protocol has been litigated several times. The first judgment was that in the *Belgian Linguistic Cases*.[36] The facts of this group of cases are complicated and they raised a number of issues; they were decided on narrow and cautious grounds. The cases were brought by French-speaking families living in Flemish-speaking areas who were obliged to send their children to Flemish-speaking schools contrary, they claimed, to their rights to free expression, freedom of conscience and their philosophical convictions and to the disadvantage of their children and their family life.

In its judgment, the Court held clearly, first of all, that Article 2 of the Protocol, in spite of its formulation in the negative, did enshrine a right to education, although only to the education that already existed. Second, it held that there was no right to an education in the language of the parents, but there was a right to education in the national language, or one of the national languages, of the country. Third, to be able to profit from education meant to be able to secure official recognition of qualifications; since such recognition was obtainable by taking a special examination, there was no breach of the Convention on this ground. Fourth, if parents sent their children away to French-speaking schools, it was they who were disrupting family life and in any case it was not the purpose of the rules on language to disrupt family life. Fifth, the Court found there was a difference between the form of expression (i.e. language as the vehicle of expression) and its content (i.e. what was expressed), and that while Article 10 safeguarded the content, the form might be subjected to restrictions. All the claims were rejected except that on behalf of a small number of children living in the periphery of Brussels who should have been allowed to attend French-speaking schools. Although the case was lost, the Belgian government did reconsider its existing rules.

Several cases have concerned the type of education to which an individual can claim a right and therefore have implications for the content of the curriculum. It has been held that the right to education applies to those educational services that already exist and is primarily concerned with elementary education and not necessarily with advanced studies such as technology or retraining programmes. The State is not obliged to recognise or continue to recognise any particular institution as an educational establishment. The State's function in education includes such matters as the allocation of places in secondary schools and the organisation of the system of secondary education. Children cannot be compelled to attend religious education in the State religion when this is different from their parents' own Protestant religion.[37]

Two other cases have had a very direct bearing on the content of the curriculum. Neither concerned girls' education, but the principles established can be applied to sex-role typing.

Kjeldsen, Busk Madsen and Pedersen v. *Denmark* concerned sex education. The parents objected to compulsory sex education at school on the grounds that it raised ethical questions and they preferred to teach the children themselves. They sought to get the children exempted, but were unsuccessful. The Court held that care must be taken to ensure that:

> information or knowledge included in the curriculum is conveyed in an objective critical and pluralistic manner. The State is forbidden to pursue an aim of indoctrination that might be considered as not respecting parents' religious and philosophical convictions.[38]

The legislation requiring compulsory sex education was intended to ensure that pupils received better information, would be able to take care of themselves and show consideration for others and did not overstep the bounds of what a democratic state may regard as the public interest. Second, the Court held that practically every subject carries some philosophical or religious weight, directly or indirectly, and that the second sentence of Article 2 of the Protocol did not permit parents to object to such teaching.[39]

The concepts of education and of philosophical convictions were developed further in *Campbell and Cosans* v. *UK*, the Scottish Tawse case. The parents of two boys objected to the use of corporal punishment. The LEA refused to give Mrs Campbell a guarantee that her son would not be subjected to corporal punishment, but in fact he never was. Jeffrey Cosans was threatened with corporal punishment for a minor offence, refused on his father's advice to submit to the punishment and was forthwith suspended from school; as a result he lost his final year of schooling. The parents claimed violation of Article 3 of the Convention (inhuman and degrading treatment)[40] and Article 2 of the Protocol. In its decision the Court gave education a broad definition:

> The whole process whereby, in any society, adults endeavour to transmit their beliefs, culture and other values to the young. Whereas teaching or instruction refers in particular to the transmission of knowledge and to intellectual development.[41]

The Court further held that discipline was 'an integral, even indispensable, part of an educational system' on which governments were under an obligation to respect parents' religious and philosophical convictions.[42] 'Philosophical convictions' denoted:

> such convictions as are worthy of respect in a democratic society and not incompatible with human dignity; in addition, they must not conflict with the fundamental right of the child to education, the whole of Article 2 being dominated by its first sentence.[43]

On these grounds, the Court upheld the complaints under Article 2.

As regards the suspension of Jeffrey Cosans from school, the Court held (Sir Vincent Evans dissenting) that his right to education had been violated. The Court reiterated that Article 2 was dominated by the first sentence, held that the right to education was the right of the child,[44] and, while recognising that the right to education 'by its very nature calls for regulation by the State', held that:

> such regulation must never injure the substance of the right nor conflict with other rights enshrined in the Convention or its Protocols . . . A condition of access to an educational establishment that conflicts . . . with another right enshrined in Protocol No. 1 cannot be described as reasonable and in any event falls outside the State's power of regulation in Article 2.[45]

As Lonbay justly observes,[46] the case is important not only in relation to the abolition of corporal punishment, but also in relation to the rights of children and of students and to the right of heads to suspend pupils from school. The decision has clearly speeded up the abolition of corporal punishment in British schools.[47]

These decisions could be extremely helpful to parents wishing to challenge sexist education in schools. Parents could reasonably claim that sexist education was contrary to their philosophical convictions. Anti-sexism is more than an opinion or idea and can properly be said to reach 'a certain level of cogency, seriousness, cohesion and importance'.[48] It is clearly a conviction worthy of respect in a democratic society; it is compatible with human dignity and it does not conflict with the fundamental right of the child to education. Although sexism is a philosophical view which runs through virtually all the curriculum, States are under an obligation not to indoctrinate, but on the contrary must take care that 'information included in the curriculum is conveyed in an objective critical and pluralistic manner' as stated in *Kjeldsen*. Sexist education does not meet this standard. The consequences of a successful action on these lines could include the replacement of existing sexist texts and materials with non-sexist texts, or at least their supplementation by non-sexist texts and by the retraining of teachers. Such measures would seem to fall foul of the UK's reservation to Article 2 of the Protocol by which the UK accepted the second sentence:

> only so far as it is compatible with the provision of efficient instruction and training, and the avoidance of unreasonable public expenditure.[49]

It may be that the reservation itself contains the answer to the plea of unreasonable public expenditure. Sexist education is incompatible with efficient education and training, as shown by the under-achievement and drop-out of girls and women.

Anti-sexist education would be contrary to the philosophical convictions of some parents. LEAs which have introduced compulsory home economics for boys have been faced with parents complaining that they do not want their boys 'turned into sissies'.[50] Such opinions, however firmly held, would scarcely meet the Court's criteria as a philosophical conviction.

The convictions of some parents belonging to traditional and orthodox religions, that girls should be educated to fulfil only traditional family roles, could not be so easily dismissed.[51] However, the right to education is the right of the child, the daughters in this case, and is a right which dominates Article 2 and hence takes priority over the religious or philosophical convictions of the parents. Furthermore, Article 17 of the Convention provides that no State, group or person has:

any right to engage in any activity or perform any act aimed at the destruction of any of the rights and freedoms . . . or at their limitation to a greater extent than is provided for in the Convention.

The establishment of girls' schools intended to prepare girls only for domestic and family life could be argued to be such an activity. The right of the child has been recognised as a right distinct from that of her/his parents,[52] and the European Commission will ensure that a minor is represented by some means.[53]

Daughters could argue that they were being discriminated against contrary to Article 14 of the Convention in their right to education, because they were denied an education equal to that of their brothers and male contemporaries and as a consequence also denied the opportunities to which education leads. Parents would have to argue that, although the education they wished their daughters to have was different from that of boys, it was of equal value.[54]

Under the ECHR, cases have to be brought against States, not individuals. It is therefore necessary to show that the State can be held responsible in relation to the matter complained of. In the case of maintained schools or schools for which LEAs or the DES have a responsibility, the liability of the State is clear, and proceedings would have to be taken in the first instance under the SDA. Since s.25 of the SDA (general duty of the public sector of education to ensure that educational facilities are provided without sex discrimination) is enforceable only by complaint to the Secretary of State under s.68 or s.69, it would appear that there are no domestic remedies should the Secretary of State decide not to act.

A private person or body responsible for both a boys' and girls' school could, it would seem, be sued under the SDA, and ordered by the Court to equalise educational opportunities open to the girls (and to the boys). It seems most unlikely that an argument of different but of equal value to the recipient could succeed. An education for domesticity clearly is not equal in value to an education that leads to marketable skills.[55] If the school were a private girls' school, it is difficult to see what remedy would exist under UK law. However, under Article 1 of the Convention, States have a duty to secure the rights and freedoms guaranteed to all within their jurisdiction and this principle was upheld in *Van Oosterwijck* v. *Belgium* and *Airey* v. *Ireland*.[56] The argument on behalf of the girls would be that the state had a duty under the ECHR to ensure that all girls received an education that did not discriminate against them. It will be readily appreciated that this argument can be applied to access to subjects as well as to the ideology of the official and hidden curriculum in many different types of school.

CONCLUSION

It is clear from the provisions of English law and of European law that the ideological role of education is recognised and considered important. This is scarcely a remakable finding. What is important is the way in which the ideological role is recognised. In England, primacy is accorded to the teaching of religion in the 1944 Education Act, but there is an absence of general principles to guide and, equally important, of legal means to challenge the ideology in education.[57] For this reason it is difficult to challenge either sexism (or racism) or the narrow, utilitarian policies of the Thatcher Government.

In the EEC, education is linked to vocational training, at first sight a narrow, utilitarian principle. However, the EEC is based on principles of free and fair competition, hence on non-discrimination. These principles have in fact been interpreted and developed to provide for women a right not only to equal pay and equal treatment in employment and training, but also implicitly to equal secondary education at least. Also the ETD includes provision for positive action. Furthermore the ECJ is giving increasing weight to the provisions and principles of the ECHR.

The European Court of Human Rights has elaborated a hierarchy of principles in relation to the right to education. First, it is a positive right to the education provided by the State to be enjoyed without discrimination. Second, it is a right of the child or individual claiming the education. Third, the State is required to 'respect the right of parents to ensure that the education it provides is in conformity with their own religious and philosophical convictions'. Furthermore, the State is under an obligation to ensure that those resident within its boundaries enjoy the rights guaranteed by the Convention.

I have discussed an important potential conflict between the rights guaranteed by the ECHR, for example between a daughter and her parents. There are also significant differences in women's right to education under the ECHR and the ECJ, and between both those jurisdictions and British law. Both the explicit and the implicit ideology in education could be brought within the ambit of the ECHR and therefore possibly of the ECJ. This is important because the enforcement powers of the ECJ are stronger and its procedures faster than those of the ECHR. The principles involved could apply to racism and other forms of discriminatory ideology. It is doubtful whether this principle would safeguard British schooling against cuts, although an argument might be made on the grounds of regional discrimination because of the arbitrary disparity in the effects of the cuts. Such an argument would also raise the difficult issue of equality of outcome in relation to non-discrimination in provision, but the provisions for positive action of the EEC might be helpful.

The development of European jurisprudence that I have suggested may seem over-optimistic in view of the cautiousness of both Courts and the exceedingly slow procedures of the European Court of Human Rights. Much might depend on how far the two European jurisdictions would apply each other's principles.

Notes

1. For example: Universal Declaration of Human Rights 1948; American Declaration of the Rights and Duties of Man, 1948; UN Declaration on the Rights of the Child, 1959; UNESCO Convention against Discrimination in Education, 1960; International Convention on the Elimination of All Forms of Racial Discrimination, 1966; UN Convention on the Elimination of All Forms of Discrimination against Women, 1979.
2. The European Convention on Human Rights and Fundamental Freedoms was signed in 1950 and entered into force on 3 September 1953. It is the first international document drafted as an enforceable legal document which made provision for a right for individuals to sue their governments before an international tribunal. Because of its early date and in spite of its innovatory provisions for enforcement, it appears now as a rather conservative document and the early judgments were extremely cautious. More recently, the Court and Commission have been bolder.
3. Sections 8, 55, 80, 50, 41 of the Education Act 1944 respectively: s.1, Education Act 1962; s.24, Education Act 1980.
4. Section 25, Education Act 1944.
5. Sections 77 and 62 respectively.
6. Sections 6, 7, and 8, Education Act 1980, Education Act 1981 respectively.
7. Sections 67, 68 and 99, Education Act 1944 respectively.
8. AC 1014.
9. G. Taylor and J. B. Saunders, *The Law of Education*, Butterworth, London, 1976, p. 80, note (a); C. Harlow and R. Rawlings, *Law and Administration*, Weidenfeld & Nicolson, London, 1984, p. 296; T. C.

Hartley and J. A. G. Griffith, *Government and Law*, Weidenfeld & Nicolson, London, 1981, pp. 369–73.

10. *Report by Her Majesty's Inspectors on the Effects of Local Authority Expenditure Policies on Education Provision in England*, Department of Education and Science (DES), London, 1984, para. 8, and 1985, para. 6; F. J. Hunt, 'Education Policy and a Constrained Economy: the Case of England', *Compare*, vol. 13, no. 2, 1983, pp. 118–19, 122.

11. Harlow and Rawlings, *Law and Administration*, pp. 272–3.

12. Many better-off middle-class parents send their sons to private-sector boarding schools (fees over £1,500 per term). Daughters are more likely to be sent to direct-grant or the better state schools as day-pupils. DES, *Statistics of Education*.

13. See *Statistics of Education*, HMSO, London, annual, vol. 2, *School-leavers, CSE and GCE*, vol. 4, *Teachers*.

14. E. M. Byrne, *Women and Education*, Tavistock, London, 1978; R. Deem (ed.), *Schooling for Women's Work*, Routledge & Kegan Paul, London, 1980.

15. G. Lobban, 'Sex-roles in Reading Schemes', *Educational Review*, vol. 27, no. 3, June 1975; several other articles in this issue are relevant to this point. D. Spender and E. Sarah, *Learning to Lose*, The Women's Press, London, 1980; A. McRobbie and T. McCabe, *Feminism for Girls*, Routledge & Kegan Paul, London, 1981; M. Rendel, 'Ideological Measures and the Subjugation of Women', *International Journal of Political Education*, vol. 5, no. 2, 1982, pp. 105–20.

16. A.-M. Wolpe, *Some Processes in Sexist Education*, WRRC Publications, London, 1977; M. Stanworth, *Gender and Schooling: A Study of Sexual Division in the Classroom*, WRRC, London, 1981, and Hutchinson, 1983; P. Mahoney, *Schools for Boys? Co-Education Reassessed*, Hutchinson, London, in collaboration with the Explorations in Feminism Collective, 1985.

17. Board of Education, *Report of the Consultative Committee on the Differentiation of the Curriculum for Boys and Girls Respectively in Secondary Schools*, The Hadow Report, HMSO, London, 1923; M. David, *The State, The Family and Education*, Routledge & Kegan Paul, London, 1980.

18. M. Rendel and others, *Equality for Women*, Fabian Society, London, 1968.

19. Central Advisory Council for Education, *15–18*, The Crowther Report, HMSO, London, 1959; *Half Our Future*, The Newsom Report, HMSO, London, 1963.

20. R. D. Barron and G. M. Norris, 'Sexual Divisions and the Dual Labour Market', in D. L. Barker and S. Allen (eds), *Dependence and Exploitation in Work and Marriage*, Longman, London, 1976; C. Hakim, *Occupational Segregation*, Department of Employment London, Research Paper No. 9, 1979; J. West (ed.), *Work, Women and the Labour Market*, Routledge & Kegan Paul, London, 1982.

21. J. Mitchell, *Woman's Estate*, Penguin Books, Harmondsworth, 1971.

22. L. Althusser, 'Ideology and Ideological State Apparatuses', in *Essays on Ideology*, Verso, London, 1984, first published 1970.

23. The Race Relations Act 1976 makes almost identical provision in relation to discrimination on grounds of colour, race, nationality or ethnic or national origins.
24. Sections 26 and 27, 25, 1(1)(a) and 1(1)(b) respectively of the SDA. Indirect discrimination is a requirement or condition applied equally to both sexes but which is such that the proportion of one sex able to comply with it is considerably smaller than the proportion of the other sex and which, furthermore, cannot be justified.
25. EOC Information Leaflet No. 7 – *Equal Treatment in Education (Class Organisation in Schools)*, March 1985.
26. Freedom from central control is rapidly disappearing. See, for example, B. Simon, *Does Education Matter?*, Lawrence & Wishart, London, 1985.
27. For example, the notorious *Building Bulletin*, 2A. Ministry of Education, 2nd edn, 1954, withdrawn in the late 1960s. On this point, see also Rendel, *Equality for Women*; Labour Party, *Discrimination Against Women*, Report of a Labour Party Study Group, London, 1972; Byrne, *Women and Education*. But the school buildings are still in use.
28. J. Whyld (ed.), *Sexism in the Secondary Curriculum*, Harper & Row, London, 1983; H. Taylor, 'Implementing a Local Authority Initiative on Equal Opportunities', in M. Arnot (ed.), *Race and Gender: Equal Opportunities Policies in Education*, Pergamon Press in Association with the Open University, Oxford, 1985.
29. G. Weiner, 'The Schools Council and Gender: A Case-Study in Policy-Making and Curriculum Innovation', in Arnot, *Race and Gender*.
30. Articles 118, 125 and 128 of the Treaty of Rome; Preamble 7th para; Art. 1(1) of the ETD, 9 February 1976, 76/207/EEC.
31. V. Hall-Smith, C. Hoskyns, J. Keiner and E. Szyszczak, *Women's Rights and the EEC, A Guide for Women in the UK*, Rights of Women Europe, London, 1983.
32. CREW Reports, vol. V(6), June 1985 (Brussels).
33. J. Keiner and A. Wickham, 'Education and Law: The Case of the EEC', *International Journal of the Sociology of Law*, vol. 8, no. 3, 1980, pp. 227–49.
34. Article 2 of the First Protocol.
35. A. H. Robertson, *Human Rights in Europe*, Manchester University Press, 1977; G. L. Weil, *The European Convention on Human Rights*, A. W. Sythoff, Leyden, 1963; J. E. S. Fawcett, *The Application of the European Convention on Human Rights*, Clarendon Press, Oxford, 1969.
36. 1474/62; 11 YB 832; and *Inhabitants of Les Fourons*, 1974, 14 YB 452.
37. *X* v. *UK*, 5962/72, DR2, 50; *X* v. *Belgium*, 7010/75, DR3, 162. *Church of X* v. *UK*, 3798/68, 12 YB 306, The Scientology Case. *X* and *Y* v. *UK*, 7527/76, DR11, 147; *X* v. *UK*, 7782/77, DR14, 179, *Karnell and Hardt* v. *Sweden*, 4733/71, 14 YB 644 & 676.
38. Judgment, 7 December 1976, Serieis A, No. 23; 1 EHRR 711, para. 53.
39. Paras 54 and 53 respectively.
40. The Court rejected the application under Article 3 on the ground that neither boy had in fact been subjected to corporal punishment.
41. Judgment 25 February 1982; 3 *Human Rights Law Journal*, No. 1–4, 1982, 221–36, para. 33.

42. *Human Rights Law Journal*, paras 34, 35.
43. Ibid., para. 36.
44. Ibid., para. 40.
45. Ibid., para. 41.
46. J. Lonbay, 'Rights in Education under the European Convention on Human Rights', *Modern Law Review*, vol. 46, no. 3, May 1983, pp. 345–50.
47. And led to its abolition in Ireland.
48. Judgment, para. 36.
49. Quoted by the Court in *Campbell and Cosans* v. *UK*, para. 1.
50. Mr Arthur Steel, Conservative opposition spokesman on education on Brent London Borough Council, was reported as saying that the reason why girls opted for biology and boys chose physics 'was prefectly clear. Boys and girls were [sic] biologically different. Efforts to change things would have no effect except to turn boys into "hermaphrodites and queers".' *Times Educational Supplement*, 25 February 1983, p. 11.
51. A case raising rather comparable issues was heard in the High Court but was referred to the Independent Schools Tribunal for decision. In this case, it was the HMI who considered that the boys' curriculum was dominated by religious subjects to the disadvantage of their instruction in a normal secular curriculum (*R* v. *Secretary of State for Education and Science, ex p. Talmud Torah Machzikei Hadass School Trust, Times Law Report*, 12 April 1985). I am indebted to the Advisory Centre for Education for this reference. A number of similar complaints have been brought by HMI against fundamentalist Christian schools belonging to an American sect: *Guardian*, 20 November 1985.

    A fundamentalist Islamic primary school has been approved for voluntary aided status by Brent London Borough Council, but at the time of writing the decision of the Secretary of State for Education is not known.
52. *Campbell and Cosans*, para. 40.
53. L. Mikaelsen, *European Protection of Human Rights: The Practice and Procedure of the European Commission of Human Rights on the Admissibility of Applications from Individuals and States*, Sijthoff & Noordhoff, Alphen aan den Rijn, 1980, who quotes Case 1527/62.
54. See below and note 55.
55. The principle of equal pay for work of equal value exists to ensure that the recipients of pay receive equal pay for work that is of equal value to the employer, and is therefore inapplicable in its context.
56. 23 YB 49; 22 YB 420, 24 YB 428 & 482 respectively.
57. B. Simon, 'Why no pedagogy in England?', in *Does Education Matter?*, pp. 77–165. Simon argues that the lack of principles underlying the English educational system gives considerable scope for undermining education.

13 Abortion Law Reform: A Woman's Right to Choose?
Joyce Outshoorn

In the 1960s and 1970s West European states reformed the law on abortion, with the exceptions of Belgium, Ireland and Greece.[1] This has meant that for women medically safe abortion has become a viable option – a 'back-up' method to the more accepted forms of birth control. Access to an abortion, however, is not evenly spread geographically.

Another consequence of this is the phenomenon, denigratingly coined 'abortion tourism', which takes place within states and across borders. Yet up to now there have been few attempts to deal with these issues at the European level. The chances for a low-price, medically safe abortion vary widely for women living in different parts of Europe.

The reforms of the 1960s and 1970s were not the outcome of a new controversy over abortion. There had been major political debates and legal changes in the latter half of the nineteenth century and at the beginning of this century which usually resulted in the tightening-up of abortion laws or the introduction of new prohibitive statutes in most of the European states. In the 1920s and 1930s there had also been a movement to liberalise abortion laws, but reforms were only achieved in the Scandinavian countries.[2]

Debates about abortion in European countries is therefore nothing new; what is novel about the recent debates is the new meaning abortion has acquired through the rise of the women's liberation movement which views abortion as a necessary condition for the liberation of women. The availability of legal abortion is considered to be a prerequisite for women's equality on the grounds that it gives her the ability to control her own life and body.

If one looks at the legislation in most of Western European states, it becomes apparent that abortion on demand, at the request of women themselves, has only been achieved in a few countries. Most governments clearly did not approach the abortion issue in order to satisfy the demands of women but rather tackled it as a social or medical problem.

A woman's right to choose was not the starting-point of the lawmakers and original reformers. Among the reasons usually stressed by these reformers, who were often liberal professionals, was the serious need to combat illegal abortion. The central argument was that abortion law reform would make abortion safer. Strict laws had led to illegal and risky abortion, driving it underground. Reform, it was suggested, would eliminate these unhealthy practices.

Other frequently cited grounds for reform included the physical and mental danger to the woman's health (the so-called 'therapeutic abortion'), damage to the foetus and pregnancy as a result of rape or incest. Another argument pointed out that abortion law reform was necessary in order to maintain respect for the law; a statute on the books which was neither being observed nor being prosecuted (as was usually the case) led to an undermining of the rule of law. Abortion law reform was already on the political agenda in a majority of countries when the women's liberation movement arose. The movement, however, was only partially successful in redefining the issue and getting its view embodied in law.

Sweden and Denmark granted a woman abortion on demand, although this only occurred in the 1970s after earlier reforms had paved the way for a gradual change. Abortion was therefore not conceived as part and parcel of a policy designed to bring about improvements in the position of women. When the European Parliament addressed abortion as a women's issue in 1981, as part of its recommendations on the position of women, this was notable and unusual. The European Commission did not follow this lead or suggest a common policy on abortion because of the widely different definitions of the problem contained in the laws of the various member states.[3] The women's liberation movement gave the abortion debate a new momentum, both in countries where politicians for their own reasons preferred to ignore the issue, and in those countries where limited reform had already taken place.

In this chapter I first discuss the abortion issue prior to the rise of the women's movement and the feminist redefinition of the issue. I then go on to examine abortion politics in Western Europe and describe how politicians reacted to the issue. In so doing, I compare women's legal and practical access to abortion in the various nations. Finally I offer brief comments on the future of the debate.

MAKING THE ISSUE

It is important to stress that social problems do not simply exist as such, but are in fact constructed, or labelled as 'problems'. Events or sets of circumstances by themselves do not automatically constitute issues. Rather, they become significant by the meanings and values people attach to them. Something has to be classified as a social problem to become identified as such; and even then it is not necessarily a problem for public policy or governmental attention.[4] Because of this social construction many definitions of a problem are possible. When abortion was illegal, public discourse about it, in so far as there was any at all, was in terms of deviant behaviour, crime and unpleasant operations. It is therefore not surprising that the medical profession was the one to make the issue. In the 1960s when abortion started to attract attention, doctors brought it to the fore. Abortion was therefore defined as a medical or psychiatric problem. Apart from some general factors such as changing views on marriage, sexuality and reproduction, and the particular impetus of the thalidomide scandal, students of the period are divided about the causes of the renewal of debate in the 1960s. It is often claimed that illegal abortion was on the increase and that doctors were alarmed by this. Statistics about illegal practices are unreliable, so there is no way to substantiate this. It is also alleged that doctors were increasingly confronted by women who, encouraged by the new openness about sexual affairs, dared to ask them for an abortion. The net effect was that the doctors felt pressurised into doing something. They debated the merits of individual cases and the grounds on which abortion should be considered acceptable. This made safer abortions possible and undermined the ethical dominance of the churches and other moral experts. But it also gave the medical profession more power in an area which was not inherently medical. It was precisely on this point that the new feminist movement challenged the medical profession's authority, claiming that a woman is her own best expert when it comes to judging her own situation – a judgement which is as good as, or superior to, that of any psychiatrist, gynaecologist or social counsellor.

The women's movement had to redefine 'the issue' which was already framed in terms of a medical and psychiatric problem, with the battle lines drawn for or against partial reform. The women's movement wanted total repeal; women should be granted an abortion on demand if they wished one. Despite different political environments and variations in the availability of abortion, this demand was broadly the same in most European countries. Women were the ones to bear children; pregnancy occurred in their bodies; and in contemporary circumstances, they reared the children. It was the woman's life which was most influenced by an unwanted pregnancy and therefore she should be the one to have the final say. Equality, emancipation or improvement in women's condition became empty words when something apparently as trivial as a contraceptive mishap could totally ruin a woman's future.

The wording of the demand differed. In a country with a strong natural rights tradition, such as the United Kingdom or the United States, abortion was defined as a woman's right. In the Federal Republic of Germany and in the Netherlands the demand was phrased in terms of control over one's own body enshrined in the German feminist slogan 'Dein Korper gehort dich' or the Dutch 'Baas in eigen buik'. However, in contrast to their opponents from the traditional 'establishment', such as the churches and the newly established anti-abortion movement, long treatises or lengthy legitimations of the demand were lacking. For the women's liberation movement, the demand was akin to the Rights of Man and considered almost self-evident. Whatever the phrasing of the demand, women stressed their competence to be moral judges and to take responsibility for the decision. They thus redefined abortion as a 'lay' affair, no longer the province of the experts. Abortion decisions could no longer be contained in a small political arena of professionals. The ground was laid for a mass movement, and – not surprisingly, given the new definition of the problem – also for a mass movement of opponents to reform. Resolution of the issue in the parliamentary arena then became inevitable, leading to protracted and often bitter political struggles.

THE ISSUE IN THE POLITICAL ARENA

It is sometimes said that abortion is a difficult political problem to solve, either because it is an issue on which no compromise is possible, or because it is a moral issue involving conflicting ethical premises. As I have argued above, abortion is not necessarily a moral issue; it becomes one through the process of issue definition. In political-science jargon, it becomes a 'position' issue; an issue on which people disagree about ends, not on means. This contrasts with 'valence' issues, where the political debate focuses on the means to reach an agreed goal.[5] Position issues are notoriously hard to solve. But this does not fully explain why abortion reform proved to be so difficult. Why cannot a parliamentary majority vote resolve the matter once and for all? This finally happened in most countries, over a period of more than ten years.

To explain this, one must take into account the structure of West European party systems. Abortion as a political issue cuts across the dominant cleavage of politics which is usually based on the socio-economic divide of society, popularly known as the left–right divide. This means that parties will not easily establish a position on abortion when it emerges as a political issue. Abortion is not usually linked to the main doctrines of right and left. The major exception to this occurs when there are parties originally organised on religious bases and therefore have a well-defined position on abortion based on Christian morality. But these parties will also tend to let socio-economic interests predominate in their policies, as they are well aware of the fact that voters usually cast their votes on bread-and-butter issues. Religious parties also have to take into account coalition-building in those countries where majority government is only possible through a coalition of several parties. As coalitions usually follow left–right divisions, religious parties may confront the dilemma of preserving their specific identity or playing down religious questions in order to make co-operation possible. The result is that issues such as abortion will tend to be organised out of politics unless strong counter-pressures exist.[6] Such pressure can come from a religiously based party or a strong pressure group, such as the Church, medical profession or a social movement such as the women's liberation movement.

Examination of the way in which abortion politics in West European states has cut across the left–right divide is revealing. Abortion politics has led to strategies intended to contain the issue – 'the politics of abstaining' is the refusal by governments, parties and leaders to take a stand. This happened in Great Britain where the abortion debate in Parliament was only made possible by a private member's bill. In such cases, to give the bill parliamentary time, there must be some measure of sympathy from the government party. This was evident under a Labour government when David Steel – a Liberal – pioneered a successful bill in 1967. Similarly, in 1980, the Conservatives were not averse to the amendment proposed by Tory John Corrie, which was unsuccessful.[7]

The 'politics of postponement' forms another strategy of containment. Here governments will delay as long as possible before allowing the issue on the agenda and acknowledging that it is their responsibility to do something about it. Political leaders rightly fear that abortion will disrupt the 'normal course of business'. Postponement was standard strategy in Belgium, where no reform has yet taken place. Moreover, in the northern part of the country the problem is exported. Belgian women from Flanders cross the border into the Netherlands for an abortion. In the Netherlands, there was also a long delay; in France and the Federal Republic of Germany, it took about ten years to get a bill passed.

The 'politics of depoliticisation' constitutes a third strategy. Here the issue is redefined as a technical matter best left to experts. These may be members of the medical profession (as was the case in Switzerland, parts of Germany and – unsuccessfully – in the Netherlands) or the judiciary (as was the case in the United States).

As well as leading to strategies of avoidance, postponement, and depoliticisation, abortion politics has caused great tensions in coalition-formation. This has been evident in those nations with multi-party systems where coalition is necessary for majority government, such as the Netherlands, Federal Republic of Germany, Italy, Norway and Belgium. Great tension during coalition-formation occurs: in the Federal Republic of Germany the position of the Liberal Party forced both socialists and Christian Democrats to take up the issue; in Italy aspirations to participate in government led the Communist Party to take a very half-hearted view of the matter in order not to damage its ambition. In the Netherlands no less than three cabinet formations were plagued by the issue. In all these nations religious parties play an important part. In Norway, the Netherlands and Italy it was the women's movement which kept the issue alive, while in the Federal Republic of Germany it was the Church and part of the medical profession.

The abortion issue, furthermore, is seldom definitively solved with the passing of a bill. Abortion became a position issue and therefore opinion polarised. Framing the issue as a right, either as a woman's right or as the right to life of the unborn, made compromise more difficult. Most bills are attempts at compromise, usually allowing several grounds for abortion. The solution is therefore never stable, as neither the women's movement nor the anti-abortion groups are satisfied and seek opportunities to reopen the issue. This is the case in Britain where since 1967 there have been no less than nine attempts to amend the law in a restrictive sense. In France, reconsideration took place three times after the original liberalisation in 1975; in Germany, abortion is still a very controversial issue; in Ireland, after the referendum of 1983 (which led to a clause forbidding abortion in the constitution) those in favour of abortion continue to press for reform. In the Netherlands, the opponents of reform are fighting implementation of the 1981 reform bill. There seems to be a definitive settlement in Denmark and Sweden – both nations having attained abortion on demand.

Field, in her twenty-two-nation study of abortion law reform, concludes that the major obstacle to change is the existence of a strong Catholic Church and a predominantly Catholic population.[8] This accounts for about two-thirds of the total variation across nations in the extent to which abortion policy is liberal. Even a small Catholic presence appears to exert strong influence. The case-studies I have drawn on for Western Europe support this conclusion.[9] This source suggests that in Catholic countries the abortion issue has tended to be treated in a formal and legalistic way – 'correct' principles counting for more than actual practice – while in predominantly Protestant countries principles and practice tend to coincide. The Netherlands, cut in two by the historic divide of the Reformation, neatly illustrates this observation. Since 1973, despite strict laws, practice has been liberal. For years, politicians and interest groups sought to promote a bill which more nearly approximated actual practice. Catholics, however, sought to preserve the old law, thereby choosing to ignore the actual situation of easy access to abortion.

KINDS OF BILLS PASSED

Reconciling very different principles has led to hybrid legislation. Nevertheless, bills can be grouped into three main types.[10] First, there is the so-called 'grounds' or indication type. Here abortion is legal if certain criteria are met, such as a grave danger to the health of the woman (England), or if certain procedural rules are observed (the Netherlands). Second, there is the 'term' type. According to this, abortion is legal if performed before a certain time-limit in the duration of the pregnancy, such as 10 or 12 weeks (France and Italy). And third, there is the 'mixed' type: indications are combined with given terms and/or procedural rules such as exist in the Federal Republic of Germany. Table 13.1 shows the type of law adopted in different states.

Table 13.1   Types and year of reform

Nation and year of reform	Model
Switzerland (1942)	indication
Sweden (1965, 1975)	on demand
United Kingdom (1967)	indication
Denmark (1970, 1973)	on demand
Austria (1974)	term
France (1975, 1980, 1982)	term
Federal Republic of Germany (1976)	mixed
Italy (1978)	term
Norway (1979)	term
Netherlands (1981)*	indication
Portugal – pending	
Spain (1985)	indication
Ireland (1983)	prohibition

* free abortion available since 1973.
Source: Data from Ketting and Van Praag, 1983; Lovenduski and Outshoorn, 1986.

Most laws also contain clauses about minors, about facilities in hospitals and clinics, conscience clauses for medical personnel not willing to co-operate and for contraceptive advice and registration. Provisions about who pays vary.

ACCESS TO ABORTION

In their ten-nation survey on abortion facilities, Ketting and Van Praag indicate that the legal changes enacted in the various nations had little impact on the total number of abortions. The major factor in accounting for the number is not so much a permissive or strict law, but the existence of good medical facilities, organised by the state or by private enterprise, and the availability of contraception and good contraceptive advice. Ketting and Van Praag underline the importance of studying the implementation stage of the policy cycle because the intentions of a law are often thwarted. This can happen in two different directions. Sometimes the intentions of the law are not strongly against a woman's right to choose, but the non-cooperation of hospitals and medical personnel, and no refund of costs by the national insurance scheme, mean that in practice a woman's choice is heavily curtailed. Often there are major regional disparities. This has been the case in the United Kingdom, France, Italy and Austria. By contrast the law is occasionally very restrictive, but women find their way around it with the co-operation of doctors. In these circumstances doctors frequently profit financially from the situation and they have a stake in the maintenance of the legal status quo. This is the case in the Federal Republic of Germany and Switzerland.

Other obstacles to a woman's right to choose are certain legal requirements. These include: a residence requirement for abortion in a province, town or state; the permission of parents in case of minors; the requirement of a second opinion. Additional obstacles include the mentality and ethics of the medical profession and the general social climate which prevents women from discussing abortion openly. A constitutional factor which forms an obstacle is federalism, characteristic of the United States, Switzerland and the Federal Republic of Germany. Here regional variations can be explained by different state statutes. In the Federal Republic of Germany and Switzerland these can be related to religious differences between states. Only in Sweden, Denmark, the Netherlands and in some regions of the United Kingdom, is a woman's right to choose more than a slogan or noble intention.

Some countries are now pursuing a policy to make abortion more accessible. In this respect it is useful to compare the United States and Sweden. Both have liberal statutes, but in Sweden there is an active policy of providing services, refunding costs, and providing contraception and advice on birth control, while in the United States of America, due to the restrictive efforts of various administrations and legal judgments, abortion on demand is becoming a purely formal right. Austria and the Netherlands are also contrasting examples. Since 1974, Austria has had a reasonably liberal law, but abortion is still a taboo subject, so that it is only by word of mouth that women can find their way to the scarce facilities. In the Netherlands it is the other way round. An old law prohibited abortion, but from 1973 a very liberal practice prevailed with widely available contraception. By the early 1980s the Netherlands had the lowest abortion figures per 1,000 inhabitants in the whole world. The French reform of 1982 under Mitterrand can be seen as an attempt to compel hospitals to organise facilities for abortion.

THE EUROPEAN LEVEL

As noted at the beginning of this chapter, abortion law reform has been attempted transnationally in the various European-level institutions. In 1971, Piet Dankert, a Dutch socialist, tried to initiate reform through the Council of Europe by asking member states to amend their statutes on abortion in a liberal direction. Even a watered-down version of his resolution had no chance of success. Several attempts at reconciling national statutes have been made by both pro- and anti-liberalisation Council members, but none has had any success. In the European Parliament there was a heated clash on abortion during the debate on the Resolution on the position of women in the European Community.[11] That the issue was debated in this context was an implicit recognition of abortion as a women's issue; it can be seen as a victory for the women's liberation movement.

This resolution contained two paragraphs on abortion under the heading of 'health and care'. It was a carefully worded document, bearing the hallmark of compromise. A more liberal text would not have reached the resolution stage. It stated that abortion was on the increase; that in nations where 'voluntary interruption of pregnancy' was not recognised in law, clandestine abortion was the rule, often with serious consequences for the women concerned; and that in nations where it was allowed, there were often insufficient facilities to have the abortion performed. The draft resolution observed that this situation resulted in women travelling to other countries for abortions; and encouraged the tendency to see abortion as 'a normal practice and one which is in itself sufficient to solve the problems experienced by women in this area'.[12] The resolution called on the Commission to press for national legislation in order to make it unnecessary for women to travel to other countries for abortion; this leads to commercialisation and makes any form of social support impossible. The draft stressed that abortion was to be seen as a last resort. The Commission was asked to encourage measures to decrease the number of abortions, through the sexual education of young people, the availability of contraception, social acceptance of unwed fathers (!) and mothers, extra help for large families, and proper childcare provisions.[13] These last sentences were inserted to appease the Christian Democrats and other conservatives in Parliament. The passages on abortion were approved against their will by pressure from left-wing members of the committee which drafted the proposal.

The debate on the resolution was held in February 1981. The

Christian Democrat group let it be known that it would oppose any amendment approving 'easier abortion' in the interests of protecting mothers and the unborn. Abortion, Ms M. Lenz argued for the group, was not a woman's problem but a human problem.[14] One Italian member, Ms P. Gaiotti de Biase, pointed out that the present ideal of motherhood is 'restrictive' and 'burdensome', which leads women to avoid becoming mothers; she suggested that abortion is caused by social contradictions and was not 'individualistic egoism'. In her view, a good feminist strategy would be to develop an ambitious social plan to provide for what she termed 'positive maternity'. Demographic considerations also entered into the argument.[15] The group combated the view that abortion was part of an emancipation strategy; letting women decide gives women sole responsibility and men are let off the hook instead of sharing responsibility.[16] Abortion is too important to be left to individual women – the legal protection of the unborn child and the woman in need are the responsibility of governments, according to the Christian Democrats.

Most of the Irish delegates were virulently opposed to the paragraphs on abortion in the resolution. According to them, such statements encouraged the view of abortion as a normal practice and furthermore were opposed to the interests of the Irish people. Insisting on the foolishness of the attempt at harmonisation, one member threatened Ireland's withdrawal from the Community if the two paragraphs were included in the resolution.[17] Ms S. de Valera stressed that the Commission had no competence in this field and had no right to propose harmonisation 'as these are exclusively matters of conscience'.[18] In her eyes, the text actually diverted attention from questions concerning women! Another member called abortion 'hideous murder of the innocent'.[19]

Most of the socialist, communist and other left-wing groups were in favour of including the paragraphs in the resolution, as were several Liberals. One Socialist member, Ms J. B. Krouwel-Vlam, stated that the full development and independence of women also depended upon their freedom to decide whether or not to have children. In her eyes it was a grave error to think that facilities would reduce the number of abortions: 'It is to misjudge women to believe the causes are material.'[20] Women, she felt, should be the ones to decide and all member states should enact legislation to this effect. The Socialists also pointed to back-street abortions, and stated that any pressure brought through European Communities' legislation was wholly justified. The Socialist Ms Y. M. Fuillet argued that the free movement of working women did not exist 'when they are subjected to different laws affecting their most profoundly personal decisions'.[21] Addressing the Irish members, Boot and De Valera, she asked, if abortion did not concern women, then whom did it concern?

Of the amendments put forward in order to remove or water-down the abortion paragraphs, none received a majority; both paragraphs were passed in the end by clear majorities.[22] The Christian Democrat group asked for roll-call votes on both.[23] From the voting one can draw the same conclusion as for many of the decisions taken in national parliaments: the divisions split most of the parties represented – not all Christian Democrats or Conservatives voted against, and not all Socialists voted in favour; Liberal and Communist dissidents could also be found.

The European Commission, however, did not act on the two paragraphs in the Resolution because the Treaty of Rome does not provide a legal basis to do so. The Commission is therefore dependent on the political will of the member states to have proposals accepted. The Commission also stated that any harmonisation of abortion laws would be impossible given the lack of political will among the member states. It seems unlikely that either the parliamentary road to further liberalisation, or the path of rescinding reforms, as the still very active anti-abortion groups demand, will be tried again. This is for the same sorts of reasons which prevail at the national level; abortion has been framed in terms of a position issue and it again cuts across the socio-economic divide. The widely varying statutes and views of the member states also tend to make action difficult.

It is more likely that various interest groups will try to press their case through the European Commission of Human Rights and the European Court of Human Rights, by bringing cases on the basis of the Convention for the Protection of Human Rights and Fundamental Freedoms of 1950. There have been three cases to date attempting to prevent or restrict reform measures, and one to widen them. The European Commission of Human Rights received a complaint in 1960 against the Norwegian reform in 1960. The Commission did not judge itself competent to pronounce *in abstracto* on the compatibility of Norwegian law with the Convention. The plaintiff was not recognised as a 'victim of violation' in the sense of Article 25 of the Convention, and therefore his appeal was not upheld.[24] In 1975, an Austrian complained about the Austrian abortion reform. Again he was not recognised as a plaintiff on the basis of Article 25 and the claim was not admitted. The Austrian Constitutional Court itself pronounced that the reform was not in conflict with Article 2 of the Convention, which guarantees 'Everyone's right to life shall be protected by law', since the Article was not held to protect 'emerging life'.[25] So in both cases there was no pronouncement by the European Commission on the meaning of Article 2.

In 1977 two women plaintiffs complained to the Commission that the German reform of 1976 was too restrictive.[26] They based their appeal on Article 8 of the Convention which covers respect for private life and the right to family life and alleged that the reform was in conflict with this article. Although both women were accepted as plaintiffs, the Commission held that the German statute did not violate Article 8.

The third case from the anti-abortion side came up in 1980, when an Englishman complained that his wife had had an abortion, which he had not been able to stop under English law. The Commission accepted him as a victim as defined in Article 25, but did not accept his invoking Articles 2 and 8. The Commission then pronounced on the meaning of Article 2. It stated that Article 2 did not cover the right to life of the foetus. 'Everyone' did not, according to the Commission, include the unborn. The Commission also pointed out that the definition of 'life' is a matter on which there is no agreement and refrained from establishing its own definition. The reasoning of the Commission on Article 8 is very interesting, since the potential father argued that his right to family life had been violated by the abortion. The Commission ruled that: 'The "life" of the foetus is intimately connected with, and cannot be regarded in isolation from, the life of the pregnant woman.'[27]

If seen as an absolute, the foetus's right to life is of a higher order than the life of the woman – someone already born. Such a position is contrary to the object and purpose of the Convention. The Commission ruled that the father of the foetus should take into account the rights of the pregnant woman as being the person primarily concerned in the pregnancy, and her private life should be respected. The abortion decision was his wife's and taken to avert injury to her physical and mental health. It was necessary, even though it interfered with the respect for his family life, for the protection of the rights of another person.

It remains to be seen if other attempts at restricting abortion law reform will take place at this level. It is probable that they will, given the success of the legal strategy in the United States of America – where anti-abortion groups have been successful in limiting the scope of the 1973 Supreme Court decision which allows abortion on demand in the first trimester of pregnancy. The tendency of European anti-abortion groups to argue their case within the framework of natural rights fits in with the basic philosophy of the Convention. But success for these groups will mean having to reverse the Commission's interpretation of Article 2.

FUTURE TRENDS – THE ABORTION DEBATE

The abortion debate in Europe is not over. Abortion law reform is still being contested in several nations. Since the problem is usually defined as a position-issue, compromise necessarily dilutes the principles held by the contestants and they are consequently dissatisfied. This produces an unstable situation.

I have argued that it is unlikely that abortion law reform through the European Commission or European Parliament will be successful. Harmonisation among member states has been seen by the proponents of abortion law reform as a weapon against restrictive statutes, rather like the third European Commission Directive on Social Security which compelled several member states to remove discriminatory charges against women from their regulations. It was precisely this that the Irish delegates feared, and it also accounted for some of the opposition of the German Christian Democrats. Demanding harmonisation may also be a dangerous strategy for nations with a very liberal law, such as Denmark and (to a lesser extent) the Netherlands. This could lead to a moderate compromise more or less like French or Italian law which would undoubtedly revive anti-abortion groups in the more liberal countries.

In addition, the abortion debate may be refuelled by several other trends. One of these is the growing influence of a pro-population-growth lobby consisting of several influential groups in the Federal Republic of Germany especially, and also in France and the Netherlands. These groups are making an issue of 'demographic decline'. The birthrate has declined so much that in several nations there is already zero or negative population growth. This may lead to new attempts to curb abortion facilities and restrict legal access. However, abortion is a very crude instrument for influencing the birth-rate and not always successful, as can be seen from the experience in Eastern Europe. Restricting abortion may then become part of a pro-natalist policy along with other measures which curtail reproductive freedom for women.

The meaning of abortion may also change and lead to new disquiet with the development of new technology such as *in vitro* fertilisation, experiments on human embryos, and innovation in prenatal diagnostics. This last trend has already led to women in the United States of America being medically examined and treated during pregnancy on the grounds that it was in the interest of the unborn child. The rights of the unborn have been widely interpreted since the advent of the anti-abortion movement in the United States of America. Further technological innovation could also push back the limits of viability of the foetus outside the womb: several laws stipulate a prohibition of abortion after viability. This will limit the options for an abortion. Similarly, *in vitro* fertilisation and experiments with embryos have touched off new debates on the beginning of human life, which may call abortion into question. These latter developments are leading to increased power of the medical profession over human reproduction. In the long run, this is probably more threatening to women's control of their own fertility than the anti-abortion groups. Redefining human reproduction as a medical problem, giving the profession a growing control, should be countered by women's liberation groups in order to defend the gains made in the 1960s and 1970s in the field of reproductive rights.

Notes

1. Switzerland also did not reform in this period, having liberalised its law in 1942. In Belgium, various reform bills have failed. In Ireland there was the reverse trend: an abortion prohibition was inserted in the Constitution in 1983.
2. Notably Sweden and Norway.
3. E. Ketting and Ph. van Praag, *Abortus Provocatus. Wet en Praktijk. Een internationaal vergelijkende analyse van de abortuspraktijk zoals die na wetswijziging in tien westerse landen is ontstaan*, Zeist: NISSO, 1983.
4. J. Outshoorn, *De politieke strijd rondom de abortuswetgeving in Nederland, 1964–84*, September 1986.
5. D. Stokes, 'Spatial models of party competition', in A. Campbell *et al.* (eds), *Elections and the Political Order*, Wiley, New York, 1966, pp. 170–1.
6. J. Lovenduski and J. Outshoorn, *The New Politics of Abortion*, Sage, London, 1986.

7. D. Marsh and J. Chambers, *Abortion Politics*, Junction Books, London, 1981.
8. M. J. Field, 'Determinants of Abortion Policy in the Developed Nations', *Policy Studies Journal*, vol. 7, 1979, pp. 771–81.
9. Lovenduski and Outshoorn, *The New Politics of Abortion*.
10. Ketting and Van Praag, *Abortus Provocatus*, p. 15.
11. *Official Journal*, Debates of the European Parliament, 1980–81 session. Report of Proceedings from 9 to 13 February, no. 266.
12. Zitingsdocumenten Europees Parlement, doc. 1-829/80-1 (29-1-81) D1. 1. *Ontwerpresolutie behorende bij Verslag namens de Commissie ad hoc voor de rechten van de vrouw over de positie van de vrouw in de Europese Gemeenschappen*, paras 5 and 36.
13. Ibid., para. 36.
14. *Offical Journal*, Debates of the European Parliament, 1980–91 session. Report of the Proceedings from 9 to 13 February, no. 266, p. 42.
15. *Official Journal*, ibid., p. 56.
16. Argued by Ms E. C. A. M. Boot, *Official Journal*, ibid., p. 76.
17. T. J. Maher, *Official Journal*, ibid., p. 79.
18. *Official Journal*, ibid., p. 73.
19. M. Clinton, *Official Journal*, ibid., p. 87.
20. *Official Journal*, ibid., p. 54.
21. *Official Journal*, ibid., p. 81.
22. Voting on para. 35: for 122; against, 99; abstentions, 17. Voting on para. 36: for, 128; against, 89; abstentions, 13. In *Official Journal Information and notices*, 9–3–81. C50, p. 30.
23. *Official Journal*, p. 108.
24. 876/70 *x* v. *Norway*, Yearbook 4, p. 270.
25. 7045/75 *x* v. *Austria*. European Commission of Human Rights, *Decisions and Reports* 7, Strasbourg 1977 (October), pp. 87–9.
26. 6959/75, *Brugemann and Scheuten* v. *FRG*. European Commission of Human Rights, *Decisions and Reports* 10, Strasbourg 1978 (June) pp. 100–18.
27. 8416/79 *x* v. *United Kingdom*. European Commission of Human Rights, *Decisions and Reports* 19 (October), pp. 244–54.

Pg 11 – Pippa Norris –Candidism (field)
+105 +107

Index